THE GOLD ROCKS OF GREAT BRITAIN AND I
CALVERT

CW01642195

Publisher's Note

The book descriptions we ask booksellers to display prominently warn that this is an historic book with numerous typos, missing text or index and is not illustrated.

We scanned this book using character recognition software that includes an automated spell check. Our software is 99 percent accurate if the book is in good condition. However, we do understand that even one percent can be a very annoying number of typos! And sometimes all or part of a page is missing from our copy of a book. Or the paper may be so discolored from age that you can no longer read the type. Please accept our sincere apologies.

After we re-typeset and design a book, the page numbers change so the old index and table of contents no longer work. Therefore, we usually remove them.

Our books sell so few copies that you would have to pay hundreds of dollars to cover the cost of proof reading and fixing the typos, missing text and index. Therefore, whenever possible, we let our customers download a free copy of the original typo-free scanned book. Simply enter the barcode number from the back cover of the paperback in the Free Book form at www.general-books.net. You may also qualify for a free trial membership in our book club to download up to four books for free. Simply enter the barcode number from the back cover onto the membership form on the same page. The book club entitles you to select from more than a million books at no additional charge. Simply enter the title or subject onto the search form to find the books.

If you have any questions, could you please be so kind as to consult our Frequently Asked Questions page at www.general-books.net/faqs.cfm? You are also welcome to contact us there.

General Books LLC™, Memphis, USA, 2012. ISBN: 9780217296441.

CHAPTER I. *Peculiarity of Gold Discoveries, — Phoenicians. — Early Discoveries.—Gold the earliest Metal.—Scotland.— Ireland. — United States. — Siberia. — California. — Australia.-- Canada.—Gold Searches.—Natal.— Greenland.—Parallel History of Silver Working.—Geological Discoveries. — Refining. — Gold Schemes. —Gold from Sea Sands. — Gold from the Basin of the Rhine. — Universal Distribution of Gold.*

The history of modern gold discoveries presents itself to us under one uniform aspect; a long preliminary working and then a sudden publication and recognition. The gold is obtained more or less openly and notoriously by individuals for years and centuries, but the fact is neglected by the community at large till some sudden recognition is obtained, and then a general working takes place, and a new epoch of enrichment is begun. Such was the case with Scotland, with Ireland, with Russia, with California, and with Australia; such may be the case with Britain at large. Perhaps, too, had we the materials for the ancient history of gold, we should become acquainted with many examples of a like state of circumstances, for history is consistent in the uniformity and parallelism of the chain of events she narrates.

In the scarcity of such data, any reference to the history of ancient gold workings for the purpose of this book must necessarily be brief. As gold is one of those metals most extensively diffused, so is it under certain circumstances

B most easily found and wrought. There are few great river beds in some part of which gold in visible particles and nuggets has not at one time existed, and the earliest inhabitants attracted at first by the chance glittering of a nugget, would be directed to a more general search to supply themselves with metal. The pure soft gold of nuggets is easily fusible, and the metal being found native can be reduced with greater facility than the mixed ores of other metals. All records point to gold as one of the earliest metals known, and it has been observed from the relics of the Iberians and others, as exemplified in the Museum at Copenhagen, for instance, that in many of the implements gold is profusely employed when contrasted with the parsimony evident in the expenditure of iron. In that Museum are swords, daggers, and knives, the blades of which are of gold, whilst an edge of iron is formed for the purpose of cutting. It will be remembered that Homer speaks even of a suit of armour of gold, besides large vessels of that metal; Mr. Jacobs, from the evidence of the Museum at Copenhagen, considers that at the unknown period and among the people who raised the barrows which antiquarian research has of late years explored, gold was a much more abundant product than iron.-

This opinion merits consideration, for, though extravagant according to the standard of a few years ago, it is perfectly consistent with our present knowledge. The amount of gold which may be acquired by one individual in a favourable district is now known to be very great. What is called Dr. Kerr's hundredweight of gold was found by an Australian aboriginal, and out of a mass of about two hundredweight, one hundred and six pounds of pure gold was obtained. Two brothers in New South Wales collected sixty pounds' weight of gold in four weeks. At Ballarat, a young man named Jacob's Historical Enquiry into the Precious Metals, vol. i. p. 3. t *Ibid,* p. 3.

Stapleton, gathered twenty pounds in one week, in February last year; and at the same place, in September, six men gathered in one day the same quantity. At Louisa Creek, a man named Brennan found a lump weighing about twenty-five pounds. Four men brought from Mount Alexander, after a few weeks' work, two hundred and ninety pounds' 'weight. From a quartz vein in New South Wales, with my own hand, I knocked off, in one day, quartz containing seventy-six pounds' weight of pure gold.

A mass of fifty, eighty, or one hundred pounds of soft metal would supply the wants of a small community in a rude state of society, and as population was scanty, the possessions of individuals would be the larger, and a large amount of gold might have been in use at a very early period. As population became denser, the demand for other metals would arise, and as the available deposits of large or visible gold had been exhausted, it may be presumed the rocks would be searched for minerals.

In a more advanced state of society, and when gold, by becoming rarer, had acquired another value, the communities would become the prey of the seafaring nations, and when these latter had exhausted this source of enrichment, they would seek new gold fields. This, there can be little doubt, was a great motive for the earlier Phoenician expeditions, in which they penetrated to these remote regions. Thus Herodotus tells us they discovered and worked the gold mines between.ZEnura and Caenyra, in Thasus, as they did those in the Greek islands; and as there is no reason to presume these countries were uninhabited, the developement of the gold workings may fairly be attributed to the Phoenicians, and not to the native inhabitants. These gold expeditions gave a stimulus to piracy for obtaining slaves to work in the gold fields.f In the earliest periods of history, Herodotus, b. vi. ch. 47.

t Thucydides, b. 1.

or perhaps we may say in the prehistoric period, we find the Phoenicians making expeditions to every quarter to obtain gold, and the adventurous spirits of the day engaged in working the river sands of the Phasis, Pactolus, and other rivers. At a later period, so anxious were the Phoenicians to obtain supplies of gold, that it is suggested they founded Carthage to get supplies of gold dust by the Caravans over the desert of Sahara, and so to compete with the Egyptians, and that they formed the treaty with Solomon to compete with the same people in the eastern supply of gold by the Red Sea. These are enterprizes not beyond what we know of the bold spirit of the Phoenician citizens.-f

Gold was a chief object with the Phoenicians and their kinsmen, the Carthaginians, and besides what has already been stated, they worked the gold of Spain and Western Europe. Thus they left little for the Greeks and Romans to glean; and the only gold these latter obtained in Europe was from mine workings, which were not very productive, while their chief source of supply was from the east. It was with the Romans, little accustomed to river washings and dry diggings, that the notion arose that rich veins and deep workings contained the mother supply of gold, a notion which more than anything has obstructed the progress of gold working. It is true PlinyJ was acquainted with the process of streaming, and the supply of gold from copper, tin, and other metals; but fantastic notions prevailed as to the miraculous origin of gold and the alchemical doctrines of production and transmutation had likewise full acceptance. The simplest facts were perverted, and the truth was overlaid and forgotten. Thus, what is called antgold, turned up to the surface by ants in burrowing, in the Indian gold fields, was said to be the secretion or produc Gold Notes, Wyld, p. *5.* t Humboldt, Cosmos, vol. 2, p. 498, by Otte.

X Pliny, Nat. Hist. lib. 33. tion of gigantic ants. Henceforth the speculations of learned men took a course as far apart as possible from the domain of facts, and for several centuries gold working was to a great extent lost sight of. Its lingering state will be well enough seen in the next chapter.

Whatever was the case with regard to the ancient discoveries, the discovery of gold in America was certainly accidental. It is very likely that the Phoenicians, as they did in Thasus, Cyprus, and Spain, found in many places gold which the inhabitants had neglected; but accident made the Spaniards, in the first instance, acquainted with the gold supplies of America, though they afterwards made systematic explorations to every accessible part for the discovery of gold fields. These explorations embraced the West India islands, the southern regions of the United States, and thence as far south as Spanish power extended. Thus all the existing localities, except California and Virginia, became known to the early Spaniards, and were worked by them, though many have been since neglected or forgotten. Among those places so enumerated by Barba is Carabaya, which, in 1850, caused so much excitement in Peru. The Spanish modes of working were distinctly those now pursued in California and Australia, and both dry and wet diggings are described as clearly as by any of our contemporaries. A whole river basin was thus worked over by sinking trial pits, taking out stuff at every few feet, washing it in trays in the river, and continuing until gold was obtained, or the bed rock was reached, f The nature of the gold in dust, scales, and nuggets, is likewise accurately described.

It is very questionable whether the processes of gold working and washing adopted by the Spaniards in America Barba's Art of Metals, ch. 26.

t Peter Martyr, Decade 1, lib. 22, p. 16; lib. 3, p. 19; Gonzalo Fernando Ovideo, West Indies, pp. 188,189,190. *X* Peter Martyr, Decade 1, lib. 10, p. 56; Acosta, History of the Indies, ch. 4. pp. 212, 213. were borrowed from the natives, as the descriptions of the ancients were familiarly preserved, and in several parts of Europe river workings were still kept up. The mode of working in the Leadhills district in Scotland, as now pursued by the local population, and as described in the sixteenth century, is exactly conformable to the usual practice, and there is no reason to imagine it was adopted from the Spaniards. A similarity of rude processes will be found all over the world among various nations, arising from the conformity of natural conditions under which the gold is sought for and obtained in the river beds.

In the more modern gold discoveries we shall find that state of circumstances alluded to at the head of this chapter, namely, that in each case gold was found by individuals for years, and that this was more or less known, but that the community at large did not acknowledge the fact till some sudden light burst in upon them, and that then extensive workings took place. Thus the imputed or supposed date of a gold discovery is commonly later than the true date. The public all at once seem to wake up to the knowledge of gold in Scotland or Australia, perhaps because they can no longer refuse to acknowledge the evidence of facts. This is, however, a state of affairs not peculiar to gold workings, but extending to most social transactions. Men are not so ready to listen to truth as to their own prepossessions, and it is almost in vain to tell them there is gold or anything else in a country, if they are disposed to believe there is not. Thus there is extreme incredulity as to everything which does not conform to these prepossessions, and extreme credulity for everything that does. Many now living poohpoohed and ridiculed steam-boats, railways, and gas, who now spend their evenings in table-turning, or hold a seance with the well-paid medium of spirit-rapping. There are, of Pliny's Natural History, book *33,* ch. 21.
course, grades in the manifestations of public prejudice; there are those who will greedily pin their faith on tableturning, who withhold their acquiescence from the relations of the spirits or their interpreters, but there is no real difference as to the operating cause.

In this way persons, learned and unlearned, having possessed themselves of certain notions as to gold, examine the facts submitted to them by the dictates of these preconceived opinions. The transmutation of gold they may be willing to receive, but the existence of gold bodily they deny. Gold is a rare metal—gold is only to be found in certain countries, gold is only to be found in hot countries—gold never was found in Britain, or in Australia, and never will be—if it were Peru, that is a different thing altogether. Peru is graciously allowed to possess gold, or perhaps guano, but the public have laid down a scheme for nature, and nature is not allowed to deviate from it.

Show them a specimen—they do not admit the presence of gold unless they cannot help it. It is pyrites, or it may be anything, but it cannot be gold. If they allow there is gold, there cannot be much of it, and it will never pay. Show them a nugget, and they will believe it is a mass of coin melted up. Thus fact after fact is got rid of, and the accumulation of numerous facts, during centuries, which otherwise would present incontrovertible evidence is effectually prevented, and the whole course of facts is forgotten, or becomes involved in doubt. Such is more particularly the case, as will be shown in another chapter, with reference to the history of gold in Britain.

One of the first incidents in modern history is the gold mining epoch in Scotland in the sixteenth century. We will pass over the allusion of Tacitus to the gold of the Caledonians, but, nevertheless, the streams at the source of the Tacitus, Agricola.

Clyde were long worked by the shepherds for gold, but the existence of gold in Clydesdale was not generally known till the workings in the reign of James IV. and V., when three hundred thousand pounds' value, having been raised from the mines, a temporary notoriety was acquired for them, and afterwards Queen Elizabeth sent Sir Bevis Bulmer, and other famous speculators, to work them for her personal purposes.

The detailed history of the Crauford Moor diggings will be found under the proper head; but, before dismissing the subject for the present, it may be worth while to notice the obscurity which has attended workings certainly among the most remarkable in Europe. A line in a manual of geology is their epitaph, and in the Statistical Account of Scotland, filling a goodly row of volumes, three or four lines in a long account of the parish alone, record the golden glories of Leadhills.

The second locality which may be adduced is likewise connected with these islands. A tradition of the bards, authentic or not, but at any rate recorded and published, pointed to the district south of Dublin as a productive gold district. An inhabitant of Wicklowshire, who, in conformity with the stereotyped formula was designated mad, is known for many years to have nuggeted at Croghan Kinshela, and others of the inhabitants had made themselves acquainted with its treasures. At length the population of the district chose to believe that gold was really obtainable, and flocking there, found what would have passed as a good digging in the now acknowledged gold regions. The government workings in due course failed, and thus the fame of Wicklow was dimmed, instead of any encouragement being afforded by it to further gold explorations.

With regard to the mad gold finder there is a singular harmony of incidents. The blacksmith who for years got gold on the Shoalhaven of New South Wales, was likewise entitled by the popular voice the " mad" blacksmith; and the gentleman who had done so much for the discovery of gold in North Wales, has been favoured with the like qualification, and until lately has been duly acknowledged as a madman. Inventors of course are always mad by public courtesy, and gold finders gain the same homage. With regard to the gold fields, there are three incidents of independent origin, and admitting of no controversy, and yet illustrating a uniformity of what is called traditions, which in due time would, in the school of Niebuhr, be resolved into one myth, and that deprived of authority; and yet so far from public credulity being in this case the author of fable, it is public incredulity which denies truth.

The history of the discovery in the Carolina, or Southern United States district, is conformable with the other cases. The gold hunters traversed it for years, but their pursuits excited no sympathy among the general population till a period comparatively recent, and yet, in 1810, a very interesting account of the Carolina gold regions was published, in which its resources were well stated. About a quarter of a century ago a mania sprang up, and the produce at times has been very large, and is still considerable. This is now an acknowledged gold district.

The rich Russian gold workings in the Ural are commonly set down as of recent date, and yet Humboldt has pretty well shown that they were known to the ancients, and has connected the evidence of the former workings with the records of the classic historians. In our own mining history there is a reference to these mines, but little known. It is contained in a pamphlet published by Thomas Bushell, a famous mining speculator of the beginning of the seventeenth century, who will be referred to hereafter. In this volume is an affidavit of Walter Busbee, assayer in the Mint, who Von Humboldt, Asie Centrale, tome 1, pp. 389, 407; Kosmos, vol. 2; and Ansichte der Natur. Herodotus.
incidentally states that in the reign of James the First he was sent to Russia to give advice as to the gold mines beyond the Ural, and that being taken prisoner by the Tartars, he was carried into Siberia and kept there some years, but at length was exchanged by the Grand Duke of Russia. These Ural workings have produced in some late years upwards of ten thousand pounds' weight of gold.

The pueblos or missions in California were founded by the Jesuits, who are reputed to have greatly enriched themselves from the gold workings, and who marked its auriferous characters on their maps.f At any rate, in the beginning of the last century, the existence of gold in California was made known by Captain Shelvocke, who commanded a privateering expedition in those seas, and in the account of the voyage, published in Queen Anne's time, he affirmed that the black sands of the rivers yielded gold largely, and that the whole country abounded with it. The like accounts were brought by the fur traders to the northwest coast, who watered there; and by the privateering expeditions which entered those seas in the beginning of this century. By these ships specimens of Californian gold sand were brought into this country, and found their way into our collections, and among others, that of the British Institution, and of Mr. Hyde Clarke. The adobe bricks, which had been taken as ballast from old buildings in that region, were found to contain particles of gold; and lately, sufficient gold has been obtained from one of these buildings to pay the expense of pounding and washing.

During the great share mania of 1825, a company was formed for the pearl fishery of the Californian Gulf, but, singularly enough, the gold escaped the notice of the spe Bushell's Book or Pamphlet, British Museum, c. 27, f. 1. This has been likewise quoted in the Mining Journal, vol. 4, 1837.
t Rev. "W. B. Clarke's Plain Statements. Sydney, 1851, p. 5. J lb. p. 6. culators, who yet went so far as to send out two ships under the command of Lieut. Hardy, R. N. Diving bells were taken out to facilitate the fishing for pearls, but unfortunately it was found that the pearls were hidden in clefts among the rocks at the bottom of the sea, which parts the men within the diving bells could not reach, on which account the undertaking was abandoned.

In that very year gold ore was washed by a Mexican in a mine at St. Isidore, near St. Diego, but through the disturbed state of the country, it was not followed up with spirit.f During the mania of 1825, although capital was found for the pearl expedition and gold companies were in particular request, of which the St. John del Rey, Imperial Brazilian and Mariquita Companies alone remain, and although every region was sought for gold mining or gold washing localities, California escaped. Nevertheless, in 1815, William Phillips had published the following:—" On the coast of California there is a plain of fourteen leagues in extent, about fourteen inches beneath the surface of which large lumps of gold are irregularly interspersed.''J This was likewise recorded in Jameson's Mineralogy, and we now know it to be true enough. The fact must have been derived from local observations, but it was soon lost sight of, both in California and in Europe. After a time it ceased to be reprinted.

In 1840, another discovery of gold was made in California, and a small thread of gold was wrought in the district of St. Barbara, but not to any extent. In 1841, Lieut. Emmens, of Commodore Wilkes's expedition, accompanied by Mr. Dana, the mineralogist, passed down the Sacramento, but they found no gold.§ Emigrant's Guide to California. Pelham Richardson, p. 10. t Gold Notes, Wyld, p. 37.
X W. Phillip's Outline of Mineralogy and Geology; London, 1815; p. 33. § Gold Notes on California, Wyld, p. 15. Mr. Dana, in his survey, certainly acknowledged the resemblance of the district to the gold-bearing formations. He says:—" The talcose and allied rocks of the Umpqua and Shasta districts, resemble in many parts the gold-bearing rocks of other regions; but the gold, if any there be, remains to be discovered."

He likewise crossed the American Fork, just above Sutter's rancho, but without perceiving that it was auriferous yet.f Dana noticed and described many of the rocks associated with gold.

In 1844, Captain, now Colonel Fremont, on a voyage of exploration, made his way into the valley of the Sacramento, and over a region rich in gold diggings, and passed along the American river in which what is called the gold discovery took place. Colonel Fremont is now a large owner of gold quartz property, in the rich Mariposa district; but, in 1844, he saw no signs of gold. J

The officers of the English navy, who surveyed the Sacramento river from its mouth, were equally deficient in their explorations.

In September, 1847, Captain Sutter, a settler, contracted with Mr. Marshall, to build a saw-mill on the American Fork, near some pine woods. In the spring of 1848, it was ready, and the dam and race constructed; but when the water washed on the wheel, the tail-race was found too narrow to let the water through quick enough. Mr. Marshall, to save work, Yankee fashion, let the water right into the race with a strong stream, so as to sweep the race wider and deeper. Having done this, a great bank of gravel and mud was driven to the foot of the race. One day Mr. Marshall, on walking down the race to this bank, saw some glittering particles on the upper edge; and, having gathered a few, examined them, and conjectured Geology of the Exploring Expeditions, p. 638.

+ Ibid. p. 639. I Fremont's Travels.

their value. He went down to Sutter's Fort, and told the captain; and they agreed to keep it a secret until a grist-mill of the captain's was finished. It so happened, however, that a Yankee carpenter, being suspicious of their visits to the mill-race, followed them, and likewise inspecting the bed of the stream, found the gold scales, of the true nature of which he was pretty well convinced, and he promulgated the intelligence.

From that time, the great Californian gold mania arose, which is a fact which has made itself well enough known to every one.

The last instance I shall give, exemplifying the way in which the public neglect facts as to gold workings, is that of Australia. And here the historical incidents have passed under my own eyes; for I did not leave Australia until gold-digging had reached its height. I well remember soon after landing at Adelaide, being shown a nugget by an overlander, which he had brought from the Morumbidgee. The nugget was pulled out of his pocket in company with his knife, tobacco, &c., and had evidently been well rubbed. Believing me to have some knowledge of mineralogy, he told me he had " a stone to show me, which he believed to be of the nature of gold, though he did not mean to say it was as valuable as a real sovereign."

Soon after that, I discovered fine gold near the present Mount Remarkable special survey. I then discovered gold opposite Mr. Foott's station, on the Gawler. Subsequently I discovered it on land where it was afterwards worked by the Victoria Gold Mining Company, and by the Montacute Mining Company. Having satisfied myself that gold existed, I was not long before I ascertained its general diffusion over the whole schistose formations of the south-eastern districts, in the neighbourhood of the intruded rocks; and for this purpose I made explorations in South Australia, Victoria, and New South Wales; in the latter, over a very extended area. My experience and pursuits were not singular, those of some of my own friends and companions were to the same effect. But since public attention has been drawn to the subject, many such facts have been brought forward. Perhaps the earliest cases of gold finding were among the convicts in the road-gangs, who were punished for the possession of gold supposed to be from watches or jewellery melted down.

The shepherd, M'Gregor, for years employed himself in getting quartz gold from a vein which crossed his master's run. Another gold finder was the mad blacksmith on Major Elkington's estate on the Shoalhaven, now the property of the Honourable Sir Charles Nicholson, Speaker of the Legislative Council. The blacksmith was supposed not to have gone, from the time he was used to start with a bag, on moonlight nights, a distance of above four miles, and having filled his bag with some mysterious substance, returned home, and went to bed. The next morning the substance brought in was put, with some admixture, on the forge; and, after some working, the cinders were removed, and he used to *find* gold at the bottom, which was believed to be done in some unaccountable way.

I remember the case of a man who left a bag of dust from the Tumut, for years in Mr. Keighran's private store, where it remained unmolested until the gold fever sprang up, when suspicion as to the nature of the hoard being awakened, it was suddenly missed.

I well recollect, as thousands of Australians do, that for years Mr. Cohen exhibited in his window a parcel of specimens labelled—" Native Australian Gold." This was in George Street, the grand street of the city of Sydney, in the daily sight of thousands.

In some cases the finders did not really feel assured of what they had secured; and Mr. Clarke relates a case of a poor fellow who carried specimens of gold about with him for years, believing it to be copper, and who offered it for sale as such during the late excitement. Some certainly believed they had found copper; because the general opinion was unfavourable to the existence of gold in New Holland. But, when gold was brought into the market, the prevalent belief was, that it was the produce of convict hoards, obtained by robbery.

This class of examples of gold finders might be very much extended, but the apathy of the public and of their functionaries in the local and imperial government, is set off more strikingly when we consider that scientific men, on various grounds, had promulgated the opinion that Australia was a gold country. The scientific world, at any rate, had due notice, though rather anomalously, of those parties who, on the evidence of geological structure, detected gold in Australia, shut their eyes to stronger evidence affecting England. The great discoverer of the Silurian system, Sir Roderick Murchison, was no exception to this. His sagacity detected in the rocks of Wales the elements of a new and extensive geological class, which he named the Silurian system. Having had the further good fortune to apply in the gold regions of the Ural his discovery to the determination of like formations there, he was in a position to generalize as to the character and constitution of the Silurian rocks. He was thus induced, on reported similarities of structure, to indicate to the scientific world, the probable existence of gold in Australia; nor was he contented with announcing his views on this head to the scientific world (as he has neglected no opportunity of doing), but he considered it his duty, occupying the high position he does, to communicate his opinions to members of the government by whom they were coldly, nay it is said, contemptuously received. He was told not to let them " have too much of a good thing."f Sir Rev. V. B. Clarke's Plain Statements, p. 7.

t *Ibid,* p. 6.

Roderick does not, however, give any place to gold in his work on Siluria;

nor although gold from that region has been offered to his inspection, has he in his public discourses, announced it as a gold district, or given any encouragement to gold working there.

In 1839, Strzelecki had hinted respecting gold, but received so little encouragement, that at a subsequent period he was silent. My late companion in a New Zealand expedition, Francis Forbes, took a more decided course. He publicly announced his knowledge and convictions, though it was not till 1849 that he published a series of papers in the Sydney Morning Herald, on gold working. The unfavourable reception these communications received, not only damped the enterprize of Mr. Forbes, but that of those connected with him, or the full discovery would have taken place in that year. Mr. Forbes, setting apart other considerations, was well entitled to attention, for he had not only studied the geological structure of the Australian Continent, but he had likewise examined New Zealand, and he was deeply interested in the gold question, which was the constant object of his conversation and thoughts. The inattention of the Sydney public very much affected him, and he went to California, and I heard, with deep regret, of his death there in 1850.

Sir Thomas Mitchell, the Surveyor General of New South Wales, met with no better reception from the colonial authorities, than Sir Roderick Murchison did from the imperial government. In 1846 the government surveyors under his direction, discovered gold deposits in the great dividing range in the northeast part of New South Wales, but the Governor General refused to allow the searches to be followed up, alleging that he had " no funds to devote to such a visionary purpose."

Col. Helmersen, of St. Petersburgh, Member of the Im Gold Notes, Wyld, pp. 31, 35.
perial Academy of Sciences, well acquainted with the Ural gold formations, expressed publicly his conviction of the existence of gold deposits in Australia, and his opinions appeared in print.
The Rev. W. B. Clarke, of St. Leonard's, N. S. W., states, that in 1841 he brought gold from the Basin of the Macquarie; that this gold was exhibited to members of the Colonial Government and Legislature, in the council chamber itself, and to numbers of persons in the community. It was, says he, spoken of openly, discussed in the public journals, was, made the ground of enquiries into the probable extensive auriferous character of the colony; and Mr. Clarke promulgated a theory, that in certain formations, gold would be found in considerable abundance. These views he republished at a later period, with a general theory of gold discoveries.

About 1849, a Mr. Smith tendered to the Colonial Secretary of New South Wales a piece of gold quartz, offering to disclose the site for a reward. Mr. Stewart, Mr. Trappit, and others, were known discoverers of gold.

In April, 1846, the discovery of gold in the Montacute North Mine was again stated, in the vein which was afterwards found to extend into the sett of the Adelaide Mining Company. This vein was worked and gold obtained from it, though the general character of the mines not proving sufficiently productive, the workings were suspended. This discovery was known both in Australia and England, and was communicated in the public journals.f

Much more evidence might be adduced to prove the discovery of gold anterior to 1851, but quite enough has been already given to show that had there been adequate inquiry by the government, the workings might have been commenced at an earlier date, and Australia, having reaped the Rev. W. B. Clarke's Plain Statements, pp. 6, 7.
t Mining Journal for 1846, pp. 376, 449.

C benefits of the discovery, would at the present moment have been in a more advanced state of progress. Who knows but that the horrors of the Irish famine might have been alleviated, had the resources of the Southern Continent been developed only ten years ago?

The gold fever in California, it might have been naturally expected, would at once have set the Australian public on the alert, revived all the floating rumours and neglected statements, and caused a general search, such as has since taken place in some other countries, Natal for instance; but it was not so. Forbes met with no attention, and the Australians flocked out to San Francisco, where many of them became impressed with similarities of structure in the gold regions to those they had quitted in the south. Among these was Mr. Edward Hammond Hargraves, who has had the good fortune to reap the honours of the discovery. He returned from California, and without being aware of what had already been done by others, instituted an independent search for gold in his own neighbourhood, and on the 12th February, 1851, he discovered the gold diggings in the Bathurst and Wellington districts, and by that time had ascertained the existence of gold sands in no less than twelve places. Satisfied with this result, he made formal application to the government, who heard him with unwilling ears, but could no longer dispute the fact. The discovery was promulgated, and on the 1st of May, 1851, on the day of the opening of the Great Exhibition at the Antipodes, it was made known that in Sydney great gold discoveries had been made, and the mania began. The government, however, were consistent, and grudgingly allowed the diggers to work, and grudgingly rewarded and employed Mr. Hargraves, though at length they did so, and commissioned him, Mr. Clarke, and Mr. Stutchbury, the government geologist, to prosecute the researches.

When the rush took place to the Victoria diggings, I was induced, in consequence of my former explorations of those regions, to offer my services to the government of New South Wales, to develope the district between the Ovens and the Tumut, with a view to open workings more accessible to the southern parts of that province, but my propositions were not acceded to, as they said they were not in a position to find funds.

Although the whole public had been aware of the existence of gold, they looked upon it as obtainable only by men of science, or accidentally, and it was not till the practical authority of Mr. Hargraves showed them that there was no barrier between them and the gold, and that any man could make large earnings by washing the soil in a pan or dish, that the working effectually began.

The discovery of gold in Canada, in 1850, is a parallel case to those already given. The place in the Chaudiere district where the gold fields exist, was actually named the Val D'Or by the first French discoverers or settlers. M. de Lery, a neighbouring seigneur, had found gold there for many years; and in 1847 it was publicly announced that gold had been discovered there in large quantities. This was, however, anterior to the Californian mania, and was therefore unheeded.

In 1850, the discoveries of gold in the Chaudiere river and in the neighbouring brooks, were confirmed, and a company was formed for working. In 1851, specimens of the stream gold were shown in the Great Exhibition by Mr. Logan, the government geologist, and by the newly formed Chaudiere Mining Company.f This district has since been found of considerable extent, and has been worked.

These examples of Scotland, Wicklow, the Ural, Carolina, California, Australia and Canada, are simply taken as in Mining Journal for 1848, p. 187. t Gold Notes, Wyld, p. 36.
stances of productive gold fields, the resources of which have been neglected for long periods, and a tardy recognition has been made. Many others might be brought forward, but they will perhaps be sufficient for those persons who are inclined summarily to dismiss the more detailed evidence which will afterwards be given as to the existence of gold in these islands. They will likewise serve as a caution to those who may be willing to receive as evidence of the nonexistence or non-productiveness of gold workings, the unfavourable opinions of men of eminence, and the negative testimony of long continued public neglect.

I am not unaware that there are instances of the discovery or promulgation of gold discoveries under other circumstances. The American discoveries were, as I have stated, at first the result of accident, and were afterwards systematically carried out. The researches made for the discovery of gold are of another class. These have resulted in its discovery in Oregon and in New Zealand, and there is a probability of their success in Natal. The settlers in Natal have not proceeded on a vague fancy that gold may be found, as coal was once sought in this country, and pit-shafts were sunk in Blackheath; but they proceed on rational grounds; first on the fact that gold was for a long period exported from the neighbouring regions by the Portuguese at Delagoa Bay; and next on the evidence of their people in Australia, that there is a similarity of structure between Australia and Natal. It might be that these explorations and workings might not result in the discovery of gold in Natal, but might prove failures. They are nevertheless fully justified. Another case of systematic exploration is by the expedition now out in Greenland, under Mr. Albert Robinson. It has been frequently reported that the Arctic Regions yielded gold; but although some of In the case of New Zealand, I discovered gold there in 1848, in company with my friend, Mr. Forbes; and in *I8i9,* in New Caledonia.
the stuff brought home failed to satisfy the assayers, such a circumstance is not conclusive. So far as Greenland is concerned, it is reputed to present resemblances of structure to the gold regions, and crystals of tin are reported from it, affording favourable indications. It is by the pursuit of researches, based on rational grounds, that we are justified in Natal, in Greenland, or in Britain, in seeking for further and conclusive evidence, which may guide us in our proceedings: at any rate, we are not obliged to rest satisfied with negative evidences; nor are we obliged, unless we choose, to shut our eyes to positive facts, because some people choose to believe there is no gold on no other ground but their own fancy, as they believe in dreams, gipsies, the Rochester knockings, or any vagaries of their imagination.

If permissible in any other branch of science, geology is at any rate a branch in which foregone conclusions and the doctrines of finality have no place. Geology, as a science, is the creation of the last half century, and its history is that of successive and important discoveries. The blackband ironstone, the anthracite coal field of South Wales, the coal of Cannock Chase, the iron districts of Northamptonshire and Cleveland, the deposits of coprolites, are all of recent discovery, and already minister usefully to the "public service. So too in manufactures dependent on minerals, there is much that is new. The soda manufacture has superseded that of kelp; the production of sulphur from pyrites has been effected on a large scale; in the iron manufacture new material, new fuel, new applications of blast, and new modes of making steel, have given it a vast extension; and so is it throughout. If the whole world of geologists tell the public there is no gold, the public are not obliged to believe them. The public may give Sir Roderick Murchison or Sir Henry Delabeche full credit for their discoveries, but are not, as a consequence, to accept their imprcssions or prejudices as of equal value, though I would show respect even to the hasty dicta of men who have rendered so great a service to the cause of science.

I have chosen to give examples in which gold, though readily discoverable, has escaped public notice; but though I have dwelt upon them at some length, as necessary for my argument, I do not wish to put it forward as a peculiarity attaching to gold. The same will be found in all mineral formations. Whole districts may be rich in a particular metal, which yet may escape recognition. Copper was only of late discovery in South Australia and New Zealand, but even in older settled countries the same circumstance may be noticed. Black-band iron-stone of course only became available from Mr. Mushet discovering the mode of its application; and Dr. Buckland's explorations for coprolites were made in consequence of the demand for guano; but Northamptonshire, which within the last two years has become an iron district, was not supposed to be a suitable locality for that manufacture. Cleveland, in Yorkshire, has likewise only recently become the seat of iron mining.

At Killarney a singular incident occurred. A gentleman discovered that the beach of the landing-place opposite the principal hotel is composed of lumps of lead ore, and obtained some of them for smelting, though he could not work the lode, as it lies at the water's edge, and a mineshaft would not be an agreeable neighbour to the hotel.

The history of silver working would, in many cases, be the parallel of that of gold working. It is true that in some places silver has been constantly worked, or at any rate worked for long periods, as in the Hartz, in Bohemia, and in Sweden; but in this country silver working has been subject to great vicissitudes. In the middle ages, and particularly in the reigns of the three Edwards, the silver lead mines, more especially at Combmartin, in Devon, were worked productively, and a considerable proportion of silver for the coinage is ascertained, from the Mint accounts, to have been of native origin. Silver workings, indeed, seem to have proved more profitable than those of gold. The latter metal, of native produce, has never been minted in England, though it has in Scotland; but silver has been coined repeatedly in special coins, from the time of the Edwards down to that of Anne. In the civil wars, Charles the First established a mint in Wales, to work up the silver with which he was supplied by Thomas Bushell; and the native silver being of better ley, was likewise most useful in coining the plate which was contributed by the royalist gentry and churchmen.-)-The silver lead mines for a time were nearly lost sight of, and the new corporation of the Mines Royal was not very successful in its exertions. Indeed the rich Welsh mines they leased to the enterprizing Sir Hugh Middleton, who thence obtained the wealth which he dissipated in the New River and other undertakings. From Middleton's hands, after a time they came into Bushell's, and then they were neglected again until Queen Anne's time.

Again, in the last century, and the early part of this century, the rich silver lead ores of Cornwall were much neglected, and there is very probably lead in existence containing five to ten pounds of solid silver per ton of metal. For that matter, copper has been turned out of the Cornish and other mines with large proportions of silver, and, as I shall have occasion to show, of gold; and at times speculators have got up and refined particular articles for the purpose of obtaining the precious metals from them. Such was the case with some heavy penny pieces some years ago, and likewise with some French copper coins.J A wellknown instance, within the last twenty years, was that of Ruding's Annals of the Coinage.

t See Bushell's Pamphlets before referred to. *X* Some persons will recollect the Mexican dollars with a yellow tinge, which have all disappeared in the melting pots of the refiners. the Spanish bells, which on the general sale of church property by the revolutionists in Spain, were bought up by some French speculators chiefly for the purpose of refining, though they were got at a low price. Such is the skill of the French refiners that it pays them for parting when there are only 3-10,000 of gold in silver; though in some continental government establishments, as much as 600-10,000 is considered requisite to meet the expense of parting gold and silver. Our own refiners are likewise very skilful, and make partings of all gold and silver ores coming into their hands. The Brazilian gold ores so treated, yield not only silver, but a considerable portion of the platinum and palladium of commerce. The supply of rhodium and of some other of the rarer precious metals is obtained from the refiners of London, Paris, and Marseilles. There is reason to believe, although London is the now great gold and silver market of the world, that much of the movement of the precious metals to the continent is not for purposes of trade, but for those of the refiners, who re-work them. Of late years, in consequence of the alterations of the London Mint, where a contract for refining is held by the Messrs. Rothschild, the processes are likely to be so effectively conducted as to produce a large revenue to this country, and limit the operations of the continental refiners. It will be kept in mind that refiners are here spoken of, and not assayers. It is the express business of the refiner of Californian gold, for example, to part the silver and other metals admixed, but it is the duty of the assayer most commonly to assay an ore or specimen for one or more metals only, without reference to the fractional quantities of other metals or elements. Thus an ore, of copper for example, containing fifteen per cent, of copper, and containing one pound of gold to the ton of metal, would not figure in the assayer's report—which would stand thus: copper 15, other substances innumerated 85, total 100; and in which the gold would only represent, say 00.005 or 00.006. In the example here taken, gold worth £50 per ton of metal would escape the notice of the adventurers.

I may perhaps properly refer in this place to some of those occasions on which the subject of the production of gold on a large scale has been prominently brought before the public. Of such a character were the schemes of the alchemists which gained such acceptance in the middle ages, but on which it is not necessary to dilate. They had the effect, as already observed, of withdrawing attention from legitimate gold working.

The extraction of gold from sand is a subject which has obtained more attention from chemists and other men of learning than from the public. Boyle, in various parts of his works, expresses the opinion that all sand contains more or less gold, and he likewise entertained the impression that gold was to be found in most ores. Like opinions as to the universal distribution of gold have been promulgated by many chemists and mineralogists; among these may be cited Becher, Lieberecht, and Cramer.

Becher. a chemist of some eminence in the eighteenth century, undertook to obtain gold with profit from the common sea sands, and entered into engagements with the States of Holland for establishing a mineral work on that foundation; but he did not succeed, as he says, through the jealousy of the mint master and assayer. A previous adventurer had equally failed. Becher seems to have been something of an alchemist, and wrote very much on what he called his mineral works. One of his books was published in London.

The basis on which Becher proceeded apart from his analysis was the existence of gold sands in rivers. Those of the Rhine have been worked by the gold washers for Becher, Minera Arenaria; Lewis, Commercium Philosophico-Technicum, p. 189.
many hundreds of years. The Roman writers do not men tion the Rhine as a gold stream, and Tacitus expressly states that the Germans had neither gold nor silver. The existence of gold there, is, however, matter of history for a long period;f according to the report of Reaumur on the gold rivers of France, presented to the Academy of Sciences, in 1718, the part of the Rhine between Strasburg and Philipsburg was chiefly worked, and the gold washers were licensed by the magistrates of Strasburg, who received as their portion four or five ounces per year; but the whole quantity obtained was supposed to be more considerable. The district in which gold is found is also more extensive as it reaches from Switzerland to below Philipsburg. The Aar and the Reuss, head feeders of the Rhine in Switzerland, are, likewise, gold streams. J According to a more recent account, the gold of the Rhine may be taken as now yielding above £1,800 yearly, that being stated as the net amount after cost of washing, &c.§

In the year 1718 the subject of the gold streams of France was brought before the Academy by M. Reaumur; in 1846 the resources of the Rhine were examined in a memoir read before the same body by M. Daubree. After detailing the many localities in which gold is found in the bed of that river, M. Daubree proceeded to an estimate of the total amount of gold contained in the bed, and this he reckoned, taking a very low average, at 36,000 tons of gold, a quantity far beyond the total amount of gold now in existence, which has been reckoned at £500,000,000 or £600,000,000, and far beyond the current resources of Australia and California. The value of these 36,000 tons Tacitus's Germania.
t Boyle's Works, vol. 5, p. 34; Reaumur's Report; Dictionnaire des Sciences Naturelles. *X* Lewis, Commercium Philosophico-Technicum, p. 185.
§ Dictionnaire des Sciences.
Mining Journal, 18i6.
would be near £3,600,000,000. M. Daubree in his memoir proposes to realize this amount, or something approaching to it, and explains his mode of working and refining, the properties of gold in the sand being very low, and confessedly below that of Siberia and Transylvania. To work out even the middle bed of the Rhine would in 1836 appear a mad and impracticable undertaking; now at any rate we may look upon it as within the compass of practicability from what we know has been done in the basin of the Sacramento, and what we know to be in progress among the tributaries of the Murray, so that it is by no means impossible the project of M. Daubree may be revived and again submitted to examination under more favourable antecedents. CHAPTER II.

CAUSES OF THE NEGLECT OF GOLD WORKING IN BRITAIN AND OTHER COUNTRIES. *Alchemy.—Discovery of America.—Geologists.—Erroneous Notions as to Gold Mining. — Want of Quicksilver. Assays.—Royalties.—Monopolies.*

In the last Chapter it was the endeavour to show that the richest gold deposits have remained neglected for considerable periods, notwithstanding manifest evidence of their existence, and that the neglect of the gold workings of Britain is not therefore to be received as a conclusive argument against their existence or productiveness. With reference to those points, I shall adduce testimony a little further on, and at present it may be useful to consider the causes, on which this neglect of gold working depends, and more particularly with reference to Britain. Some instances have been already given incidentally, but many circumstances have concurred in producing a result so prejudicial to social interests, as the neglect of Australia exemplifies. Among these causes may be classed:

Alchemy.

The Discovery of America.

Rival Mining Interests.

Want of Information as to Gold Workings, &c.

The course taken by Geologists and Geological Writers.

Erroneous Notions as to the Nature of Gold Deposits.

Erroneous Notions as to the Modes of Working.

The Scarcity of Quicksilver.

The Deficiency of Assays.

Government Royalties and Claims.

Monopolies.

At a period when, on the revival of learning, there was a disposition to resume the ancient modes of working, the contemporaneous revival of alchemy had a most prejudicial effect. It seemed useless to look for gold deposits supposed to be rare, when metals so abundant as lead and copper could be converted into gold. We cannot well doubt, from the accounts which have come down to us, that the alchemists in some of their experiments and public trials, did produce gold, it may be in some instances wittingly, in others unwittingly, having used metals in which gold existed, and having, in reality, performed the process of parting. We have ample testimony that, in modern times gold has been extracted from the inferior metals as delivered by the smelters, and as manufactured; and it must be reasonably assumed that gold was likewise found in them in the middle ages, and might very well be extracted from the large quantities used, and in the course of the various processes tried. Gold has great powers, and great virtues attributed to it in modern times, it is the greedy object of pursuit, and the ruler of souls, but, by the alchemists, the most extravagant qualities were attributed to this metal. Being supposed to represent the sun, it was designated Sol, the Great King, the Old Man, and various fanciful epithets in the devotional language of the adepts. Liquid and drinkable gold was thought to have wonderful virtues, and the mode of making it was long eagerly sought. In many minds all rational science was annihilated by these superstitions, and even by the greatest, alchemy was believed, as astrology was by the astronomers. Thus, even in the seventeenth century, Bacon and Boyle expressed their hankering for alchemy, and Newton and Flamsteed cast horoscopes, as it is said some eminent philosophers have done in this. The prevalence of alchemical pursuits certainly had a prejudicial effect on gold mining.

To show to what an extent extravagant notions were carried, a few extracts from writers of the seventeenth century may suffice. Bacon suggests an experiment for trying to make gold, and another experimentalist absolutely asserts the making of gold, and describes the process, though he avows he got only a few grains. Gabriel Plattes says, " And the reason why the hotter the country is, the richer the minerals are, can be no other but the same, that roasted meats are sweeter than boiled meats or raw meats." This sagacious lucubration passed through more than one edition.

Another writer enforces his views by names of weight. Moses Stringer says, " The products of all natural bodies may be reduced to two classes, viz. animal and vegetable, of which the latter comprehends not only plants, &c., but metals, minerals, &c., for the philosophers of this and the last age tell us (and that, too, with good reason), that 'tis highly probable they have a vegetable power; and that as the beds are emptied by the miners, so, after some time they recruit. Mr. Boyle has been already very large on that subject. Vide ejus Scept. Chym. Part 6, p. 962; Qualities of the Air, p. 18.f "

This certainly was Boyle's opinion,J as it had been Bacon's.§

The discovery of the American mines, likewise, withdrew the attention of the public from the home mines, and the more especially as very wrong ideas prevailed of the nature of the gold operations. From that period gold enterprize Gabriel Plattes' Discovery of Subterranean Treasure, ch. 8.

t Opera Mineralia Explicata, p. 8. *X* Boyle's Works.

§ Busbell's Pamphlet.

RIVAL MINING INTERESTS. 31 was directed abroad; and, whether in the shape of Sir Walter Raleigh's wild expedition to Guiana, the voyage to Hudson's Bay, or the general gold crusade of 1825, the tendency was equally adverse.

Home mining pursuits have had a like influence. At one time there has been a mania for copper mining, at another time for silver-lead mines. The interests, too, of those engaged in special mining, or in local mining, have been arrayed against gold workings, as against other mining enterprizes. The copper or tin interest opposes silver-lead working, the Cornishman speaks with prejudice and contempt of Welsh, Irish, or Scotch mining, and the native interest is arrayed against colonial and foreign enterprizes. When anything has been published on gold in Britain, or a company been brought forward for gold working, every mining captain gave his practical opinion against it, every mining man felt it his bounden duty to protest against it; and the more zealous published hostile letters and communications in the newspapers. Thus the market has been virtually closed against gold mining ventures, some have been stillborn, the prospectus being the epitaph; and those now in the field have to contend with every prejudice. The gold companies which have been projected have been mostly under the cover of being partly, or principally, copper companies, so great has been the indisposition against anything having gold for its pursuit.

One very great difficulty the public have had in arriving at accurate conclusions with regard to gold working, has arisen from the want of a special literature on this subject. While, as will be seen under the next head, there have been most erroneous notions propagated, there has been a want of standard works on gold. The best works embrace silver or other metals in their scope, and gold is treated with less attention than it merits. This defect is seen in every department. Thus there is no good enumeration of gold sites. The fullest are in Jacobs's History of the Precious Metals, and in Gold Notes, but they are far from complete. But, of nearly a hundred recognized gold sites in Britain, some half score only are enumerated in the latter work; and, on the Ordnance Geological Survey, the gold mines of Wales are reduced to one spot. The situation of the gold workings of America is, so far as the authorities are concerned, left in obscurity, dependent on the generalities or old statements of Humboldt. There is no full account of the geology of the several gold regions, the works treating on the subject being cheap digests for Californian or Australian diggers. In such works, too, the operations for raising and reducing gold are treated. In the numerous works on mineralogy, to which I have referred, the accounts of gold ores are by no means copious enough for the right understanding of the subject, or for the use of practical men. Thus the public have not access to the requisite information, and those who do learn must learn piecemeal, although there are ample materials from the works of the Greeks and Romans down to those of the present day, and some of the older works will be found the most valuable. Those who know how different the metallurgy of gold is from that of silver, may conceive that it is not compatible to treat of the two metals together. The finding of gold in dry and wet diggings, and in the state of dust, scales, and nuggets is a peculiarity of gold, as much as its chemical characteristics, and the working of the two metals is in few points similar. The remarks that I have made I do not mean to apply to English writers only, but equally to the French, German, and Spanish, so far as I have the opportunity of judging.

Gold metallurgy has, however, suffered as much from those who have written upon it as from those who have neglected it. The geologists and geological writers have, as a general rule, adopted the notion that gold is only to be found in particular districts, and is not to be found in Britain. From circumstances connected with its development, geology has become to too great an extent a study of classification and of fossil zoology, where it has not been pursued for geognosy alone. At all events, mineralogical considerations have less influence now than at a former period, when geology was less advanced, and oryctology, palaeontology, and the sciences of fossils less understood. Even those works which treat of the application of geology to engineering and mining, by treating mostly of the chief deposits of minerals, give very imperfect ideas of gold at any rate, nor do they give a complete view of any metal. Some parts of the subject are considered to belong to mineralogy, some to metallurgy, and some to chemistry. This is not from want of ability in the writers, for had gold been as favourite a subject as coal, it would have been as well treated.The public will find, in geological text books but little to guide them as to gold, and very little as to the gold regions of Britain, nor will the most eminent geologists give them any better encouragement. In the first place, they have not fully considered the subject; in the next, they act from preconceived notions; and, in the third place, even such as have seen gold districts, have not practically followed up gold explorations and gold working. As Professor Sedgwick very candidly stated in addressing the Geological section of the British Association at Hull, in comment on my paper, although he had found gold in some parts of Cumberland, he had paid little attention to the subject, because his inquiries were more directed to fossils.

It is partly owing to the geological writers that the prevalent impressions as to gold deposits have-been formed, though the alchemical writers broached the notion of the mother of gold. Till California and Australia forced parties Ansted's Geology; Rooke's Geology as a Science, applied to Engineeyng, &c.

D to alter their convictions, river deposits and gold sands were little considered, and attention was directed to find the central deposit, the mother vein, the mother of gold, from which the river basins have been supplied, and from which alone it was supposed was any solid or permanent result to be obtained. The search for the mother of gold has been a delusion for ages, and has withdrawn attention from those sources of wealth, which were available, and might have been advantageously worked.

Foiled in finding the mother of gold, or rich bunches as of copper or even silver, and finding the veins of gold in many places mere strings and specks, a reaction has taken place in opinion, and it had become till lately a settled opinion, and it is one still very generally entertained, that gold ores will not pay for working, and a discredit already attaches to quartz veins. Certain pattern ideas have been adopted from other metals for gold, and gold is expected to conform to them. Copper and lead are worked in large veins and lodes—therefore gold is only to be found in such a state. Coal, it is allowed, is of different geological constitution, and is admitted to be distributed in strata, but gold is not expected to present itself in any unfashionable condition, but only as theorists have prescribed for it. The theorist sketches out a generalization, to which nature is to conform, and the practical man does the same. As Canute laid down laws for the ocean in obedience to his courtiers, so do Cornish captains and miners lay down laws for the mineral kingdom. Tin at one time was tabooed to a western part of Cornwall, and its existence in the eastern districts was nullified. The Cornish authorities have pronounced their ukazes as to the existence of copper in other countries. Men who stood on the rich slabs of the Lake Superior district, or of Australia, pronounced that it was a bad enterprize to work for copper there, as the ore was so rich it could not hold down or be continuous. Undoubtedly the practical knowledge of a Cornish miner is most valuable, but from the want of the higher scientific instruction, which the government for so many years neglected to afford, this practical knowledge cannot safely be applied in other districts, indeed becomes absolutely mischievous. The chief causes of the disappointment which befell the American gold and silver mining companies, founded in 1825, was sending out such men, who contemptuously neglected the native processes, and unprofitably expended the shareholders' money. Those companies which survive, and which are at length worked with some profit, do so because they have at a fearful cost to themselves trained a staff. Between the Cornish miners who had empirical knowledge only and the Germans who had school knowledge, hundreds of thousands of English money have been wasted, and unless care be taken, the same process will be gone through by the new Californian and Australian gold companies. It is a fact which cannot be denied, that small companies are profitably working quartz in California with the Chilian mill, and yet none of the English companies are doing anything effective, and only the Agua Fria has remitted gold. There are many reasons why local or native processes in America or Cornwall should be effective, while more refined processes fail, just as in malting or in brewing, practice has ascertained, apart from science, the actual degrees or stages of temperature at which the operations should take place. Trevithick, it is true, by introducing the steam-engine into South America, unwatered the deep mines and enormously increased the produce, but it may be questioned whether since his day, and since the English have engaged in mining on that continent, they have really introduced improvements equivalent to the old modes of working, and certainly they have not got up to the old rates of produce.

Abbot on the Mines of England, p. 6; S. H. Thomas, Mining Journal, vol..10, p. 114.

The Gornish captain depends wholly on local incidents of country, capel, mundic, gossan, pryan, killas, elvan and cross-courses, with a tinge of superstition as to the divining rod, and though he has made Cornwall one of the finest mining districts in the world, and has shown a capability for mining elsewhere, out of his element he must be treated as a learner and not as a teacher. He has learnt a great deal of late years; he may learn more. He has learnt to work silver-lead and sulphur ores at home, copper in Cuba, Chile and South Australia, silver in Mexico, and jacotinga in Brazil: he may yet learn how to work gold in California, Australia and Britain.

While the search after the mother of gold leads the miner away from the gold fields, his prejudices equally beset him when he has got the gold ore to his hands. He knows how he treats copper and how he treats tin, and he has an indistinct glimmering that gold is to be treated in the same way, and if he cannot so obtain it, he neglects it. Gold is, however, distributed in such minute particles and atoms in many cases, that it is not under the same conditions, nor will the strongest stamps of Cornwall prove, in every case, the best apparatus for reducing gold ores. The miner cannot always tell when he has found a gold ore; for not being accustomed to its characteristics, he may pass by a very rich gold formation, and gold is found precisely in those rocks which he is accustomed to consider as waste and deads. I have seen many very rich gold ores in Australia and in England, which do not show a particle of gold to the naked eye, and barely reveal it to the microscope. Nothing, therefore, but a longer and more varied experience, and more liberal attainments than the common miner is likely to receive, will make him conversant with gold ores, and gold being so generally diffused in nature, its ores are very numerous indeed. Thus, undoubtedly, gold ores of very rich quality have escaped notice, or been rejected, as tin, copper, silver, lead and other ores have confessedly been lost sight of. Beyond this, as already observed, metal has been turned out of the smelting-house with large quantities of gold and silver left in it for the profit of refiners who may speculate in auriferous copper or argentiferous lead. Mr. Abbott says of Cornwall—" There is no doubt but there are now many mines throwing away silver ores, as copper has been, and no doubt gold."

The miner is not expected to be an assayer, but the mine assayer is not the most refined practitioner, f and the London assayer is not often called upon to display his skill. The London assayer, as has been stated by one of them having a very great practice, has ore sent to him with directions to make an assay for lead or copper only, to which he restricts himself, being limited to a moderate *fee,%* and although his experience may detect indications worthy of further study, he is not in a position to follow them up. It may be that the local assayer is likewise so limited, but at all events there is a great deficiency in the number of assays and in the scope of those that are made. It might be expected that the companies would maintain an assay establishment, and that assays would be made of every mineral found, but the directors grudge money spent in assays, and the mine captain would consider it as so much taken out of the pockets of himself and clan, and therefore the money of the shareholders is expended in what is called making discoveries, when minerals in sight would yield good returns. Mr. Mitchell, just referred to, who makes a great number of assays for mining companies and proprietors of minerals, states, " Iron and other pyrites are in many cases succesfully worked for the precious metals, yet in this country the mineral is seldom or ever employed, excepting in the manu

Abbot's Essay on the Mines of England, p. 16.

t Watson's Mining, p. 20; Abbot's Mines of England, p. 17.

J J. Mitchell, Mining Journal, 1847, p. 260.

facture of arsenious and sulphuric acids, and that only within the last few years, but many of the samples contain both gold and silver." Rich gossans, containing sixty ounces of gold, or two hundred and forty pounds worth to the ton, are neglected, and the same of other rich ores of gold. This is no new notion as to the neglect of gold. Boyle observed it,f and Cramer not only alluded to the neglect of gold ores, but he states distinctly that gold is dissipated by the bad processes employed,J for it may be observed that there are processes which crush the gold, and leave it so that it can be washed away, or that actually dissipate it in the very operation of reduction, and then it is said there is no gold, or the gold does not pay. I have no doubt this is now taking place in California.

By using wrong processes or neglecting old processes, gold ores are much maltreated, and the opportunity of realizing good workings is lost. The mode of sinking trial pits for gold to reach the bed rock is a process as well established in gold working as costeaning is in Cornwall, and yet it is mentioned with ridicule by English mining writers. It is considered by them perfectly absurd to sink pits in a river bed on the chance of finding gold,§ although there are hundreds of thousands of gold diggers who have done it, and who find it answer. Mr. John Phillips, who spent many years at the Real del Monte mines, in Mexico, considers however that great prejudice has arisen from neglecting the rude local mode of amalgamation, which he looks upon as the most effective.

The want of quicksilver, or the high price of it, consequent on the Almaden monopoly, and the enterprises of the J. Mitchell, Mining Journal, 1847, p. 266.

t Boyle's Works in various places.

X Cramer, p. 259; Becquerel, Comptes Rendus de 1" Academie de Science. § Abbot's Essay on the Mines of England; Manlow's Bargemoot Court. Phillips on Amalgamation; Railway Register, vol. 4.

Messrs. Rothschild, have interfered with the reduction of gold ores where it is necessary to resort to the amalgamation process.

The crown and government rights and claims have had a prejudicial effect on gold working, particularly in Britain. These pretensions resolve themselves into a prerogative right to all gold and silver mines, claim of exclusive working, claim to allow persons to work mines on their own lands on paying a royalty, or portion of the metal obtained, claim to allow persons to work for mines on the property of other people, claim to exclusive refining and minting, claim to the preemption of gold.

All these claims have been made and enforced in Britain, and several of them still exist, and have been used as arguments against gold companies. In all cases of the discovery of gold, it becomes doubtful whether the landowner, or lord of the manor, can grant a lease or obtain royalties, and whether the crown, the holder of royalties, or the grantees of the crown may not step in. The unsettled state of rights to gold workings is indeed as injurious as that to waste lands reclaimed from the sea or rivers. The crown made the corporation of Liverpool pay a sum of £100,000 for lands recovered by them from the Mersey, on the Birkenhead shore. The reclaiming of forty thousand acres from the sea has been prevented by the dispute of the crown and Duchy of Lancaster as to who should seize the land when the capitalists have succeeded in recovering it. The crown is such a hard taskmaster that few choose to come within its clutches. From a petty case of treasure trove to a gold mine, nothing comes amiss to the Exchequer. Much of the gold nuggetting has been carried on secretly for fear of the crown rights, and many Roman and medieval coins and relics have been melted to prevent the authorities from claiming them. In the case of the Wicklow gold field, the crown sent down a company of soldiers to take possession. In the case of working for precious stones near Cork, the same was done. The mines of most of the English districts have been made the subject of grants at various times, those of Cumberland and Wales have been claimed from the holders of the soil and of manorial rights, and even from crown grantees. As the seizure involved the loss of the inferior metal, as well as of the gold, it became the interest of landowners and miners not to disclose the existence of gold. In the case of gold mines, there are repeated cases of writs issued for inquisitions and of seizures made, affording precedents for the Wicklow case. A writ was issued in the 34th year of king Edward III. to John Jugg and Henry of Wisbeach, as follows: " Whereas, we are informed that certain mines of lead mixed with gold and lead ore, are found in the county of Salop, we will that the Barons of the Exchequer and the Treasurer may be certified of the manner of finding the said mines, and whether any metal hath been transported, and by whom." King Henry IV., by writ of Mandamus, dated the 11th of May, in the second year of his reign, commands Walter Fitzwalter, upon information of a concealed mine of gold in Essex, to " bring all such persons as he in his judgment thinks fit that do conceal the said mines, and bring them before the king and his council. " The High Commission Court and the Star Chamber, have ceased to exist, but these are the precedents on which lawyers act, and the arbitrary claims of the crown are well enough known even to miners, for they are enforced or attempted to be enforced, in all parts of the world. When I was in South Australia, the newly found copper mines were jeopardized by the prerogative claims of the crown; and, again, when the proclamation of the Wellington gold fields took place, the crown made pretensions, which the rapid march of events alone prevented it from enforcing. To go back; on the discovery of gold in Gloucestershire and Bedfordshire, in the last century, the crown grantees Sir John Pettus' Fodinie Regales, p. 34.

seized the mines and worked them. One argument used against the proprietor of the Cwmheisian mines, and those who attempted to work them, was, that the gold veins constituted a mine royal, and would be seized by the crown. Further on, the subject of crown rights will be more fully treated. Here they are brought forward to account for the indisposition towards the working of goldmines and deposits caused by the operation of these claims.

The last cause affecting gold mining, to which I shall advert, is the operation of monopolies. For five centuries the right to gold and silver working in England has been the subject of monopolies created by the crown, and one, or rather two of these in one, still subsists. This is the corporation of the Mines Royal Company, the amalgamated representative of the old Mines Royal Company, and of the Mineral and Battery Company, created and incorporated by Queen Elizabeth, and which, by the grants and powers of the two corporations, claims the gold and silver mines of England, Wales, and the greater part of Ireland. It was this corporation which seized the Gloucestershire and Bedfordshire gold mines. In some districts there are competing claims to royal mines, as those of the crown and Duchy of Lancaster, in Lancashire, and the representatives of these conflicting pretensions might embarrass persons attempting to work gold. The Duchy of Cornwall department has taken upon itself to lease the working of gold ores on some of its properties.

There are also conflicting claims of paramount lords, lords of manors, and freeholders, and as to the operation of former crown grants.

The causes already brought forward as affecting gold mining, at one time or another, are numerous enough, and it may be affirmed quite sufficient to account for the little that is done in gold mining in Britain, and the apathy shown towards it.

CHAPTER III. HISTORY OF GOLD IN BRITAIN. *Iberians.—Phenicians.—Discovery of Tin through Gold. Romans.—Queen Boadicea.— Cunobeline.—Irish Kings. Henry III.—Edward I.—Edward II.—Edward III. Scotch Kings. — Henry IV.—Alchemists.—Henry VI. Henry VII. —Lanarkshire.— Grants by Queen Elizabeth. Thomas Bushell.—Lord Bacon. —Charles tlie Second's Laboratory.—Prince Rupert.—Boyle.—Acts of William and Mary to encourage Gold Working.—Mania in Queen Anne's Time.—Sir Alexander Murray.— Wicklow.— Victorian Gold Workings.*

Of the existence or working of gold in England at an early period, we have no definite record. The doubts which have been entertained as to the existence of gold, and the neglect which has commonly prevailed, have prevented researches from being made on this subject.

The earliest writings we have at all referring to gold in Britain, are those of the Romans, but the arrival of that people, in the island was only a comparatively remote event. The Belgians, in the south, were acknowledged to be an immigrant population, but even the Celts, Britons, or Welsh of the rest of the island, were not aboriginals. Earlier populations have been indicated. Relics have been found of a low Scythic or Tartaric population, possibly allied to the Laps, and who occupied the whole of Scandinavia, and probably a greater portion of the north of Europe. With this low population, members of another branch of the same race, but of a higher type and more cultivated minds, came in contact, by invasions from the south. These were the Euskardians, or Iberians, who at one time occupied the whole south of Europe, and were the authors of its earliest civilization. To the ruder members of this race, what are commonly called the Druidic monuments, to be found from India to the far west of the British world, have been assigned. Among the more cultivated members of this race have been reckoned the Phenicians, Carthaginians, and Etrurians. By these Iberians, and not by the Celts, it is supposed the rivers have been named.

Traces of this Iberian population are supposed to be found in the Silures of South Wales,f and in the so-called Spanish population of the west of Ireland, and it is to the Iberians, and not to the Phenicians, that the earliest commerce with these islands has of late been attributed. Of the tin trade we have records, but it has been suggested that the first expeditions of the Iberians were for gold and not for tin. Whether Iberians or Phenicians, came here, and whether they exported gold or tin, there must have been some motive for the expedition. The common assumption is, that the Phenicians came here for tin, the Phenicians being, with many writers and antiquaries, the ready instruments and available and assignable cause for everything, as with the vulgar in many countries Solomon Ben Daoud, Alexander or Iskander, and Napoleon, are the grand authors and constructors of everything natural or constructed, for which a maker is to be named. It has, however, been well observed, that the Celts, supposing them to be the aborigi Hyde Clarke, in Wyld's Popular Atlas; Von Humboldt, Essays on the Euskardians; James Fergusson, Dissertation on the Iberians, in the Introduction to his Architecture.

t Ibid. nals of Britain, were not in such an advanced state as to be the discoverers of tin, nor were they a seafaring people, likely to carry the metal so found on a chance speculation to the south. The Iberian race, if the Phenicians and Etrurians be rightly included in it, were addicted to seafaring pursuits. Of these populations, the western branches were much more likely to make expeditions from Spain or South Gaul to Britain, than the Phenicians were, to whom it would have been a distant and protracted enterprise.

In the view taken, the Iberians of Spain came to Britain on a gold finding or nuggetting expedition, as the Spaniards in after centuries made the round of every river and country of America. It is observed, " River washings, there can be no doubt, were the chief ancient sources of gold and tin. Stream working could be rudely carried on in the bed of the Phasis, or in the rivers of Spain and Cornwall, as in this age, in the streams and valleys of the Murray and the Sacramento. These workings were, however, more difficult to carry on, as the metal washers, in a rude state, went through greater hardships, and could less readily get food than even the gold finders of California. The moment, too, that a gold finding became productive, then, as the Indians have done in Sonora, in our days, wild tribes would pour down, strip the miners, and drive them away, but never set to work in their stead; thus the sources of supply must have been precarious.

It was, however, to Spain that the Phenicians directed their chief efforts. The discovery of that great country, rich in the precious metals, gave them an independent source of supply. It may be that the Phenicians, like the Etruscans, were members of the great Iberian or Euskardian race, and that they were drawn to Spain by ruder members of their race, or to support some declining tribe, yielding before the wild forefathers of the Basques, or before a Celtic invasion." Gold Notes, Wyld, p. 4.

On this view, the known facts admit of a much more satisfactory explanation than any other yet proposed. The original visit to Britain, and the regular intercourse with it, is accounted for. It may seem strange to suggest that the ancients were engaged in gold nuggetting expeditions, but there is no good ground for disputing it. That they did obtain gold from rivers their naturalists and geographers tell us, that they resorted to Spain for such purposes, admits of as little question, and the voyage of the Argonauts to the Phasis, if involved in more obscurity, may still be admitted as a proof. When a new excitement for gold working sprang up in the sixteenth century, the Spaniards sent out expeditions for like purposes, and now, in the nineteenth century, zealous adventurers prospect every stream of California and of Australia, and gold-finding expeditions search in Texas, Oregon, Vancouver's Island, Peru, New Zealand, and South Africa.

On this view, too, the discovery of tin, and the trade in it, are more readily accounted for. Gold was then known to be a widely distributed metal, tin a rare one, and unless Banca tin first arrived from the east, would not be known in the old seats of civilisation until the discovery of Britain. The presence of gold in tin washings is one of the acknowledged facts in the history of gold, and we shall again have occasion to refer to it for other purposes, but it may be here remarked that tin is found in gold countries, not only in Britain, but in Malacca, in Bohemia, in Wicklow, and in Chile, and myself and others have lately found it in the gold workings of Australia. Gold finding would be the natural precursor of tin workings in a stanariferous district. At an early age, gold mining did not exist, nor did tin mining. It was gold nuggetting or washing, and it was tin washing or streaming, and from stream works was for a long time the chief supply of tin as of gold.

The expeditions made to Britain for gold, became the Dr. Aquila Smith, Mining Journal, vol. 11, p. 47.

origin of tin streaming, and of the Iberian or Spanish settlements in Cornwall, South Wales, and in Munster and Connaught, which were principally in the western or gold district. When the rivers in these islands had been well nuggetted, or richer diggings elsewhere had drawn off the adventurers, the gold trade would fall off, and in time be forgotten by foreigners, but the tin trade would remain. Events in Spain weakened the connection of the Iberians with their settlements in these islands, and the Celtic invasions must have materially affected them, so that in the time of Tacitus the Silures alone remained in Britain to represent the Iberian race, as the Basques, in Spain, now represent it there. The Romans, who succeeded to the dominion in Spain, would hear little of the gold trade, and the intercourse of the Iberians, or Spanish Phenicians, would be attributed to the tin trade alone.

It is not without probability that gold was still produced in small quantities, but that it was used solely for domestic purposes. It would be obtained from the tin streams and occasionally in nuggets and scales, from the rivers of Wales and North Britain. It has been supposed that the gold ornaments and weapons of the Iberian and British and Irish chiefs, found in tombs and elsewhere, are of metal obtained from river washings. I have not had the opportunity of trying and assaying any of these torques or other ornaments, but so far as can be judged from description and appearance, they seem to be of very pure gold, and being softer, would be more readily worked. It may be assumed that the gold ornaments of the nations of antiquity were generally of this character, and that alloy for the purpose of hardening and adulteration was of later introduction. It is possible that the strange pits, close to each other, commented upon by Mr. W. D. Saull and others, may be in some cases the remains of gold workings.

Gold Notes, Wyld, p. 24; Kane, Industrial Resources.

The opinions of the Romans as to the existence of gold in Britain seem to have been much divided. The hope of obtaining the precious metals has been attributed to them on the ground of passages in Strabo and Tacitus. The words put into the mouth of Agricola, by Tacitus, are, *Fert Britannia aurum et argentum et alia rnetalla, pretium victorice.*

The allusion of Tacitus is ambiguous, but it does attest the existence of gold and silver in Britain, and it may be that it admits of the interpretation, that the gold treasures of Lanarkshire and Aberdeenshire were worked at an early period. It is possible that the Iberians may have nuggetted the streams of Cornwall, South Wales, and the basin of the Shannon, and left little for the Romans, but except where there was such a river as the Shannon they are little likely to have penetrated far inland. We know that they did not rifle the Lanarkshire gold field, for large treasures were obtained from it in the sixteenth century, and yet the Caledonians may have got gold where it was to be found in every stream, and have offered Agricola inducements for such an expedition.

The strongest evidence of the acquaintance of the Romans with the existence of gold in Britain, is to be found in the circumstance that Pliny knew that gold is found in tin, and expressly states so in his Natural History.f He would not learn this in reference to the Banca tin mines; it is little likely that this fact was obtained from the supposed tin workings in Spain, and we may very fairly refer it to the observations of the Romans in Cornwall.

Cicero, writing at the time of the original invasion, so far gives countenance to the idea that the Romans were brought here by traditions of the precious metals, for he writes to Atticus, in stating the news of the expedition, to inform him how those expectations were disappointed, and what little Tacit. Vit. Agric.

t Plinii Hist. Nat., lib. 35, o. 16. hope there was of Quintus Tullius, a chief officer in the expedition, getting anything by it. He writes:—" *Etiam illud jam coynitum, neque argenti spiculum esse ullum in ilia insula, neque vllam spent procda; nisi ex mancipiis.*" " This," says Cicero, " is already found out that there is not a fragment of silver in that island, nor any hope of prize-money, except from slaves." Again, " *A Quinto fratre et a Ccesare accepi ad 9 Kalend. Novemb. literas confectas Britannia; obsidibus acceptis, nulla prceda, imperata tamen pecunia, datas a littoribus Britannia;.*" " I have had letters from Britain, both from my brother Quintus and from Caesar, and hostages have been taken, and requisition made for money, but there will be no prize-money."

Although we cannot absolutely identify the ancient workings, there are assertions that the Romans worked gold in four localities: at the Poltimore mines, in Devonshire; at the Oogofau mines, in Carmarthenshire; at the Gold Scoop mine, in Cumberland; and the Lanarkshire Hills. The two latter places I have been in, and I have seen full accounts of the Poltimore works, but of the Oogofau I know nothing. That the works are ancient workings is evident, but whether they are of the Romans, or of some more ancient civilized people, may be matter of conjecture, but I was much struck by the circumstance that the Lanarkshire gold field is encircled by strong Roman camps, and is passed by a road, as if the workings were under military protection. The local legend is, that the lead was found in seeking for gold, and Glengonnar, which in Erse signifies poisonous waters, is stated to have its name from the poisonous qualities given to its waters by those lead workings, and which they always resume on the lead workings being put in activity, causing death to the sheep and other animals which may drink of the waters. It should be observed upon this, that in the time of the Romans that Epistle to Atti-

cus.
district was not occupied by an Irish speaking people. The workings I have seen are well cut by hammer and chisel, and from the shape it is my opinion that the mine produce and deads were carried out in bags on the shoulders of men. To economize labour, the form of the galleries or level is such as will just clear a moderate sized man, being narrow at the feet, wide at the shoulders, and falling in again at the head. Those of Gold Scoop, which I carefully investigated, were very beautiful and even. Where the rock becomes too hard, or a considerable obstacle is met with, the gallery takes a sharp turn. It is very desirable that what are called Roman workings in Britain should be examined by some one conversant with the *cloaca;* and *emissaria* of the Romans in Italy.
A legend that occupied the attention of the antiquarians of the seventeenth and eighteenth centuries, though on what evidence does not appear, was, that Queen Boadicea obtained gold in Essex. Moses Stringer says, " That the mines of these parts were early known," appears yet further, from what some authors write of Queen Boadicea's extracting much gold out of English minerals and earths. To this may be added the testimony of another author, who was well acquainted with the product of his country, who says, " *Calles Britannia; fertiles sunt auri," i.e.* "The lands of Great Britain contain great quantities of gold." Mr. Stringer does not state his authorities. It is elsewhere asserted that Cunobeline, Prince of the Trinobantes, coined at Cameloduhum gold obtained from a mine in Essex.f

The authenticity of the Irish legends is not perhaps greater, but they are precise as to the existence of gold in a locality where we know it has been obtained, for they refer to the neighbourhood of the Wicklow workings. J Opera Mineralia Explicate, p. 8.
t Sir John Pettus' Fodinae Regales, p. 32. *X* Moore's History of Ireland, vol. 1, p. 10!).
K

We have no evidence, or even tradition or inference, as to gold workings in the old English or Anglo-Saxon times, except an obscure statement of Muses Stringer about King Canute. Had gold been accessible, the old English or Anglo Saxons would have sought for it, but Celtic slaves seem to have been the chief booty and the chief trade in the north. Whether the English or so called Danish invaders of Ireland, were prompted by the Irish gold, is equally undeterminable.

During the middle ages nuggetting must occasionally have taken place, but the Norman claim to gold and silver, as royal peculiar property, checked open gold working. In the time of Edward I. however, we get abundant evidence that the existence of gold was well known, both pure and in combination with other metals, as silver was. From this time for above a hundred years, we may trace a strong feeling for gold and silver mining, of which there is evidence enough in the records; but towards the time of Richard II. the alchemists had obtained a hold of the public mind, and gold mines were less looked after than the transmutation of gold from other metals, till at length the ignorance of the alchemist was combatted by the ignorance of the priest, and the multiplication of the precious metals was first anathematized by the church and then by the legislature. Whether the mania for gold or silver mining in England, in the thirteenth and fourteenth centuries, originated at home or was imported from abroad, does not appear, though miners from Bohemia were certainly invited. One result of the mania was the determination of a number of gold sites; indeed the gold districts were better known in the fourteenth century, than in the eighteenth or nineteenth. With regard to the produce of gold, we have no record, but the produce of silver was con

Opera Mineralia Explicata, p. 9.
siderable. The coinage accounts do not appear to me to present any indications of a large home supply of gold, nor is there any mention of native gold coined. Most of what was produced was very likely smuggled and worked up by the jewellers, and that some was produced is to be inferred from the sedulous attention to gold mining in districts known to contain that metal, and where I myself have identified it. With a few exceptions, none of the eastern counties are referred to in gold grants, and it is to be presumed, therefore, that the speculators proceeded on facts, and not on imagination.

The earliest record we have as to gold mines, is a writ (the 47th Henry III.) directed to the Sheriff of Devon, requiring him not to allow gold and copper mines to be occupied until the King shall give orders.j-It is stated that in this reign the Keswick gold was discovered. There is a grant of mines of gold and silver in Devon of the 27th of Edward I.J In the 29th year of this reign is a doubtful reference to the mines royal in Birland, in Devon,§ and a commission of inquiry as to mines royal in that county.

The reign of Edward II. is also scanty in records; in the 12th and 15th year of that reign, however, there were grants to prospect for gold and silver in Devonshire.

The proceedings in Scotland, as to gold mining, are considered under the head of that country, but they show that there was a concurrent movement in favour of gold and silver mining.

In Edward Ill's, reign we get fuller records. In the 11th of that King, G. Suthrop or Southrop was appointed warden of the mines of gold and silver within the counties of Cornwall and Devon.If In his 28th year he Ruding's Annals of the Coinage, vol. 1. p. CI; Jacobs on the Precious Metals; Plowden's Reports, pp. 319, 327.
t Ruding's Annals of the Coinage, vol. l,p. 60. *X* Cottonian MSS. Otho Ex. § *Ibid. Ibid.* If *Ibid.* leased his mines of gold and silver to John Hanner and Herman Kainsthorpe, of Bohemia. This has only the authority of Holinshed. In his 32nd year he granted to John Ballanter and Walter Bolbolter all his mines of gold, silver and copper in the county of Devon, for two years.-f-At the expiration of this grant another was made. J In the 37th year of this reign there was a grant of all mines of gold, silver, lead and tin in the county of Gloucester,

to Wm. Nottingham, for seven years.§ In the 37th year was a grant of mines of gold and silver, in the counties of Devon and Somerset, to William Nottingham, by indentures between him and the King. This grant is twice recorded.If

Copper was generally claimed as a mine royal on account of its containing gold and silver; the tinners however were privileged to work within the Duchy of Cornwall, and the lead miners in Peakland. Ballanter, and Bolbolter paid the first year of their royalty, which was a fixed sum, but they made no return in the second year, as they were reported dead. It must be observed, that this grant, for a short date, was in the nature of a commission of inquiry, or right of prospecting for gold and silver. Some of the grants which are referred to, were absolute grants of existing gold and silver mines for long periods; others were simple permissions of the class just defined. If the evidence of gold mines rested solely on these medieval writs, their existence would be open to doubt, for we do not find that the prospectors or grantees made any return to the Exchequer for gold, though they did of silver, of which two instances are mentioned.ff Holinshed Chronicles.

t Plowden's Reports, p. 16; Pettus' Fodinae Regales, p. 34; Opera Mineralia Explicata, p. 17. *X* Cottonian MSS. Otho E x.

§ Cottonian MSS. Otho E x. *Ibid. Ibid.* Plowden's Reports, p. 319.

tt Plowden's Reports, pp, 319, 317; Ruding's Annals of the Coinage, vol. 1, p. 61.

The grants are seldom made, except to districts such as Cornwall and Devon, where we have independent evidence of gold deposits, and therefore the remainder may be considered as affording fair presumption of gold having likewise been found. Many of these grants may be presumed to have originated in the knowledge that gold had been found in particular districts by the tinners, miners, and local population, and by the desire to get possession of the localities, and reach the mother vein of gold. Some seem to have been granted to foreigners, with particular privileges of refining or parting gold from gold bearing ores, and then parties may have obtained such grants on the knowledge or speculation that gold was to be obtained from particular ores.' The negative fact, that no native gold was returned to the Exchequer, or mint, is not worth much, for gold workers, where there are royalties, or workmen or slaves employed in gold working, are always desirous to conceal or smuggle gold, for which they have great facilities. The sands of the Rhine, which have been worked for centuries, have only yielded paltry royalties. Workings, which have been known to realise six hundred ounces in one year, have paid three or four ounces in royalties to the magistrates of Strasburg. The river washings of India yield no revenue, or an inconsiderable one to the English government, the gold washers representing themselves as too poor to pay. The Indians of South America have long smuggled gold, and those employed in the mines there pilfer all they can. In Australia, those who can evade licenses do, and even the optional charge for escort is not willingly met. Without an ounce entering the Exchequer, many pounds' weight of gold might have been yearly raised in Britain, as they have since. It is possible that some of the alchemical operations were carried on by refiners to evade the royalties or interference of the government authorities. Where the crown claimed the right of minting, although the process was rude, and the coins hammerstruck, it would be a long while before the holder of gold would get it back; in coining a delay takes place even with the modern mints. Governments, in those days, were not always punctual in paying debts, their functionaries were well exercised in extorting fees and bribes, and where there was a preemption right, the trader would not get the best price.

In the case of the grant to Ballanter and Bolbolter, it is noticeable that they paid the first year's royalty, so that it is to be presumed the grant was considered worth something.

In the 7th year of Edward III. the government was informed that a mine of copper, mixed with gold and lead, had been found on the lands of Robert Brown, in Shropshire, and enquiry was directed accordingly to ascertain the facts and enforce the crown rights. In the 34th of the same reign, another like writ is found as to a reputed gold mine in Essex.f No answer to these mandates is recorded.

According to Prynne, a statute was passed, by Edward III., in the 12th and 15th years of his reign, giving greater liberty for mining, and so far limiting monopoly. This statute allows all persons to dig for gold and silver in their own lands, and refine and coin it, on paying half the gold and one-third of the silver, under inspection of such officers as the king should appoint. This is a very important measure, and of course limits all subsequent grants for working and prospecting. This statute is not in the books, and was not brought forward in the Earl of Northumberland's case, which is so fully reported,§ but serves to some Plowden's Reports, p. 324.

t Pettus' Fodinse Regales, p. 34.

X Cottonian MSS. Otho E x.; Prynne's Aurum Reginae, p. 128; Ruding's Annals of the Coinage, vol. 1, p. 61. § Plowden's Reports.

extent to explain the discrepances in the contradictory precedents adduced for the crown and the earl. A grant of mines was therefore only of those in the possession of the crown, or of those which might be discovered, and a permission for prospecting might or might not convey the right of working gold mines on any one's property. It is possible that private gold and silver mines were worked and held under this statute, and which would be one circumstance accounting for the absence of crown receipts of gold.

Altogether, the reign of Edward III. is as remarkable for its mining history, as it is for so many characteristics, and affords good proof of the energy of that prince. Holinshed says that Edward III. paid great attention to his gold and silver mines. It must be observed that the incidents here narrated are only scraps, as it were, from the records of a long reign, writs without any return, scattered accounts of partial receipts, discovered by the industry of individual antiquaries,-and hereafter, it is to be hoped, to be increased, when public attention becomes more closely interested in the subject of gold. Although I have brought together many facts, which form a large aggregate, I shall most likely be told of many that I have neglected; but I shall be satisfied to bear this blame, if a foundation is laid upon which others can more profitably work.

Although we have so little to guide us as to the actual receipt of gold and silver, yet it is to be presumed that the grants of such minerals were worth something, as reversions of such grants were actually obtained before the subsisting grants run out. The grantees, too, are by name the most powerful in the land, princes, regents, kingmakers, and where a person of less note is named, it is a learned priest, or some skilled foreigner, in whose speculations the mighty would have part.

In the 1st year of Richard II., we find a grant made, Ilolinshed's Chronicle.
by the infant king and his council, of certain mines of gold in the county of Devon. In the 2nd year of this reign, is a grant to Henry Burton, of mines holding gold and silver, in the counties of Cornwall, Devon, and Somerset, f In the 5th year is a giant of mines of gold and silver, in the counties of Devon, Somerset, and Gloucester.J In the 8th year, by letters patent, dated 11th June, is a grant to Richard Wake, Clerk, of the right of digging and searching for mines of gold and silver, in the county of Devon.§ In the 11th year, is a grant of mines of gold and silver in the counties of Gloucester and Somerset. In the 20th year, is a grant of mines and gold and silver, in the kingdom of England, to Henry Derby, for the term of five years.1f

The grants made of the rights to gold and silver had no doubt the usual prejudicial effect of monopoly, in checking enterprise, as they have now, and the proceedings of the alchemists gave, as it were, the finish to the gold mining mania. Many ludicrous statements were made of the production of gold by the alchemists, and very much money was spent in idle essays. In various quarters alarm was created, the king was afraid he should lose his royal monopolies; the church, that the devil was using the alchemists as the stalking horse; and even parliament was frightened for the public liberties, if that very loose authority, Moses Stringer, is to be trusted. He says, " After Raymond Lully and Sir George Ripley had so largely multiplied gold, the Lords and Commons, conceiving some danger, that the regency having such immense treasure at command, would be above asking aid of the subject, and might become too arbitrary and tyrannical, made an act against multiplying Cottonian MSS. Otho Ex. t *Ibid. Ibid.*

§ Plowden's Reports, p. 317; Cottonian MSS. Otho Ex.; Pettus' Fodina; Regales, p. 317.
Cottonian MSS. Otho Ex. *Ibid.* gold and silver, which made it death to attempt it, or use such tools, instruments, vessels, and furnaces, as were then used about such operations."
The only other incident of the reign of Henry IV. in relation to gold, was the presumed discovery of a gold mine in Essex, f

Henry VI. granted a monopoly for twelve years to the Regent Duke of Bedford, or rather the Duke did to himself, of all the gold and silver mines in England, (or, according to one account, in Devon and Cornwall,J) as the boy king, his nephew, was only seven years old.§ This grant was worked effectually, so far as silver was concerned, for in one year the royalty paid into the Exchequer amounted to thirty-six pounds; but there was no gold.

In the 6th of Henry VI. was a grant of mines, holding gold and silver to Richard Carson, for the term of twenty years,1f but, in the 17th, is a record of a reversion of the Duke of Bedford's grant for Devon and Cornwall, to John Sollers, for twenty years, including gold, and silver, and lead, containing gold and silver.

We have seen one record of an appointment of warden of the king's mines; but, in the time of Henry VI., we find that the mining department was regularly organised. In the 21st year of this reign, is an appointment of Robert Burton, as comptroller of mines of gold, silver, copper, aurichalch, and lead, and mines containing any gold and silver.j-f The office of comptroller had reference only to Opera Mineralia Explicata, pp. 9, 255.
t Ruding's Annals of the Coinage; Pettus' Fodinae Regales, p. 37; Opera Mineralia Explicata, p. 18; Plowden's Reports, p. 317. *X* Cottonian MSS. Otho E x.
§ Opera Mineralia Explicata, p. 19; Pettus' Fodinae Regales, p. 38; Plowden's Reports, p. 317.
Plowden's Reports, p. 320. *H* Cottonian MSS. Otho E x.
Plowden's Reports, p. 324; Pettus' Fodinae Regales, p. 39. tt Cottonian MSS. Otho E x.
mines royal. In the 23rd year, is an appointment of the Marquess of Dorset, as seneschal of the king's mines of gold, silver, copper, lead, &c., and of mines containing gold and silver. In the 29th year, Adrian Spenke, a priest, was made governor of the king's mines in Cornwall and Devon.f

In the 30lh of Henry VI., John Bottwright, a priest, the king's chaplain, was made comptroller of all the king's mines of gold, and silver, copper, brass, and lead, within Cornwall and Devon,J and in the next year provost and governor of all mines of copper, tin, and lead, containing gold or silver in those two counties.§ The separation of silver from lead ores was a recognised operation carried on to a considerable extent, and it seems to have become a practice to obtain gold from such silver, and likewise from the silver contained in copper, or from the copper direct. These two metals, with occasional nuggets from tin streams, seem to have been the chief source of gold in the south; and in the north some must have been obtained from nuggets. Whether the gold was parted or separated by private refiners, or at the mint, seems uncertain. At any rate, Bottwright was required to refine the gold and silver at his own expense, though in some cases persons were required to bring the gold and silver direct to the mint, and the mint did work up native silver.

In the 27th year of this reign, is a demise of mines of gold and silver, and of lead and copper, holding gold and silver, for fifty years.%

In the 34th year of his reign, Henry VI. granted to the Duke of York all mines of gold and silver, and all other Cottonian MSS. Otho Ex. + *Ibid. X* Opera Mineralia Explicata, p. 20; Watson's Compendium of British Mining, p. 58; Pettus' Fodinas Regales, p. 40; Plowden's Reports, p. 325. § Opera Mineralia Explicata, p. 20.

Plowden's Reports, p. 320; Ruding's Annals of the Coinage. If Cottonian MSS. Otho E x. metals containing gold and silver, within the counties of Cornwall and Devon, for twenty-one years. The royalty is not named. Richard was then Duke of York, and his son Edward, afterwards King, seems to have paid considerable attention to gold and silver mining, and perhaps extorted this grant from his weak rival. In the 38th year is a grant to John Ormond, of the mines of gold and silver in Devon, for twenty-two years, j

Prynne says, that notwithstanding the severe statute of Henry IV. his grandson, Henry VI. countenanced alchemists, and gives examples of commissions.J The King thought it safest to include priests and monks among the commissioners.

The statute was not altogether a dead letter, for in the 7th year of Edward VI. one Eden was found guilty of felony on his own confession, for practising to make the philosopher's stone.§

The wars of the Roses interfered with mining and every other pursuit; but Warwick, the kingmaker, obtained from Edward IV. another of those pernicious monopolies, in a grant for forty years of all mines of gold and silver on the north of Trent. In the 1st year a grant had been made to John Nevill de Montacute, of all mines containing gold and silver in the counties of Devon and Cornwall, for the term of his life, being the only example of a life grant. 1 In the 12th of his reign, the same King gave a concession to Gallius Lynn, Wm. Marriner, and Simon Pert, to dig and search within the counties of Somerset and Gloucester for Sir John Pettus' Fodinae Regales, p. 34; Plowden's Reports, p. 325; Opera Mineralia Explicata, p. 21. t Cottonian MSS. *X* Wm. Prynne Aurum Reginae; Cottonian MSS. Otho E x. § Sir John Pettus' Fodinae Regales, p. 85. Plowden's Reports, p. 326; Pettus' Fodinaa Regales, p. 42; Opera Mineralia Explicata, p. 22; Cottonian MSS. H Cottonian MSS. Otho E x. mines of lead, tin or copper, containing silver or gold, for the term of five years. It seems from these grants that the gold fever had rather revived. In the 18th year of his reign, Edward granted to Wm. Goderswick and Dodderick Waverswick or Naylerswick, who seem to have been Netherlanders, all mines of gold, silver, copper and lead in Northumberland and Westmoreland, for ten years.f

As the history of gold mining in the middle ages has been but little treated of, and it will be requisite to refer to these records again under the several counties, it may be useful to publish a document, which gives a much fuller list than has yet appeared. The following is a summary of writs and records, preserved in a mutilated and burnt Latin MSS. of the Cottonian Library in the British Museum,J from which an abstract is made of those relating to gold, which may be found useful for reference. This was perhaps drawn out for the use of the lawyers, in the case of Queen Elizabeth against the Earl of Northumberland.

(47th Henry III. writ as to gold mines of Devon.—Ruding i.p.60.)§ 27th Edward I. grant mines gold and silver in Devon. 29th Edward I. reference to the mines royal in Birland, in Devon, and ordering enquiry as to the contentions of the abbot and miners.

Ditto commission of enquiry into the state of the mines royal in the county of Devon.

12th and 15th Edward II. grant to prospect for gold and silver in Devon. Plowden's Reports, p. 326; Pettus' Fodinae Regales, p. 42; Opera Mineralia Explicata, p. 22. t Plowden's Reports, p. 318; Pettus' Fodince Regales, p. 44; Opera Mineralia Explicata, p. 23; J. Y. Watson, Compendium of British Mining p. 58.

J Otho E x.

§ Insertions made between ( ) are from other authorities, to make the list more copious.

(7th Edward III. gold mine found in Shropshire.—Plowden, p. 324.) 11th Edward III. G. Suthrop appointed warden of the mines of gold? and silver within the counties of Cornwall and Devon. 12th Edward III. King granted in parliament permission for persons to work gold and silver on their own lands, under inspection of the crown officers. (32nd Edward III. grant to Ballenter, &c. of gold, &c. mines in Devon.—Plowden, p. 316.) (28th Edward III. grant of gold and silver mines to Hanner and Kainsthorpe.—Holinshed's Chronicles.) (34th Edward III. writ as to supposed gold mine in Essex.—Pettus' Fod. Reg. p. 34.)

Ditto, ditto, Shropshire.—Plowden, p. 316.

34th Edward III. grant to H. B. and R. C. Henry de Brytell and Richard Colle of all mines of gold and silver in the county of Devon. 37th Edward III. grant mines of gold and silver in the county of Devon to Henry de Brytell and Richard Colle. 44th Edward III. grant of all mines of gold, silver, lead and tin in the county of Gloster, to Wm. Nottingham, for seven years, on paying ninth part of gold and silver, thirteenth part of lead, and tenth part of tin. 47th Edward III. grant of mines of gold and silver in the counties of Devon and Somerset, to Wm. Nottingham, by indentures between him and our Lord the King. 47th Edward III. another grant of mines of gold and silver in Devon and Somerset, to the same William Nottingham. 1st Richard II. 1377 grant of part of a mine of gold in the county of Devon, by the King and his council. 2nd Richard II. 1378 grant of mines holding gold and

Insertions made between of words wanting.

silver, in the counties of Cornwall, Devon and Somerset, to Henry Burton. 5th Richard II 1382 grant of mines of gold and silver in the counties of Devon, Somerset, Gloucester and West

Wales? 8th Richard II. 1385 grant to Richard Wake of right of digging and searching for mines of gold and silver in the county of Devon. 11th Richard II. 1388 grant of mines of gold and silver in the counties of Gloucester and Somerset. 20th Richard II. 1397 grant of mines of gold and silver in the kingdom of England to Henry Derby, for the term of five years on a royalty of one ninth part. (Henry IV. writ as to a supposed gold mine in Essex.) 5th Henry VI. grant of mines of gold and silver in the counties of Devon and Cornwall? to John Duke of Bedford. 6th Henry VI. grant of mines holding gold and silver to Richard Carson, for the term of twenty years. (17th Henry VI. grant of John Sollers, of Devon and Cornwall.—Plowden, p. 324.) 21st Henry VI. appointment to mines of gold, silver, copper, aurichalch and lead, and mines containing any gold and silver of Robert Burton as comptroller. 22nd Henry VI. permission to John Coll to practise the art of transmutation of gold and silver, provided he does nothing contrary to law. 23rd Henry VI. appointment of the Marquess of Suffolk as seneschal of the King's mines of gold, silver, copper, lead, &c. and of mines containing gold and silver. 24th Henry VI. permission to Worsely to transmute gold and silver by the art of philosophy, and a similar permission to Richard Trafford. 27th Henry VI. demise of mines of gold and silver, lead, copper holding gold and silver to for the term of fifty years. 29th Henry VI. the governance and rule of all the King's mines in the counties of Devon and Cornwall, committed to Adrian Spenke, Clerk. 30th Henry VI. permission to John Misteldon, to transmute gold and silver. (30th Henry VI. Bottwright appointed comptroller of mines. —Plowden, p. *325.)* (31st Henry VI. Bottwright appointed provost and governor.—Plowden, p. 325.) (33rd Henry VI. Alured Cornborough appointed comptroller of the mines of gold and silver in Cornwall.—Plowden, p. 325.) 34th Henry VI. grant to Richard, Duke of York, for twenty years, of the mines of gold and silver, and metals holding gold and silver in the counties of Cornwall and Devon. 38th Henry VI. grant to John Ormond of the mines of gold and silver in the county of Devon, for the term of twenty-two years. 1st Edward IV. grant to John Nevill de Montacute of all mines containing gold and silver in the counties of Devon and Cornwall for the term of his life. 4th Edward IV. " Letters patents of license graunted to G. de Lynn and others, for to forge and digge all manner of ground within the counties of Somerset and Gloucester, for the finding of all mines of lead, tynne or copper, bearing either sylver or gould." 8th Edward IV. grant to Richard Earl of Warwick of all mines of gold and silver and lead bearing gold and silver, in all England beyond Trent. (12th Edward IV. grant to G. Lynn?) (18th Edward IV. grant to Goderswicke, &c. of mines of gold and silver in Northumberland and Westmoreland, for ten years. —Plowden, p. 318.)

In the very first year of his reign Henry VII. created a company or corporation of Jasper, Duke of Bedford and others, under the title of commissioners and governors, to work all his mines of gold, silver, tin, lead and copper in England and Wales, for twelve years. Sir Wm. Taylor was made comptroller of the mines.

In Scotland, about this time, the mines in Lanarkshire were largely worked, and above £300,000 value obtained.

The discovery of America for a time withdrew attention from the gold mines of Britain, but the reign of Elizabeth was prolific in schemes, speculations, adventures, joint-stock companies, and monopolies; and gold obtained some share of the queen's notice. In the 7th year she granted patents to William Humphreys, assay master of the mint, Christopher Schutz, a Saxon, Cornelius Devoz, and Daniel Hochstetter or Houghsetter, other foreigners, and Thomas Thurland, to seek for gold, silver, quicksilver, or ores containing them, in eight picked counties of England, in Wales, and in the Pale of Ireland, with monopolies for alum, copperas, drawn wire, sheet copper, and other manufactures. These grants became the foundation of two corporations, the Mines Royal, and the Mineral and Battery Works, afterwards united, and now known, and still subsisting, as the Mines Royal Company. In this company a number of the leading speculators of the day were concerned, but we know little of their proceedings as to the search for gold or quicksilver, nor were they successful in their operations generally, beyond the establishment of factories and the working of the silver lead mines in Merionethshire.

A scheme of Elizabeth, much more remarkable and fraught with the craft of the day, was that for surreptitiously working the mines belonging to the king of Scotland,: taking Plowden's Reports, p. 19; Pettus' Fodinae Regales, p. 44; Opera Mineralia Explicate, pp. 2, 23; J. Y. Watson's Compendium of British Mining, p. 58.

t Pettus' Fodinae Regales, pp. 46, 48.

J Opera Mineralia Explicata. Watson's Compendium, p. 59.

advantage of his minority, of the troubled state of that country, and of Elizabeth's influence. Of this, particulars will be found in the chapter on Scotland.

In the 10th year of her reign, Elizabeth resumed the mines of Keswick, which were in the hands of the Earl of Northumberland, and Plowden asserts, " she took from the Earl of Northumberland his rich copper mine of Keswick, because of its holding so much silver and gold in the copper." Others, however, state, that she only obtained copper from the mine, but that in abundance; but the Earl acknowledged to the existence of gold, which, in this very year, I have identified in the copper of that mine.

In James I.'s time the Mines Royal Company had such influence that all private enterprise was extinguished. That king made a further and fuller grant to them, and the Lord Chancellor Bacon not only took part officially as a member of the corporation, as his father had done, but likewise an active personal interest in the management; with the universality of acquirement and versatility of talent which distinguished him, as it has a modern possessor of the great seals, he betook himself to mining. He had something of a prepossession for the transmutation of gold, but he chiefly busied himself in silver lead mining, if we are to trust Mr. Bushell's account. Mr. Bushell was one of the remarkable characters of the revolutionary era, and many curious facts are to be gleaned from a book or congeries of petty pamphlets to be found in the British Museum, but which chiefly relates to silver lead mining. Bushell states that he was private secretary to Bacon, and trained by him in what is dignified as the Baconian system of mining, which consisted in running long adits, and in ventilating them by bellows and leaden pipes. The field of operation recommended by Plowden's Reports, p. 318; Dr. Fuller's Worthies of Cumberland; J.Y.Watson's Compendium of British Mining, p. 58; Pettus' Fodinae Regales; Dugdale's Baronage, p. 283; Camden's Britannia.

F

Bacon was Merionethshire. Sir Hugh Myddelton had worked these mines with £2000 a-month profit, as Bushell did afterwards, as also those at Mendip Hills, and Bushell being at first a virulent royalist, largely supplied Charles with lead for shot, and with silver, which was minted in Wales; clothed a large body of troops, advanced a large loan, and defended Lundy Island, of which he was governor. He raised a regiment of horse, commanded by his brother, John Bushell, afterwards beheaded on Tower H ill. Thomas Bushell was treated very liberally by the Parliament and the Lords Protector Oliver and Richard Cromwell, but did not succeed in obtaining the necessary capital to work his mines effectively. On the accession of Charles II., he was in prison for debt, but obtained his release, and attempted to get reimbursement for his royalist claims, but ineffectually, only receiving a mining grant, for which he endeavoured to raise capital, by issuing gold medals of Lord Bacon and prospectuses of the Baconian system of mining, not very well calculated to keep up the prestige of the great philosopher's reputation. Bushell, indeed, seems to have fallen into second childhood.f

The influence of Bacon had diverted attention to silver mining, nor did the exertions of another great philosopher, who had also a fancy for mining, restore gold seeking to favour. Boyle, who in the Philosophical Transactions and various of his works, called the public notice to mining, does not seem to have considered gold mining as offering a good field for enterprize. He was, nevertheless, aware of the existence of gold in tin and copper. As to the latter he narrates, " A friend of mine found in his own land a parcel of ore, which seemed to be copper. After fusion it yielded very good copper; but the person to whom he committed Opera Mineralia Explicata, pp. 245, 258.

t Bushell's Pamphlets; Letters of Frederick Burr in the Mining Journal. the examination, being extraordinarily skilful, found besides the copper a considerable quantity of silver, and in that silver a good portion of gold." By this time the notion had beset every one's mind that gold was to be obtained only by deep working, as in other mining, and the mother of gold was the great object of search. As usual, all evidence that contravened this assumption was overlooked, as it is to this day. Boyle, nevertheless, did not as Bacon did, foster the monopoly of the Mines Royal Company. This had been revived with new energy under the auspices of Prince Rupert, but with no more success than before, though it got deeper into debt. The Earls of Shaftesbury and Dorset and William Penn, the Quaker, were members, jA fashion for chemistry and philosophy distinguished the age of Charles II. and in which that king showed, perhaps, to the best advantage. Moses Stringer gives a statement of these proceedings, after his own fashion:—" King Charles," he says, " nursed the corporations of the Mines Royal and united them, set up a laboratory in Whitehall, and worked in mineral affairs with his own hands; and many worthy peers and gentlemen imitated his example, erected laboratories in their own houses, and laid their hands to the crucibles and melting-pots; namely, the Duke of Buckingham, Lord Chesterfield, Lord Dorset, Lord Capel, Lord Byron, Lord Ashley Cooper (Earl of Shaftesbury,)—Sir Thomas Williams was the King's laboratory keeper; the Honourable Robert Boyle, Sir Clement Clarke, Sir Talbot Clarke (his cousin), and Col. Ashburnham assisted in the work; when the King, to strengthen these corporations for mines and mineral works, erected two royal societies or companies, one called the Royal Society, whose office was to encourage arts and inventions, and to entertain such foreign artists as Boyle. Useful Philosophy. t Opera Mineralia Explicata, p. 7. should come over, and to that end there is or ought to be a ball and entertainment for three days, while such an artist can show a specimen of his performances, and this is at Gresham College, in Bishopsgate Street." According to Stringer's account, the Royal Society was a kind of Society of Arts, and held a kind of World's Fair, accompanied by such entertainment as seems more suitable for the dancing Lord Chancellor, than for Newton, Wren, Barrow, Hooke and their compeers. Stringer's views were, however, rather loose; he had himself constituted first Mineral Master General and Chancellor of the Mines Royal Company in 1703, Deputy Governor in 1705, Treasurer in 1709, and afterwards Governor, f to such a state of decrepitude had that corporation fallen. His son, Hermes Hippocrates Stringer, was constituted a kind of viceroy, under the title of Principal Register and Secretary to the aforesaid Chancellor, and Mr. Richard Stringer was a member of the corporation. % Appended to Moses Stringer's book are various proclamations, offering rewards on the part of the corporation for those who shall discover mines of gold, silver and quicksilver, and denouncing interlopers; forms of writs appointing inquisitors and bailiffs on behalf of the corporation; a scheme for relieving the necessitous poor, by stationing them on waste lands and mineral districts, under the guidance of the said Moses Stringer and the Mines Royal Corporation. It is proclaimed that the said Mineral Master

General will raise the price of nails and iron wire, claimed as monopolies for the corporation, and " the said Mineral Master General will furnish the said industrious workmen, &c. with raiment and necessaries for household goods, at prime cost, and much cheaper than they can buy for ready money. For example, a good fashionable hat, *2s. 6d.* His wife a fashionable gown and petticoat, for 13s. or 14s. N. B. Opera Mineralia Explicata, p. 276.

t *Ibid.* p. 9. *X Ibid.* p. 7.

Likewise, for such as want health, are the following provision made, viz. Advice in any distemper, *gratis.* Choice medicines very cheap. Elixir Renovans, Elixir Febrifugum Martis, *2s. 6d.* per bottle, with several other sovereign medicines, extremely cheap. Which may be had of Moses Stringer, chymist and Mineral Master General, at his laboratory in Black Fryers."

The successors of this dignitary and quack medicine vendor still subsist as a corporation, and make the same claims to the monopoly of the gold and silver mines.

In the reign of William III. Boyle, although a member of the corporation, taking advantage of the decrepid state of the mines royal, obtained an Act to be passed giving greater latitude in working royal mines, under the plea of repealing the statute of Henry IV. against multiplying gold and silver, his object being not to encourage gold working, but silver lead mines. In the first year of William and Mary an act was therefore passed under which mines of tin, copper, iron, or lead shall not thereafter be reputed royal mines, although gold and silver be extracted out of them. The Act recites that the statute of Henry IV. had prevented the home refiners from extracting gold and silver out of English ores, but that the Act is exercised in foreign parts, to the great loss and detriment of this realm.f In the fifth of William and Mary a further or explanatory statute was passed under which a preemption right is given to the Crown of purchasing all ores and metals raised under protection of the statute at certain fixed rates.J In the next year, being the 5th and 6th of William and Mary, Boyle obtained the passing of a third Act. This recites that by several statutes of the 28th year of the reign of Edward III., 38th year of Henry VIII., and the 2nd year of Edward VI. iron, copper, and bell metal are prohibited to be exported Opera Mineralia Explicata, p. 307.

t *Ibid.* p. 158. *X Ibid.* p. 161.

out of this realm. It is therefore enacted, for the better encouragement of the working of copper mines, that it shall be lawful to ship and export iron, copper, or mundic metal out of this realm. Boyle was probably doubtful of the home refiners engaging in the parting of the ores, and desirous of legalizing the export of ores, perhaps because the foreign refiners were more accustomed to parting gold. It will be particularly noticed that mundic ores are specified, which, though they may have been exported for other chemical purposes, may have been in reference to the rich gold ores of that mineral. In the present obscure state of gold history it may be useful to mention any fact or hypothesis, upon which subsequent investigations may throw light.

Boyle's enactments were successful in restoring the working of the silver lead-mines, which in the reign of queen Anne were actively prosecuted; and attention was diverted from gold working, for a mania sprang up for silver-lead shares. It is commonly considered that the Stock Exchange had its beginning in the reign of queen Anne and from the financial operations of William III., but share speculation was very much earlier. Not to go further back, the reign of Elizabeth was rife with joint-stock undertakings. Charles II.'s time had enough of them, and all classes of society were engaged in them; but it was in the time of queen Anne the speculators adjourned from the Royal Exchange to Jonathan's. A furious paper war sprang up between the Mines Royal and its champion, Moses Stringer, and the new companies in Cardiganshire, Montgomeryshire, and Merionethshire, represented by Sir Humphrey Mackworth, Sir Carbery Price, Mr. William Waller, Mr. Shiers, and others. Many of these pamphlets are preserved in the British Museum, and are interesting documents for the study of the mining captain and manager of the present day. Mr. Waller published a prospectus with maps, which for alluring calculations would pass muster in any era of share speculation. He likewise gives examples of those weekly mining reports, in which the lode always is going to be cut, and in which the sinking of the shafts and of the shareholder's money is duly recorded.f These ingenious documents, in which captains and pursers show so much skill, are therefore of greater antiquity than is commonly imagined, and the art must have attained great perfection in the time of Mr. William Waller. Sir Humphrey Mackworth was a very enterprising man, who first engaged in large iron works at Neath, in South Wales, and introduced many improvements. He worked his minerals down to the shipping-place by sails on the waggons, as is now sometimes done by the railway porters in the neighbourhood of goods' stations. Waller induced Sir Humphrey to engage in the silver-lead mines, in which he invested a large capital, and the shares rose to a high premium. In due time there was a panic, discontented shareholders, a newspaper war, and a parliamentary inquiry into the conduct of Sir Humphrey Mackworth, who was made a scapegoat, and, according to the now established practice in joint-stock eras, was accused "of rendering mining, &c., scandalous, and of having set up prodigious stock-jobbing, to the prejudice and ruin of so many families.";:

In the reigns of the elder Georges, speculation was again alive, it was the time of the South Sea bubble, and mining A Familiar Discourse concerning the Mine Adventurers of England; The Mine Adventure laid open by William Shiers; The Projector of the Mine Adventure laid open, 1712; Proposal to the Governors and Company of the Mine Adventurers of England for raising a stock of £20,000; Essay on the Value of the Mines late of Sir Carbery Price.

t William Waller, Essay on the Value of the Mines late of Sir Carbery Price,

London, 1702.

I Opera Mineralia Explieata, p. 2iS. had its share in the operations of the day. The mania was, however, still for silver mining. Dr. Woodward, who wrote in 1729, the most eminent mineralogist of his day, and who had a very large collection of English fossils, says nothing of gold in Britain in either of his works. Sir Alexander Murray, of Stanhope, a great speculator in that day, is equally silent. He employed many persons in making surveys in Scotland, and discovered many mineral districts, but names no locality for gold, though he does say that he had been accused by the Highlanders of writing letters to the king, informing him that all the Highland hills were full of rich mines of gold and silver, and that the Highlanders, being savages, must be exterminated.f

The Mines Royal Company, in this century, seized the Gloucestershire and Bedfordshire gold mines, and worked them, but not profitably.

The reign of George III. is marked by only few incidents relating to gold, that of the discovery of the Wicklow deposits is the chief. Borlase, indeed, in his Mineral History of Cornwall, gave a very strong opinion that gold existed extensively in English ores.J There was a reputed discovery of gold in Bedfordshire, which turned out to be iron pyrites.§ Several writers gave accounts of the discovery or history of gold deposits. Pennant described the Clydesdale district. Gough, in his edition of the Britannia, likewise stated that the valleys there were still worked. 1f

The Wicklow deposits engaged the public attention for some time, but the government workings proving unsuccessful, the excitement was allayed, and gold again forgotten.

Natural History of Fossils; Outline of a System. t Letter of Sir Alexander Murray, of Stanhope, to Sir Robert Walpole. X Borlase's Natural History of Cornwall, p. 215.

§ Pennant's Tour in "Wales. Pennant's Scotland.

If Camden's Britannia, by Gough.

The events of George IV.'s time were unfavourable to home gold workings, on account of the mania of 1825 for foreign gold and silver mines. The hopes raised by this mania were so extravagant that our home mines would not have been looked at, the disappointment that followed was so severe that the very name of gold working would have caused alarm.

Since 1830, home gold working has, however, received more notice, and has been partially prosecuted. The nature and localities of our gold ores have met with more attention; very rich ores have been discovered, and some workings have taken place, though not on a considerable or profitable scale. In 1840, the working of the Wicklow mines was resumed for four months. The discovery and working of gold in North Wales also took place. Gold has been ascertained over a considerable district, and its existence is acknowledged even by the Ordnance Surveyors. The mines at Cwmheisian and Dolfrwynog have produced gold, which was shown at the World's Fair, in 1851. The gold ores of Cornwall and Devon have been worked by five companies. At this time gold is raised in several mines in different parts of the island.

CHAPTER IV. GOLD REGIONS OF ENGLAND.—CORNWALL AND DEVON.

Enumeration of Counties.— Cornwall. —History of Gold Mines.— Geology.—Localities.— Stream Works.—Carnon. Trereife. — Ladock. — Devon. — History. — Geology.— Localities.—Gold Companies. —Exmoor.—Dartmoor.— Poltimore.—Britannia.

The known gold deposits of England extend over a considerable area, chiefly in the western district, and in those shires which are the seats of mining industry. The direct evidence of these deposits and workings has been continued by successive discoveries from the middle ages to the present day. As part of the evidence is of ancient date, and imperfect, the shires only are in some instances indicated without the precise locality being stated. The most convenient course will, therefore, be to give the enumeration by shires.

The shires in which gold is known, or reputed to exist, are:— 1. Cornwall. 2. Devonshire. 3. Somersetshire. 4. Gloucestershire. 5. Worcestershire. 6. Shropshire. 7. Bedfordshire. 8. Derbyshire. 9. Cheshire. 10. Lancashire. 11. Westmoreland. 2. Cumberland. 13. Northumberland. 14. Durham. 15. Yorkshire.

There are several other reputed districts, the claims of which will be examined. The number of enumerated gold localities in England is above forty, besides numerous tin streams, including which the places in England that have produced gold must be above one hundred in number. The nature of the deposits will be described in the chapter on the nature of the gold found in Britain; the history of English gold mining has been given in the last chapter.

I. Cornwall, being the seat of an intelligent mining population and a tin district, affords the greatest number of known gold localities and some of the richest gold ores. This is the supposed earliest seat of gold working in Britain, in which the Iberians and perhaps the Phoenicians discovered gold and tin. Whether the Romans worked gold here, is matter of hypothesis and is discussed in the foregoing chapter. Polwhele thinks that the gold coins of Carnbrae were of Cornish gold.f It was for Cornwall and Devon that most of the grants of gold and silver mines and the rights of prospecting were made out in the middle ages, so that the existence of gold in tin streams must have been as well known then as it was to the Romans.J It is to be noticed that in the confirmation made of the tinners' privileges by King John and Edward I., although leave is given to dig for tin, nothing is said about gold, which from the See ante Chapter 3, p. 44; Polwhele, vol. 3, supplement p. 48.

Polwhele's Cornwall, vol. 1, p. 178.

X Pliny, Nat. Hist., lib. 35, c. 16.

tenor of subsequent documents must have been a reserved right.

In the reign of Edward III. are various grants. In the 34th year of his reign and in the 37th two conveying the right of working gold in Cornwall. In the 11th year of that king is the first notice of a comptroller, Suthrop being appointed warden of the gold and silver mines in Devon and Cornwall.

In the reign of Richard II. is a grant of mines for twenty years.

Henry VI. granted these rights in his 5th, 6th, 17th, 27th, and 34th years. By the first grant he conveyed all his mines containing gold and silver to the Duke of Bedford, his uncle. As this was a general grant, it cannot be stated how far the produce raised by the Duke of Bedford and his assigns belonged to Cornwall. As besides the royalty to the king, dues were reserved to the lord of the soil, it is possible that under the act of Edward III. private workings of gold and silver were then carried on. On the expiration of the Duke of York's grant for twelve years, a new grant for twenty years was made to John Sollers for Cornwall and Devon only, of mines of gold and silver and of all mines of lead holding gold and silver.-)-The dues were the same as, before.

There seems to have been some breach of this contract, for before the expiration of the grant, the king, in the thirtieth year of his reign made John Bottwright comptroller of the mines, and in the next year provost and governor, granting to him all mines of copper, tin, and lead whereout any gold or silver should be fined. Bottwright's tenure was only during good behaviour.J Bottwright exercised the Opera Mineralia Explicata, p. 19; Pettus' Fodina; Regales, p. 3S; Plowden's Reports, p. 317, 320.

t Plowden's Reports, p. 324; Pettus' Fodinae Regales, p. 39; Opera Mineralia Explicata, p. 20. *X* Pettus' Fodinas Regales, p. 40; Plowden's Reports, p. 325; Opera powers of his office, as appears by a complaint made by him in the thirtieth year of the king, that Robert Glover had taken away 144 bowls of glance ore from Beerferris mines in Devonshire. Nevertheless, the king made a grant in his thirty-fourth year of the mines of gold and silver to the Duke of York, to hold at the pleasure of the king for twenty-one years." In this grant the rights of the miners seem to be reserved.f

Whether there was a conflict of interests in the civil war is not known, but although Bottwright was acting in the thirty-sixth year, in the thirty-third year Alured Cornborough was made comptroller of the mines of gold and silver in the County of Cornwall.J It may have been that Cornborough succeeded Bottwright in the office of comptroller only.

In the first year of the reign of Edward IV. a grant was made of the gold and silver mines. As the king himself had held this grant when Duke of York, it may be presumed to be of some value. Devon seems to have been a more favourite district than Cornwall for gold working in the middle ages.

From this time these special and temporary grants ceased, and the system of corporations began. In the first year of his reign Henry VII. created Jasper, Duke of Bedford, and other earls, lords, and knights, commissioners and governors of all his mines of gold, silver, tin, lead and copper in England and Wales for twelve years, Sir William Taylor being comptroller Of the operation of this commission no

Mineralia Explicata, p. 20; Watson's Compendium of British Mining, p. 58.

Opera Mineralia Explicata, p. 21. t Plowden's Reports, p. 325; Pettus' Fodinae Regales, p. 34; Opera Mineralia Explicata, p. 21; Cottonian MSS. Otho. E x. % Plowden's Peports, p. 325.

§ Plowden's Reports, p. 319; Pettus' Fodinae Regales, p. 44; Opera Mineralia Explicata, pp. 2, 23; Watson's Compendium of British Mining, p. 58.

account is given, but it cannot have been satisfactory as it was not renewed.

Queen Elizabeth by various grants and indentures, consigned the Cornish gold and silver mines to the patentees of the Mineral and Battery Works, now incorporated as the Mines Royal Company. In this corporation a number of the great dignitaries and speculators of the day were concerned, with extensive and arbitrary privileges of mining and preemption of gold, which must have prevented operations by other parties; and as the corporations were chiefly engaged in manufacturing operations, Cornish gold mining was for the time effectually stopped, although Carew f and Camden expressly stated that gold was found by the Cornish tinners in hops, prills, or nuggets.

With occasional notices of this kind by every historian of Cornwall, and more particularly by Borlase, gold continued to be gathered for centuries by the tinners, but without attracting any particular attention till the present reign, during which the local institutions and mining publications, have afforded opportunities for making known many gold localities.

In Cornwall, gold is obtained from

Tin streams.

Copper ores.

Lead ores.

Mundic and gossan ores.

Granite.

There is magnetic iron ore in Cornwall, but the locality has not been examined for gold. It is worked at Penryn.J

Gold has been found in granite at S. Just.§ I also obtained it from the Roach Hill granite by my Electric analysis.

Opera Mineralia Explicata, pp. 3, 4; p. 27 (27), 43. t Carew's Survey of Cornwall, book 1; Camden's Britannia (Damnonii). *X* Watson on Mining, p. 50.

§ Mr. Stutchbury's Report on Wellington district.

The geological structure of Cornwall roughly defined, consists of clay-slate, killas, or greywacke, pierced by large protruding masses of granite, and traversed by granitic and felspar porphyry dykes called elvan.

The granite has a material influence in determining the gold bearing properties of this district. It is distributed in principal masses and smaller outlying patches.

1. The most westerly mass is at Land's End. *2.* A large mass lies in the west, midland near Falmouth and Penryn. *3.* A mass lies in the east, midland between S. Austell and Lostwithiel. 4. A northerly mass lies north-east of Bodmin.

The chief outlying patches are at St.

Michael's Mount, Tregonning and Godolphin Hills; Car n Brea and Cam Math, near Redruth and No. 2; Cligga Point, near St. Agnes; Castle an Dinas and Belovely Beacon, outliers of No. *3,* near St. Columb Major; and Kit Hill and Hingston Down, near Callington, outliers from No. 4.

The composition of the rock is generally a mixture of quartz, mica, and felspar, the latter not unfrequently prevalent, and often occurring in crystals unusually large, in the more common aggregate of the three minerals, thus rendering the granite porphyritic. Schorl is also frequently found in it, but this character is chiefly exhibited at the confines of the several masses.

These masses of granite run out veins into the neighbouring rocks, at the points of junction.. In addition to the masses, smaller patches and veins of granite, there are long lines of granitic and felspar-porphyritic rocks, termed *elvans,* cutting the slates and granites, occasionally traversing both in one continuous body of rock, which in their general mode of occurrence are said by Sir Henry Delabeche strongly to resemble trap dykes, and from which they chiefly differ in mineral composition. Delabeche's Report, chap. 6, p. 156.

These elvan dykes vary from a few feet to three hundred or four hundred feet in breadth, and though comparatively narrow, many can be traced satisfactorily for several miles.

One of the largest yet known, has been traced for twelve miles, from Wheal Darlington, near Marazion, to Pool, sending off a branch near Hayle, about five miles long. I have seen such in Australia. I traced a series of elvan dykes governing the metalliferous character of a system of quartz veins, which seemed to take one general direction from south to north for upwards of fifty miles. From one vein I knocked off the dense mass of gold already referred to.

Generally speaking, these elvans are composed of a felspatho-quartzose base with crystals of felspar or quartz, and occasionally of both these minerals in the same rock. They sometimes acquire a more granitic structure in the central parts of the dyke.

Around the granite of Cornwall there is abundant evidence of the alteration of the various rocks in contact with it, such alterations depending, in a great measure, on their original mineral structure.

The clay slate groupf is chiefly composed of sedimentary deposits, varying from the finest roofing slate to conglomerates, some of the component parts of the latter weighing more than half a ton. In some districts beds of greenstone and other solid trappean rocks are found, which seem to have formed sheets or streams of melted rock, amid the mud, silt, sand or gravel, then in the course of formation, and which now constitute associated beds of slate, sandstone and conglomerates of various forms.

As gold has chiefly been found in Cornwall in the stream tin works, it will be useful to give some account of them. + The tin stone pebbles are found at the base of the mass of Delabeche's Report, p. 32. t *Ibid.* p. 37.

J Delabeche's Report, chap. 9, p. 395. gravels and sands in the valleys containing them, in the like manner to gold in our Australian diggings, and are worked in much the same way. They rest in the subjacent rock, in Cornwall called the shelf, but in California and Australia the bed rock, and they force their way when the tinstone grains are fine into all the chinks and crevices on the surface of the bed rock as gold does. It is observed that occasionally, at the meeting of two valleys or below a bar, as we should say, the end of one stream tin deposit, coming down one valley, overlaps the stream tin coming down the other, so that for a short distance a thin intermediate portion of nonstanniferous gravel may occur. A like phenomenon occurs in the gold regions. Another circumstance which bears resemblance to gold, reported by Sir H. Delabeche, is that the stream tin is always found in greater abundance where eddies might be supposed to be produced in a body of water pouring down the stanniferous valleys.

It has been remarked of the tin of Cornwall, that all the productive streams are in the valleys, which open to the sea on the southern side of the Cornish peninsula; whilst most of the richest veins are situated near the northern coast, where all the valleys open towards the north. Most of these valleys have been explored; but, although small portions of tin have been found in many of them, no extensive beds have ever been discovered. The mines, for instance, of the marshes of Lelant, Gwinear, Camborne, Illogan, St. Agnes, and Perranzabulo, are all near the northern coast; but there are no productive streams in any of those parishes. On the southern side, however, are the streams of Perranarworthal, Ladock, St. Stephen's, Roche, St. Austell, Luxillian, &c. Now, on looking at the direction, which the streams bear from the mines, Mr. Carne considered that a flood current had swept the tin from its original situation,

G and had come from north to south, or from N.N.W. to S.S.E.

Gold is reported as found in Perran Zabulo, but nearly all the southern districts named by Mr. Carne, are reported for gold. Among these are Ladock, St. Stephen's, Luxillian, and St. Austell. In fact, generally speaking, the reported gold localities are on the south coast, but then this arises from nuggets being found in the streams only.

Polwhele says, " The principal stream works of the present day are in St. Mewan, Creed, Probus, Ladock, Carnon, and Perranzabulo. The Carnon stream is nearly a mile in length, and three hundred yards broad. An adit, a little above Carnon stream, which has been driven to the west part of North Downs, a distance of nearly ten miles, drains by its various branches the mines of Chacewater, North Downs, Wheal Unity, Wheal Garland, Wheal Pink, Wheal Jewell, Wheal Hope, Wheal Daniel, Poldice, Wheal Virgin, the United Mines, Native gold is found in all our stream works. Mr. Rashleigh's piece of gold (which Mr. Wills shewed me about four years ago, at Truro,) was less in weight than Mr. Lemon's. It was from Carnon."f

The tin streams in which gold is stated to have been found, are St. Mewan, Creed, Probus, Carnon, Perranzabulo, Crow Hill, Lanliving, and Treworda.J

There is, in the Museum of Practical Geology, in Jermyn Street, a specimen of native gold, from a tin stream, near Truro. Mr. Cole, of Lostwithiel, showed me some native gold from near that town.

The gold localities reported are:—

Probus,§ near Grampound, (1).

Mr. Carne, in Transactions Geological Society of Cornwall, vol. 4, p. 110. t Polwhele's History of Cornwall, vol.4, p. 133. *X* Mining Almanack, 1849. Borlase, p. 213.

§ (1). Lysons' Magna Britannia, m, cxcv; Mining Almanack, 1849; Borlase's History of Cornwall, p. 213; (2). Lysons'; Mining Almanack; Borlase; (3). Lysons'; Mining Almanack; Borlase; (4). Lysons'; Mining Almanack;

Ladock, near Truro, (2).

St. Mewan, (3).

Carnon, or Carnon Vale, in Feock Parish, (4).

Perran Zabulo, (5).

Creed, near Tregony, (6).

Crow Hill, (7).

Lanliving, near Lostwithiel, (8).

Treworda, near Penryn, (9).

I nee Castle.

Wheal Sparnon, near Redruth (10).

Gwennap, near Wheal Garland, (11).

River Fal, (12).

Luny St. Ewe, (13).

Wheal Samson, St. Teath, (15).

St. Stephen's, on the river Fal, near St. Austell, (16).

Kenwyn/near Truro, (17).

Redruth, (17).

Castlepark, near Lostwithiel, (18).

Glynnford, (19).

St. Just, (20).

Luxullian, (21).

Roach Hill, or Belevely Beacon.

Generally gold is to be found in all the tin stream works.

Carew says, " Tynners doe, also, find little hoppes of gold among their owre, which they keepe in quils, and sell to the

Watson's Compendium of Mining, pp. 41, 69; Delabeche's Keport, p. 403; Transactions of the Geological Society of Cornwall; Polwhele's History of Cornwall, vol. 4, p. 133; (5). Lysons'; (6). Lysons'; Mining Almanack; (7). MiningAlmanack; (8). Mining Almanack; (9). Mining Almanack; (10).Borlase, p. 214; (11). Mining Review, vol. 6, p. 96; (12). Watson's Compendium, p. 41; (13).Borlase, p. 214; (15). Mining Journal, 1847,p.222; (16). Borlase, p. 214; (17). Borlase, p. 214; (18). Mining Journal, 1846, p. 158; (18). Pryce's Mineralogia Cornubiensis, p. 52; (19). *Ibid.* p. 52; (20). Philips on Gold Mining, p. 23; (21). Royal Cornwall Geological Society, vol. 4, p. 109.

Plowhele's History of Cornwall, vol. 4, p. 133. Borlase, p. 213. goldsmithes oftentimes with little better gaine then Glaucus exchange."

A general description of the Formation of the tin bearing valleys has been given already. The following account of an individual district will further illustrate the formation of these deposits.

The Carnon or Carnan stream receives several rivulets from the hills of Stythians and Gwennap, and falls into Falmouth harbour. The vale is about three hundred yards in breadth, the hills on the south being rather steep, whilst on the north their declivity is very gradual. The largest quantity of tin ore was found where the Stythians Vale and a glen called Smelter's House Vale, open into the Carnon Vale. Tin to the amount of £8000 a year was formerly raised from this vale.f The tin stream works have been carried up the vale nearly to St. Day.J

In this valley many nuggets have been found.

Some of the hills of Stythians, are of granite, some of clay slate, and in a few of them there is a junction of both these rocks. The composition of the Gwennap Hills is similar to Stythians and they are a rich mining district.§

The following is a section of the Carnon stream, by Mr. Henwood:—

Feet. In.

Carew's Survey of Cornwall, 1G02, book 1; Pryce's Mineralogia Cornubiensis, p. 52. t Watson's Compendium of Mining, p. 41. *X* Delabeche's Report, p. 403.. § W..T. Kenwood, Transactions of the Royal Cornwall Geological Society, vol. 4, p. 57; Mr. Came in ditto, p. 108. Transactions of the Geological Society of Cornwall, vol. 4, p. 58.

Feet. In.

7. Silt in some places containing stones 18 to *22* 0 8. Wood, moss, leaves, nuts, &c. all of a dark colour, much resembling what has been charred; a few oyster shells; animal remains and some human skulls.. 16 9. The tin ground, consisting of rounded masses of tin ore . .... *12 0* This latter bed is sometimes mixed with a matrix of quartz, or quartz and schorl, with rounded pieces of slate, granite and quartz, and is sometimes only a few inches thick. The bed rock is here a dirty white and pale blue clay slate.

Another section of Carnon Valley was obtained by Mr. Edward Smith, in 1807. It is as follows:—

Feet.

1. Mud and sand 7 *2.* Granite, gravel, mingled with small pieces of a substance like charcoal, and a few shells.. 4 3. Fine gravel, mud and shells, with irregular strata of oyster shells, sometimes five feet thick *12* 4. Closer mud, mixed with shells... 17 5. Tin ground varying from... 1 to 6 In No. 4 stratum have been found several branches and trunks of trees, some of which had evident marks of being cut with an axe or other sharp instrument, horns and bones of stags, likewise human skulls. This fact of the finding of the skulls has been confirmed by many witnesses, but is attributed to the fact of a previous search for tin having been made. If, as supposed in the second chapter, Cornwall was worked by the ancients for gold, diggers may have been lost, as now in the western gold regions, by their holes falling in.

At Braidwood, in Australia, I found, at a depth of about Royal Cornwall Geological Transactions, vol. 4, p. 404.

fourteen feet in the debris of the granite, a bullock's horn containing gold, taking its shape from one of the interstices of the honey combed part of the horney matter.

The only workings for stream gold were those made on a small scale by Sir Christopher Hawkins at Ladock, of which he presented a specimen to the Royal Geological Society of Cornwall. He says it was found in streaming for tin in a moor near the church. The specimen was intermixed with quartz, and was rare. The gold was commonly found alone. The ancient beds of the river were turned over for tin and gold, and the gold, when taken to Sir Christopher, was purchased by him at an adequate price. He does not state the amount, but it must have been small. In Ladock the gold is not found north of a certain line, j

John Garby, Esq., of Trereife, in a communication to the Royal Geological Society of Cornwall, announced that in 1845 he had discovered native gold in a mineral vein.

In 1840 he discovered it at Wheal Sparnon, near Redruth, in a cross course in killas or clay-slate, which ranges along the north-western side of Car n Math (one of the outlying patches of granite), within three or four hundred fathoms from the granite upon the surface. Its underlay is about *5.%* This point of junction of the two formations I consider a favourable place for gold.

The district last mentioned seems a favourable one for gold, as it is frequently found in veins in a tin stream in the valley beneath Wheal Sparnon, leading to Laity Moor, north of Redruth, where also grains of gold have been found.

On walking up a lane near Bodmin, in October, my notice was attracted by blocks of quartz, which were built in with clay slate as a fence, and on examining the quartz, I found a beautiful but small piece of gold.

Transactions, vol". 1, p. 235. t *Ibid.* vol. 4, p. 109.

J Mining Journal, 1846, p. 158.

Gold ore has likewise been found and slightly worked at Wheal Samson in St. Teath, near Port Isaac, by the East Wheal Rough Tor and by the Great Wheal Rough Tor Mining Companies, but little was done with it.

At St. Just gold is found in granite in veins.f And I found it this year in the Roach Hill granite.

II. The county of Devon has contributed in the present day, as in the middle ages, more than any other region to the history of gold working. As a tin locality it would participate in the earliest operations.

The earliest writ relating to Devon is of the 47th Henry III., directed to the sheriff, and requiring him not to allow gold and copper mines to be occupied until the king shall give orders. J

In the 27th of Edward I.'s reign we have a grant of the mines of gold and silver in Devon,§ and in the 29th a reference to the Mines Royal of Birland, and a commission of enquiry.

In 12th and 15th of Edward II. was a grant to prospect for gold and silver in Devon.If

In the 11th Edward III., G. Suthrop was made warden of the mines of gold and silver in Cornwall and Devon.

In the 28th was a grant to Hanner and Kainsthorpe, High Dutchmen, of gold and silver mines.

King Edward III., in the 32nd year of his reign, granted to John Ballanter and William Bolbolter all his mines of gold, silver, and copper in the County of Devon for two years, with liberty to dig and search, they paying twenty marks the first year and the fifth part of the produce the second year, and all other persons being excluded from digging there.ff Mining Journal, 1847, p. 222.

t Phillips on Gold Mining, p. 23.

J Ruding's Annals of the Coinage, vol. 1, p. 60.

§ Cottonian MSS. Otho. E x. *Ibid. % Ibid. Ibid.* tt Plowden's Reports, p. 316; Pettus' Fodinas Regales, p. 34; Opera Mineralia Explicata, p. 17.

On the expiration of this grant for two years, another was made in the 34th year to Henry Brytele and Richard Colle of the mines of gold and silver in the county of Devon, and in the 37th year this was renewed to the same parties. In the 47th year we find a grant for seven years to William Nottingham.

His successor, Richard II., in the 1st year of his reign, (1377), gave to the discoverer the thirtieth part of the profits of a gold mine which had been discovered in Devonshire and declared to the king and his council. This grant was made for two years, and is a singular instance of such a reward. It may have been to an informer or a discoverer of gold on another man's land, and shows the anxiety of the crown to enforce its prerogative claims. Had it been of mixed metal and on the land of the discoverer, it would under the statute of the late king have been workable by the owner.

In the 2nd year of his reign in 1378, the king made a grant of the gold mines in Devon to Henry Burton. In the 5th year another grant was made.f

In the 8th year of his reign this king, by letters patent, dated the 11th June, granted to Richard Wake, Clerk, leave to dig for gold and silver in the county of Devon. J

In his 20th year he made a general grant to Henry Derby.§

Henry VI. in the 5th year of his reign granted the mines of Devon in a general grant to the Duke of Bedford; and in the seventeenth of his reign granted to John Sollers all the mines of gold and silver in the county, and all mines of lead holding silver and gold.f Bottwright was made comp Cottonian MSS., Otho E x.; Ruding Annals of the Coinage, vol. 1, p. 62. t Cottonian MSS.

X Plowden's Reports, p. 817; Sir John Pettus' Fodinae Regales, p. 30. Cottonian MSS. Otho E x.; Opera Mineralia Explicate, p. 18. § Cottonian MSS. Otho. E x. Plowden's Reports, pp. 317, 320; Opera Mineralia Explicata, p. 19; Pettus' Fodinae Regales, p. 38. f Plowden's Reports, p. 324; Pettus' Fodinae Regales, p. 39; Opera Mineralia Explicata, p. 20. troller, provost, and governor of the mines of gold and silver, and mines of copper, tin, and lead, whereout any gold and silver shall be fined.

In the 34th year of this reign Devon was granted with Cornwall for its mines of gold and silver to the Duke of York.f In the 33rd year it was granted to John Ormond.

In the 1st of Edward IV., the gold mines of Devon were granted to John Neville de Montacute for his life.

In the reign of Henry VII. Devon was included in the grant of the first year of that king to Jasper, Duke of Bedford and his brother commissioners.J

Devon is included in the general grant of gold mines to the Mines Royal Corporation by Elizabeth.§

The sources of gold in Devonshire, are:—

Tin streams.

Copper ores.J

Lead ores.

Granite.

Gossan and Mundic.

The localities reported for gold, are:—

North Tawton, Pettus' Fodinae Regales, p. 40; Plowden's Reports, p. 325; Opera Mineralia Explicata, p. 20; J. Y. Watson's Compendium of British Mining, p. 58.

t Plowden's Reports, p. 326; Pettus' Fodinae Regales, p. 84; Opera Mineralia Explieata, p. 21. *X* Plowden's Reports, p. 319; Pettus' Fodinae Regales, p. 44; Opera Mineralia Explicata, pp. 2, 23; J. Y. Watson's Compendium of British Mining, p. 58.

§ Opera Mineralia Explicata, pp. 3, 4, 27, (27), 43.

Polwhele's Devon; Camden Britannia. f Cramer's Mineralogy, p. 158. Phillips on Gold Mining, p. 23.

Dartmoor, at Sheepstor, and elsewhere.

Arundell mines, in Ashburton district.

The Exmoor, or Molton district, is remarkable as being that district in which gold has been most wrought in Britain of late years, but, until now, little has been raised. The gold here was known in Polwhele's time, for he expressly states it was obtained from copper oresf at North Molton.

At North Tawton gold is found in granite in veins and nests. And from Dartmoor granite I obtained gold by my electric process.

Magnetic iron ore, a formation found in Wicklow and elsewhere, associated with gold, is worked near South Brent. J Hematite iron, another associated mineral, is worked in Devon, and micaceous iron ore is found on Dartmoor.§

Some of the gossan ores of North Molton have been reported as yielding twenty-seven per cent, of gold. Mr. Massey found eleven ounces per ton in picked specimens from Poltimore.

The geological structure of Devon is intermediate, between that of Cornwall and Somersetshire. The western part partakes of the character of Cornwall, consisting of killas, clayslate, or greywacke formations, with a large intruded mass of granite, constituting Dartmoor forest. This is the largest mass of it in the west of England, being about twenty-five miles from east to west, and as much from north to south, and covering eighty thousand acres. It consists, as a whole, of a coarse grained mixture of quartz, felspar, and mica, the latter sometimes white, at others black, the two micas occasionally occurring in the same mass. It is frequently porphyrinic, from the presence of large crystals of felspar, and here and there schorlaceous, but the latter Mining Almanack. t Polwhele's Devon, p. 69.

X Watson on Mining, p. 50. § *Ibid* Useful Knowledge Geography of Great Britain, by G. Long, G. R. Porter, and Hyde Clarke, p. 458. character is chiefly confined to the outskirts, where the Dartmoor granite adjoins the slates. The schorl not unfrequently occurs in radiating nests of variable size and abundance. A complete passage may generally be traced between the compound of schorl and quartz, usually termed schorl rock, and the ordinary granite. The mica usually disappears as the schorl begins to be abundant, but sometimes, though not very commonly, beyond limited areas, the granite rock is a mixture of mica, schorl, felspar, and quartz, in nearly equal proportions after the absence of mica; the next mineral which commonly disappears is the felspar, leaving the compound a mixture of schorl and quartz, the former sometimes occurring in radiating nests in the latter, but more commonly the two minerals form an aggregate in nearly equal proportions.

The granite is sometimes cut by granitic veins, which are tortuous in their courses, and, in general form resemble those on the outskirts of granitic masses intruding into the slates.f

Gold was found at Sheepstor, on South Dartmoor, about the beginning of this century. A miner, named Wellington, brought in about £40 worth, at different times, and sold it to a silversmith of Plymouth, named Pearce. Tin has been found in nearly every southern stream, but is not now found in sufficient quantities to pay.: There are five principal rivers, twenty-four secondary rivers, and fifteen brooks, with names, besides those without names.

On the south the Dartmoor granite comes in contact with the clay slates already described under Cornwall. On the north the granite is bounded by the carbonaceous deposits which are traversed by numerous trappean rocks conforming Delabeche's Reports, 157. t P-171.

X Mining Almanack, 1851, p. 305. W. J. Henwood's Transactions of the Royal Cornwall Geological Society, vol. 5, p. 141. to the outline of the granite. Gold has been found in the stream proceeding from Dartmoor through North Tawton. At North Tawton comes in a tongue of red sandstone and conglomerate, in which Sir Henry Delabeche says he has detected pebbles like some variety of Dartmoor granite.f

The carbonaceous rocks consist of sandstones, for the most part siliceous, occasionally with an argillaceous cement varying in colour from almost white to black, and shales, also, of various tints compose the bulk of the rocks. The sandstones and shales are very irregularly interstratified with each other, or rather one is often found to fine off amid a more largely developed mass of the other.J

The Exmoor district lies at the junction of the clayslate, killas or greywacke formation and the carbonaceous series of Devon. It is about eight miles from north to south and about twelve from east and west, with a surface of about twenty thousand acres. The summits of the hills, especially on the north and west, contain great swamps of many acres in extent; hardly a tree is to be seen, except on the banks of the numerous rivulets which pour their waters into the chief streams, the Barl and the Exe. Dunkerry beacon is one of the highest points. A bed of limestone is said to run through the forest from east to west. Iron and copper have been discovered on this high land, and slate has been got at Simonsbath, in the centre of the forest.§

The Britannia Mine was first worked as a gold mine under the name of the Prince Regent Mine. It is near the river Mole, and lies north of the Poltimore Mine.

The gold bearing lode is gossan, and it passes through Delabeche's Report, p. 122.

Ibid. p. 166. *X Ibid.* p. 124.

§ Useful Knowledge Geography of Great Britain, by G. Long, G. R. Porter, and Hyde Clarke, p. 59.

into the Poltimore Mine, it is also supposed closely to resemble the latter in structure, and to run parallel with it about one mile to the north. It has yielded gold stones of great richness.

The mine is worked for copper likewise.

In 1853 the company contracted for the erection of works for crushing and amalgamating their auriferous gossan under the direction of Capt. W. Moorsom and Mr. Mitchell.

The Poltimore Mine is south of the Britannia; and between that mine and the village of Heasly Hill, near the river Mole, on the property of Lord Poltimore. The Poltimore was previously worked as the Prince Albert Mine, but no attempt was made to obtain gold. The mine contains a good copper lode. In the adit level, east, are old workings for two hundred fathoms in length, and it is conjectured that this lode was worked for gold, as there is there a gold gossan lode from twelve to fourteen feet wide; and there are many hundred tons of gold bearing gossan dispersed over the surface of the mine. Malachite is found here, as in our South Australian mines which have copper and gold lodes. The gold was discovered at the Poltimore Mine in 1852, by some gentleman who took away lumps of gossan to London for assay. This mine has now produced several pounds' weight of gold. The first piece was nearly three and a half pounds: namely, twenty-six and a half ounces from twenty tons of red gossan. Some of the red gossan yields one ounce seven pennyweights per ton, and the brown six pennyweights per ton. The average yield of fifty-four tons eighteen hundred of dry ore was sixteen pennyweights per ton; the total being one hundred and two ounces five pennyweights. It is to be observed that this gold is nearly twenty-four carats and worth 83s. *6d.* per ounce.

The old works are of a very large character, and are judged to have been found by the Romans.

The gossan lode is reported on the western side as about four and a half feet wide, between two well-defined walls, undulating north, about eighteen inches in a fathom. On the eastern side the lode is from fourteen to twenty feet wide.

CHAPTER V. OTHER GOLD REGIONS OF ENGLAND. *Somersetshire. — History. — Mendip. — Gloucestershire. — History. — Worcestershire. —Shropshire. —Bedfordshire. —Derbyshire. — Cheshire.—Lancashire.— Westmoreland. Cumberland. — Keswick. — Northumberland. — Alston Moor.— Durham. — Yorkshire.— Unauthenticated Localities.—Essex.—Suffolk.— Bedfordshire.—Lincolnshire.*

In this Chapter will be embraced the remaining gold localities of England, as to which we have less information than in the western mining counties.

III. Somersetshire is a gold district enumerated by several writers.

Writs relating to gold mines in this county were issued in the 47th Edward III. to "William Nottingham; 2nd, 5th and 11th of Richard II.; they were likewise included in a general grant of the 20th of the latter king.

In the 1st Henry VI. it was included in a general grant to John, Duke of Bedford. Of the intermediate grants we have no records. From what is subsequently mentioned, as we know that the Mendip Hills were worked by Edward III., it is probable the gold was then discovered, though it is not included in the grant to Houghsetter.

There is reason to believe that earlier grants must have Pettus' Fodinae Regales; Opera Mineralia Explicata, pp. 9, 19.

been made by Edward IV. as there is one alluded to of the 4th year of that monarch, but the first grant of that king, of which we have particulars, is by letters patent of the 12th year of his reign, to Gallias Lynn, William Marriner and Simon Pert to dig and search for mines within the county of Somerset, of lead ore, tin or copper, holding silver or gold for the term of five years. In this grant, differently from the terms of those given for Cornwall and Devon, the gold is evidently considered a subsidiary object, and there seems no reason to believe that the gold of Somersetshire could have been of importance, during the middle ages. In conformity with what we know, there are many gold sites and workings in Devon and Cornwall, and only one in Somerset, and it seems to have been so understood formerly. The gold too is not found native, but in combination with lead ores. It seems fair to admit, from the tenor of the grant, that this was known in Edward IV's. time.

In the 1st year of Henry VII., Somersetshire was included in a general grant to Jasper, Duke of Bedford.

In Queen Elizabeth's time, Somersetshire had not the reputation of a rich gold county, for it is not included among the eight select English counties granted to Houghsetter and Thurland. It passed, however, into the monopoly of the Mines Royal Corporation, by means of the grant to William Humphry and Christopher Shutz, in the 7th year of that queen's reign.f The Mines Royal do not seem to have worked gold here, which was parted from the silver in the rich silver lead mines of the Mendip Hills; but Thomas Bushell seems to have raised gold as well as silver. Speaking of the Welsh mines, Stringer says, " After him the famous and most loyal chemist and mineralist, Mr. Thomas Bushell; who thence and also out of the Society's Mines at Plowden's Reports, p. 326; Pettus' Fodinae Regales, p. 42; Opera Mineralia Explicata, p. 22.

t Opera Mineralia Explicata, p. 26.

Mendip, extracted so much silver and gold as kept several mines at work, clothed King Charles I's. army, raised a regiment of horse for the King's Life Guards, and put his brother, John Bushell, at the head of them, and sent him to York to the King, who for his loyalty had his head cut off by the regicides on Tower Hill, and the other fled for his life." This may seem ambiguous, as the passage may apply to the Cardiganshire mines, rather than to those at Mendip, but it is made clear by what Stringer says in another part: " Gold, silver and quicksilver have been largely produced in Great Britain and Ireland. Gold hath been and now may be found in the hills of Mendip, in Somersetshire, called the Golden Rake; in certain rivers in Scotland; and in Ireland good gold in perfect form, like to the Arabian gold, and collected the same way after hasty rains."-fStringer is here clear and explicit as to the Somersetshire locality, and it is strange that it is the only English locality here enumerated. He not only says gold hath been found, but goes further, and says gold now may be found in the hills of Mendip. It will be further observed that the locality is designated the Golden Rake, which signifies in lead mining phraseology the oblique vein of gold,J rake being a mining term, and it may be considered that the vein had been found and worked.

Stringer does not state who worked the Mendip Hills property in Queen Anne's time, but the existence of gold was a fact fairly within his cognizance.

Houghton, in his collection of mining laws, includes those of the Mendip Hills lead mines, but these have no reference to gold or the right of working gold.§

There are no recent references to the working of gold in the Mendip district.
Opera Mineralia Explicata, p. 845. t *Ibid.* p. 9. *X* Watson's Glossary.
§' Houghton's Compleat Miner. Ancient Laws of Mendip, 1687.

H

Sir John Pettus, in his " Fodinae Regales," expressly includes Somersetshire as having copper mines, containing some gold and silver.

The Mendip Hills run in a general westerly direction for above twenty miles, a large part forming a high flat. The north and south slopes are tolerably rapid. The greatest breadth of the range is about five miles, and Blackdown Hill, the greatest elevation is stated at about eleven hundred feet. The axis of the Mendip Hills consists of old red sandstone, rising in four distinct ridges above the mountain, limestone on each side of it, and forming the highest summits of the range. Lead to a small amount, and lapis calaminaris, are still produced in the Mendips.f

The Exmoor region on the west, containing several gold mines in Devonshire, is perhaps auriferous within the borders of Somersetshire. This is described under Devonshire.

IV. Gloucestershire.—Gloucestershire attracted more attention as a gold district, in the middle ages, than might be expected. In the 44th year of his reign, Edward III. granted all his mines of gold, silver, lead, and tin, in the county of Gloucester, to William Nottingham, for seven years. J. This Nottingham seems to have been a regular mining operator, as he afterwards obtained a like grant for other counties. In the 2nd of Richard II., a like grant was made to Henry Burton,§ and in the 5th of the same king, another.

In the 5th year of Henry VI. the gold rights within Gloucestershire, passed in the general grant, to John, Duke Bedford.

There was a grant in the 4th year of Edward IV. In Pettus' Fodinae Regales, p. 6.

t Useful Knowledge Geography of Great Britain, by G. Long, G. R. Porter, and Hyde Clarke, p. 56.

J Cottonian MSS. Otho Ex. § *Ibid. Ibid.* the 12th year of that king it was included in the letters patent with Somersetshire, to Gallias Lynn, William Marriner, and Simon Pert, to dig and search for mines of lead ore, tin, or copper, holding silver or gold, for the term of five years.

In the 1st year of Henry VII. this was included with other counties in the general mining commission granted to Jasper, Duke of Bedford, and others.

By the time of Queen Elizabeth, it had acquired the reputation of a district containing the precious metals, for it is enumerated in the grant to Houghsetter and Thurland, of the choice districts in England and Wales, although singularly enough Somersetshire is not so enumerated.

The ground of the opinion that Gloucestershire contained gold does not appear, but it is included by Sir John Pettus in the list of counties having copper mines containing some gold and silver, f

This is one of the counties in which the Mines Royal Corporation exercised their monopoly as to gold. In the seventeenth century, about 1680, a gold mine was discovered at Little Taunton, in this county. " The Society of Mines Royal seized them this and another and granted two leases of them to some refiners, who extracted some gold, but they did not go on with the work, as the gold sometimes would not repay or requite the charge of separation though often it did.J" It appears by this account that the gold must have been mixed with some other metal, as it says expressly it was obtained by the process of parting.

V. Worcestershire.—Of gold in Worcestershire we have very little evidence. There are no records known as to gold workings in Worcestershire in the middle ages, but Opera Mlneralia Explicata, p. 26; Pettus' Fodime Regales, p. 46. t Pettus' Fodinae Regales, p. 6.

X Abbot's Essay on Metallic Works, p. 203; Watson's Compendium of British Mining, p. 60. it is here enumerated on account of its being included in the grant to Houghsetter in the 7th of Elizabeth, as one of the eight select counties in England rich in gold, silver and copper, along with York, Lancashire, Cumberland, Westmoreland, Cornwall, Devon, and Gloster, in all of which gold localities are known. As we find that the other counties were worked in the middle ages, and that gold has since been found there, it is fair to presume that some evidence existed in the sixteenth century showing this to be a gold bearing district.

In the negative evidence against it, is that Sir John Pettus does not enumerate it as a gold district, f but then his list is of districts in which gold is found with copper and not with other metals.

VI. Shropshire.—The only evidence we have of gold in Shropshire during the middle ages are, writs directed to the authorities of Salop, one in the 7th of Edward III., in consequence of a mine being found on the lands of Robert Brown, of copper mixed with gold and lead. J In another of the 34th year the king directs that the Barons of the Exchequer and the Treasurer may be certified of the manner of finding the said mines, and whether any has been transported, and by whom, and empowers John Jugg and Henry of Wisbeach, to inquire upon oath, and commands them to certify the Treasurer and Barons of the Exchequer thereof, so that further order may be taken.

This is the only direct evidence of gold in Shropshire, and the locality cannot be defined. It is, perhaps, on the evidence of this case that Shropshire is included by Sir John Pettus in the enumeration of counties in England having copper mines, containing some gold and silver. § A Opera Mineraiia Explicata, pp. 26, 27; Pettus' Fodinas Regales, p. 46. t Pettus' Fodinae Regales, p. 6.

J Plowden's Reports, p. 324; Opera Mineraiia Explicata, p. 17; Pettus' Fodinse Regales, p. 34.

§ Pettus' Fodinae Regales, p. 6, 13.

rich copper mine is now worked at Eardiston, near Oswestry, in this county.

Shropshire passed in the general grants to John, Duke of Bedford, and Jasper, Duke of Bedford, but is not included in the select gold counties conveyed to Houghsetter.

VII. Bedfordshire.—Of gold in Bedfordshire we have no record during the middle ages.

About the year 1680, it is stated gold was found and worked at Pollux or Pollox Hill, near Silsoe. Of this mine and another it is stated " the Society of Mines Royal seized them and granted two leases of them to some refiners who extracted some gold; but they did not go on with the work, as the gold sometimes would not repay or requite the charge of separation, though often it did." f

In the eighteenth century there was a report that gold had again been found near Ampthill, and it seems to have created some excitement. Pennant, however, states that it was only pyrites. J Whether this or the former one was gold pyrites does not appear.

VIII. Derbyshire.—As to gold in Derbyshire no medieval records have come down to us, though gold was most likely found there as well as in the other gold regions.

It passed in the general grants to the Duke of Bedford (5th of Henry VI.), Earl of Warwick (8th of Edward IV.), and Jasper, Duke of Bedford (1st of Henry VII.).

In queen Elizabeth's time it had no reputation as a gold region, and was not therefore included in the patent to Houghsetter, but it passes to the Mines Royal Corporation by the grant to Humphreys and Schutz.

The earliest reference to it as a gold producing region is by Sir John Pettus in the seventeenth century. He J. Y. Watson's Compendium, p. 62.

t Abbot's Essay on Metallic "Works, p. 203; "Watson's Compendium of British Mining, p. 60; Camden's Britannia, vol. 1, p. 330, ed. 1789. Pennant's Wales.

names it as a county having copper mines containing some gold and silver.

The laws of the lead miners of Warksworth and Peakland, contained in Houghton's collection, have no reference to gold.

That there is gold in Derbyshire, independently of the gold mines, I had occular testimony. In July this year, with the view of calling attention to the subject of gold mines in England, I threw open to the public my collections illustrative of that subject, when a gentleman brought to me a small button of gold obtained from Derbyshire.

IX. Cheshire.—The only authority we have for Cheshire being a gold district is the statement of Sir J ohn Pettus, thatit has copper mines containing some gold and silver. The other counties named by him are Cornwall, Devon, Somersetshire, Gloucestershire, Derbyshire, Shropshire, Northumberland, and Cumberland. As to all of which we have evidence independent of Sir John Pettus of the existence of gold. In the case of Derbyshire, likewise enumerated by him, I have alluded to the recent confirmation, and I therefore feel justified in retaining Cheshire in the list.

X. Lancashire.—Lancashire is named as a gold locality by several authorities. f

Lancashire is one of the selected counties granted to Houghsetter, and so passing to the Corporation of the Mines Royal, but there is no evidence as to gold in this district in the middle ages.

It would pass under the grant to the Earl of Warwick of mines to the north of Trent.

XI. Westmoreland.—We have only one record as to Pettus' Fodinse Regales, p. 86.

'f-Opera Mineralia Explicata, p. 27; J. Y. Watson's Compendium of Mining, p. 54; Leake's Coinage, p. 287, 288; Ruding's Annals of the Coinage, vol. 1, p. 60.

gold in Westmoreland in the middle ages, but it was often included with Cumberland.

In the 18th of Edward IV. letters patent were granted to William Godersweek and Doderick Naylerswick, seemingly Dutchmen, conferring all mines of gold, silver, copper, and lead in Northumberland and Westmoreland for ten years. It will be observed that this is different from the common prospecting licenses, and is an absolute conveyance of existing mines.

That it had some reputation for gold is shown by its forming part of the grant to Houghsetter of select English counties.f

It would pass under the general grants to the Duke of Bedford in the 5th of Henry VI., the Earl of Warwick in the 8th of Edward IV., and to Jasper, Duke of Bedford, in the 1st of Henry VII.

This slight mention embraces all that is known, and it gives very vague indications as to the existence of gold in Westmoreland until it was discovered by me in the present year.

Westmoreland on the north closely touches the ascertained gold districts of Alstone Moor on the east, and of

Keswick on the west, to which the reader can refer. Westmoreland contains many formations which are suitable localities for gold. J XII. Cumberland.—I have seen ancient workings at Goldscoop, attributed to the Romans, which afford me strong grounds for the opinion that the gold was worked with the copper. The ancient records are few. The gold Pettus' FodiniE Regales, p. 44; Opera Mineralia Explicata, p. 23; Plowden's Reports, p. 318.

t Sir John Pettus' Fodinas Regales, p. 46; Opera Mineralia Explicata, p. 26.

J Rooke's Geology of the Lake District.

at Keswick is said to have been discovered or rediscovered in the reign of Henry III.

In the 5th of Henry VI. it passed in the general grant to John, Duke of Bedford. It was included in the grant of the 8th of Edward IV. to the Earl of Warwick, the Earl of Northumberland, and others, of all mines of gold and silver, and all mines of lead containing gold and silver, on the north side of Trent. In the 15th of the same reign was a grant to Richard, Duke of Gloster, the Earl of Northumberland, and others, of several mines, including Keswick, but nothing is said about gold.

Cumberland passed in the general commission to Jasper, Duke of Bedford, and others, in the 1st year of Henry VII.

The first reference to gold in Cumberland is in the reign of Queen Elizabeth. She resumed the mines of Keswick on account of their containing so much gold and silver; and granted them, among the other select mineral districts, to Houghsetter, and so to the Mines Royal Corporation. Hence arose that famous trial between the Queen and the Earl of Northumberland, which is so fully reported by Plowden, and which forms a repertory of evidence as to gold and silver mining in the middle ages, a great variety of records having been brought forward on both sides. The Queen carried the day rather on the ground of prerogative, than of valid right.f The copper containing gold and silver was found at Newlands, in Derwent Fells,J the present Goldscoop mine, which I visited.

Camden says in his Britannia: " This is certain, that both gold and silver were formerly extracted from several of our mines in Devon, Cornwall, and Cumberland." Opera Mineralia Explicata, p. 23.

t Plowden's Reports, p. 310; Pettus' Fodinae Regales, p.46; J.Y.Watson's Compendium of British Mining, p. 59; Abbot's Essay on Mining; Camden's Britannia; Opera Mineralia Explicata, pp. 23, 27; Jacob's Precious Metals, vol. 1, p. 297.

J Plowden's Reports, pp. 310—323.

In the seventeenth century Sir John Pettus enumerates Cumberland as having copper mines containing some gold and silver.

Alstone Moor gold district is partly in Cumberland. At Skiddaw, in Cumberland, we have a granitic protruded mass with a group of clay slate superimposed. Above the clay slate is a group of quartzose and chloritic roofing slates, but alternating with innumerable igneous rocks, which partake of all the accidents of the slates. This Cumbrian slate formation in some places passes into greywacke.f

In August of this year I made an exploration of Cumberland and Westmoreland, identified the old site, and discovered some new places. Some accounts of these discoveries have had extensive circulation in the local and other papers.

Gold is found in Cumberland.

In river deposits.

Associated with copper ores.

„ „ lead ores.

In gossan ores.

In iron pyrites.

In quartz.

The known localities are:—

Goldscoop, in the Vale of Newlands.

Borrowdale.

Buttermere.

High Ireby.

Bassenthwaite.

Caldbeck Fells.

Keswick.

In Borrowdale I found gold. This was rather water worn.

Pettus' Fodinas Regales, p. 6. t Sedgwick's Letters on the Geology of the Lakes; Ansted's Geology, vol. 1, p. 96; Rooke's Geology of the Lakes.

The gold I found near Buttermere was rather of an angular character. It was in the ferruginous earth, lying on the surface of the clay slates and greenstone slates that I obtained the metal.

Near Bassenthwaite Lake and Peel Wyke, I found a small sample of beautiful gold in the reddish earth, resting on the clay slates.

In a mine, near High Ireby, I found small particles of gold in the hard gossans, but the softer gossans did not appear to contain any.

I found, on examining one of the lead ores at Caldbeck Fells, gold disseminated in small specks.

The Goldscoop mine, in the Vale of Newlands, attracted my particular attention, and I carefully examined the workings, ores and metal. I found gold in the gossans, and in some metal from this mine I likewise ascertained it. The ancient workings were very interesting, and I have stated my opinion, that, so far as I can judge, the Romans not only obtained copper from these mines, but likewise gold. Mr. Clarke, the proprietor of this mine, gave me kindly every assistance in carrying out my researches.

Near Keswick, there is gold in iron pyrites.

On the road which leads from Buttermere Lake and Crumnock Water to Keswick, I found a specimen of quartz containing gold.

The most remarkable specimen I collected was near the road from Kendal to Keswick, not far from the borders of Westmoreland and Cumberland. I found, on a slight undulation on the crest of a hill, a mass of gossan, and where there seemed to be a small accumulation of silica. In this gossan was what may be termed a nodule, or bunch of gold, encircling small particles of silica, and generally embedded in, or tinged by, the oxide of iron. The gross weight of the specimen was about fifty-seven ounces, fifteen ounces of which might be quartz and earthy matter. It would not have had the appearance of gold to the unpractised eye, being very dirty, with a coating of iron; until a blow from my hammer revealed some of the most beautiful specimens I have in my cabinet.

I left Cumberland and Westmoreland with the firm conviction that gold will be found generally diffused in the clay slates, and locally over the greenstones.

What will strike some as a strange and perhaps a trivial incident is, that the late Samuel Irton, Esq. of Irton, member of Parliament for West Cumberland, found a piece of gold, in carving a pullet, which gold was supposed to have been picked up in a rivulet on the estate. This is an incident, however, having many parallels in mining annals. The mules in the Mexican mines are opened after death, and sometimes as much as seven pounds of silver is found in the stomach. The Rev. Mr. Clarke relates such an occurrence as happening in Australia,f and Mr. Henwood, of gold being found in the coop of a duck in Brazil. I remember the case of a duck, at the Bathurst diggings, which was found, on being cut up, to have gold in its gizzard. The fullest account of the swallowing of precious metals by animals, will be found in a popular work of the seventeenth century, " Jonston's History of the Wonderful Things of Nature." J

Gold has been ascertained throughout the south border of Cumberland, from Alstone Moor to the sea.

XIII. Northumberland. — Northumberland has enjoyed the honours of a gold region for a long period, though there are few records referring to it, and those comparatively late. In the 5th of Henry VI. it passed in the general grant to John, Duke of Bedford, and again in that to the Earl of Warwick, Earl of Northumberland, and others in the 8th of Edward IV. for forty years. This latter grant was, however, resumed, and in the 18th year Arcana of Science and Art, edited by John Timbs, 1831, p. 217, quoting the Magazine of Natural History; Mining Journal, vol. 12, p. 354. t Rev. W. B. Clarke's Statement, p. 20. I Jonston, English Translation, p. 117. of his reign Edward IV. granted, by letters patent, to Wm. Goderswick and Doderick Naylerswick, all mines of gold, silver, copper, and lead, in Northumberland and Westmoreland for ten years. This is a grant of absolute mines and not a prospecting license. Northumberland was included in the general commission to Jasper, Duke of Bedford, in the 1st year of Henry VII. It is to be presumed that the Dutch adventurers worked gold at Alstone Moor, or elsewhere, for Houghsetter, and his brother patentees picked it out as a favourable locality, and obtained a grant from queen Elizabeth.f

In the seventeenth century it was enumerated as a county having copper mines containing some gold and silver.J

Alstone Moor is a tract at least one thousand feet above the level of the sea,§ in which rise the Tyne, the Tees, and several considerable rivers of the north.

In later times the existence of gold has been likewise ascertained. There is a statement in the " Annual Register," that about 1765, a lump of gold weighing eighteen pounds was found in this county by a shepherd. According to another account this gold was the produce of workings in Northumberland, and may have been from Alstone Moor.

XIV. Durham.—There is no reference to gold immediately within the bounds of Durham, but it includes part of the Alstone Moor district, in which gold has been recognized within the bounds of Northumberland.

Durham-passed in the general grant to John, Duke of Bedford, in the 5th of Henry VI., and in that to the Earl Plowden's Reports, p. 818; Pettus' Fodinae Regales, p. 44; Opera Mineralia Explicata, p. 23.

t Pettus' Fodinae Regales, p. 46; Opera Mineralia Explicata, pp. 26, 27. *X* Pettus' Fodinae Regales, p. 86.

§ Useful Knowledge Geography of Great Britain. By George Long, G. R. Porter, and Hyde Clarke, p. 28. B Annual Register, vol. 12, p. 95.

of Warwick, Earl of Northumberland, and others, in the 8th of Edward IV. XV. Yorkshire.—Of this county we have very imperfect indications, only the circumstance that it was selected by Houghsetter's patentees, and the monopoly conveyed to them in the 7th of Elizabeth.

In the 15th year of his reign Edward VI. appointed a master finer and assayer for the northern parts,f P. Barsonhowson, perhaps, Barsenhausen, some High Dutchman.

' There are no records referring to gold in Yorkshire in the middle ages now known; but the grant to Houghsetter, is a strong presumption of the county being known to contain gold, as the districts selected by Houghsetter were most of them then known, as they now are, to have gold in them. There is, however, no known gold locality in Yorkshire. It is, nevertheless, to be observed that the North Riding approaches very closely to the gold region of Alstone Moor, and may, perhaps, be included in it.

Unauthenticated Gold Localities.—Besides those counties as to which we have evidence of the existence of gold, there are several places in which gold has been asserted to exist, as to which there is no evidence, or opposing evidence.

Among these counties are:—

A. Kent.

B. Essex.

C. Suffolk.

D. Lincolnshire.

A. Kent. Sir John. Pettus, on what grounds he does not state, intimated that he expected to find gold in Kent.J

B. Essex, has a considerable share in the legendary his Pettus' Fodinae Regales, p. 46; Opera Mineralia Explicata, pp. 26,27; Watson's Compendium of British Mining, p. 59.

t Cottonian MSS. Otho, Ex. *X* Pettus' FodjnEe Regales. tory of gold. According to the loose antiquarians of old, Boadicea worked gold mines in Essex, and so did Cunobeline, king of the Trinobantes, who minted it at Camalodunura. There is no historical basis for this, but it is referred to more at large in Chapter III.

In the reign of Henry IV. a rumour arose that a gold mine had been found in Essex, and accordingly, by letters of mandamus, in the 2nd year of his reign, he commands Walter Fitzwalter, upon information of a concealed mine of gold, to apprehend all such persons as he in his judgment thinks fit, that do conceal the said mine, and to bring them before the king and his council, there to receive what shall be thought fit to be ordered.f

In the sixteenth and seventeenth centuries it was commonly believed that gold existed in Essex, and a passage in a work of Agricola, " Naturalia venarum signa observavi,"J was supposed to refer to this, but by others is considered to refer to ruddle.

In the year 1700, an author, reputed to be of some experience in mining operations, expresses his surprise " that more pains are not taken to search Essex for mines of different metals;" and, in 1843, Mr. J. Y. Watson expressed his opinion, that " the veins of iron pyrites might occasionally produce very small quantities of gold."§

C. Suffolk.—In an old manuscript there is mention of a writ issued to Suffolk respecting a gold mine, but the terms of the writ are obscure.

Camden, in the " Britannia," says that king Henry VIII. dug for gold at Norton, in Suffolk, but without effect.

Sir John Pettus' Fodinse Regales, p. 32; Opera Mineralia Explicata; Abbot's Essay, p. 202; Watson's Compendium, p. 59. t Plowden's Reports, p. 317. Pettus' Fodinae Regales, p. 37; Opera Mineralia Explicata, p. 18; Watson's Compendium of British Mining, p. 59. *X* Agricola de re Metallica.

§ Watson's Compendium of British Mining, p. 59. Cottonian MSS. Otho E x.

D. Lincolnshire.—Some confusion has prevailed respecting a gold locality. The majority of authorities call it Brickhill Hill, near Spilsbury, in Lancashire; but one old writer otherwise describes it. Gerard Malynes says, " I have seen the like spar of gold which was found in England in the county of Lincoln, at Brickel-hill, near Spilsby, by Lincoln."f Leake's Coins, p. 287; Ruding's Annals of the Coinage, vol. 1, p. 60. t Lex Mercatoria, p. 182.

CHAPTER VI. GOLD REGIONS OF WALES.

History.—Iberians.—Silures.—Gold Ornaments.—Tribute of Gold.—Henry VII.—Mines Royal.—Bushell.—Gold Localities.—Merionethshire.—Cumheisian. — Carnarvonshire.—Flintshire.—Cardiganshire.— Carmarthenshire.— Pembrokeshire.

Although Wales presents strong evidence of its being a considerable gold region, its history in that respect is more obscure than that of any part of these islands.

That the Silures of South Wales were an Iberian people has been already expressed on the evidence of Tacitus, and the connection of the Iberian and Phenician nations with these islands, has. been discussed in the third chapter, where it is suggested that Siluria was included in the gold expeditions of those nations.

Many gold ornaments of Iberian and British chiefs have been found in Wales, supposed to be the produce of native gold; and Sir Samuel Meyrick,f on the strength of passages in the Triads, is of opinion that native gold was worked, but the extracts quoted by him are not conclusive.

There are no writs during the middle ages as to the working of gold in Wales, but this is accounted for by the disturbed state of the country, throughout the reigns of the Tacit, Agric. Vit.

t History of Cardiganshire.

Edwards, and indeed for a much longer period, so that the developement of the resources of the country was not likely to receive much attention.

Besides the presumptions from the bardic legends, when Athelstan, about the year 937, subdued Ludwal, the chief prince of Wales, and made a peace, it was on condition of a tribute being paid, consisting of twenty pounds weight of gold, and three hundred pounds weight of silver, a large amount for those days.

In the reign of Henry VII. we find the first mention of the mineral resources of Wales, when it was put under the jurisdiction of Jasper, Duke of Bedford, and the Mining Commissioners.

Hochstetter and his co-patentees obtained a grant of Wales along with the eight gold counties of England.f We cannot, however, fairly assume, as in the case of the English counties, that Wales was sought for as a gold district, because it might have been on account of the silver mines, which were among the earliest works of the Mines Royal Corporation. The Corporation, in James I.'s time, leased these rich silver lead mines to Sir Hugh Myddelton, J who worked them most profitably, and thereby directed attention to the resources of Wales as a silver district, and diverted the public mind from all consideration of gold working, had any such plan been contemplated.

Lord Bacon, although he conceived plans for the production of gold, does not seem to have embraced in his projects mining or working for gold in Wales, if we are to be guided by the statements of Thomas Bushel, while he had a very high opinion of the silver lead mines of Cardiganshire, and recommended Bushell to undertake them, which, as more Jacobs' Hist, of the Precious Metals, vol. 1, p. 325. t Sir John Pettus' Fodinas Regales, p. 46; Opera Mineralia Explicata, pp. 26, 27, 54.

X Roht. Hunt's Memoirs of the Geological Survey, vol. 2, p. 631. than once stated, the latter did very effectually. According to Stringer, the latter obtained gold from these mines; for he says of them, that, after Sir Hugh Myddelton, the famous and most loyal chemist and mineralogist, Thomas Bushell worked them, and thence, and also out of the Society's mines at Mendip, extracted so much silver and gold as kept several mines at work, and enabled him to render great assistance to Charles I. The mines were afterwards leased by Mr. Shepperd, but nothing is said as to the_gold.

Sir John Pettus, in his enumeration of districts having copper mines containing some gold and silver, includes Pembrokeshire alone,-)-but he spoke of copper mines only, and not of lead.

From that period till the reign of Queen Victoria, nothing transpired as to gold in Wales, when the discoveries and workings in Merionethshire took place; and gold has also been discovered in Carnarvonshire, Flintshire, and other counties. The accounts of these localities will be given under their respective counties.

The only gold mines at work in Wales are those at Berthllwyd and Cwmheisian, near Dolfrwynog, in Merionethshire, but gold has just been discovered in another.

The known gold counties in Wales are:—

I. Merionethshire.

II. Carnarvonshire. III. Flintshire. IV. Cardiganshire.

V. Caermarthenshire.

VI. Pembrokeshire.

There is, however, no reason to consider that these are the only gold districts in Wales; Denbighshire, for instance, connected with the Flintshire and Caernarvonshire districts, may very fairly be presumed to belong to the number, but I have not yet seen any gold from that county.

Opera Mineralia Explicate, p. 245. t Pettus' Fodinae Regales, p. 6.

Wales has been fortunate in having been examined by some most eminent geologists, including Sir Roderick Murchison, the author of the Silurian system, Sir Henry Delabeche, and Professor Sedgwick; but the gold regions of Wales have received no acknowledgment from them. On the Ordnance Geological Survey only one gold locality is marked.

I have seen no nuggets, scales, or dust from Wales, the specimens that I have seen or heard of being in mineral formations in quartz, slate, granite, &c. In many of the rocks the gold is visible to the naked eye in specks; but in others the gold is not to be so discerned, though the specimens are nevertheless rich in that metal. Indeed, the gold ores of Wales, that have come under my notice, are among the richest in the world, only surpassed by a few Australian and Californian specimens.

I. Merionethshire.—This may properly be taken first in order, not as the earliest known gold district, but as that latest worked. Indeed, there are no early records as to gold in this county, and nothing until the last few years; and the date and authors of the discovery are matters of controversy. Mr. James Harvey, proprietor of the Cwmheisian mine, is one claimant; Robert Roberts, captain of the mine, is another; and Mr. Arthur Dean is a third, over whom each of the others claims priority.

Mr. Harvey called in Mr. Dean in 1843 to report on the mine, his object being to form a company to work the gold ores; and Mr. Dean having seen the gold there, read a paper on the existence of gold at Dolfrwynog and the neighbourhood before the British Association for the Promotion of Science in 1844; and on a notice of this appearing in the " Mining Journal," Captain Roberts claimed to have made the discovery in 1836, and to have pointed out the gold to Mr. Dean.f Some time after, Mr. Dean con Mining Journal, 1844, Nov. 2, p. 383. t *Ibid.* tested this, but was met by counter statements of Captain Roberts.f

The gold localities known in Merionethshire are:—

Cwmheisian Issa.

Moll Gwyn Cynydd Hill.

Dolfrwynog Mine.

North Dolfrwynog Mine.

Berthllwydd.

Cacquernog.

Tydden Gwladus.

Prince of Wales' Mines.%

Great Cambrian Mines. In 1846 an attempt was made to form a company, for the purpose of working these mines; but the statement of the rich gold ores was received with such derision that the endeavour was unsuccessiul. Discredit was thrown on the claims of the project by several writers, and cordially received, as no one was prepared to believe in the existence of gold ores at home. The assays were in particular held up to ridicule.§

The project was again brought forward in 1847, but the promoters took counsel by their former discomfiture, and gold was no longer made so prominent a feature, the company being called the North Wales Silver, Lead, and Gold Mining Company. After some further controversy, the company was got into work, but never received support adequate for the proper development of the mines.

Various propositions have been made for carrying on the works, and among others, to sink a shaft two hundred or three hundred feet. Gold has been found wherever sought for, and is now to be seen in no less than seven shafts Or Mining Journal, 1845, p. 6. + *Ibid.* pp. 37, 38. J *Ibid.* 1853.

§ Mining Journal, 1846, pp. 470, 482, 498.

Mining Journal, 1847, pp. 156, 163; and 1849, p. 33. workings. The reduction of the ore has caused as much dispute as the mode of obtaining it. In 1849 a proposition was made to refine the ores at a factory in Holywell, where some of the gold was obtained. Some ore was actually reduced in the works. At one time it was proposed to adopt Mr. Langmaid's process of fusion. In these various trials, about seven pounds of gold of good quality was obtained, worth about £350, and a lump of that weight was shown in 1851, in the Crystal Palace, in Hyde Park.

The company worked Cwmheisian, Dolfrwynog, and Berthllwydd, and obtained terms from the government. One of the obstacles they had to contend with was the assertion that their mines, containing gold ores unmixed with other metals, constituted royal mines, subject to the claims of the crown or the Mines Royal Corporation, not being entitled to the privileges of the act of William III., except for such gold as might be mixed with lead, and subject under that act to the crown claims to preemption of the gold at the fixed rates stipulated in that statute. The government, however, agreed to compound for the royalties at five per cent, for Dolfrwynog being on private lands, and at ten per cent, for Berthllwyd, being on crown property, and to compound for the crown preemption rights at five per cent.

Mr. Arthur Dean's paper, read before the British Association, states, that towards the close of 1843 he had occasion to examine professionally the Cwmheisian and other mines, and that at the Cwmheisian he discovered some ore in a shallow pit, which, on analysis, proved to contain seven ounces of fine gold per ton of ore as broken. Induced

by this discovery to prosecute the inquiry, he found that a regular system of auriferous veins exists in considerable abundance throughout the whole of the Snowdonian group Mining Journal, 1849, p. 613.
of strata belonging to the Lover Silurian system of Sir Roderick Murchison, or the Protozoic series of Professor Sedgwick.

The veins of the auriferous series, he stated, traverse or pass through the veins of the two other series in the district, and are for the most part small, varying from one-eighth of an inch to six inches, but sometimes attaining a width of two or three yards. Occasionally they are filled with hardened and partially laminated clay, and are then called by the miners flookans; at other times, with various oxides of iron, iron pyrites, decomposed blende, and soft clayey matter. It is in these veins that the gold is found, and chiefly where they intersect quartzose veins of the first series. In such cases, if the quartz be of an open cellular texture, the gold, accompanied by oxides of iron, blende, &c., is deposited in the cells bordering the sides of the gold veins. At other times the gold assumes the appearance of a coating upon the spar, forming the sides of the veins, and is also frequently found in detached fibrous pieces, mixed with the other substances filling the vein, in which case, if the grains be large, they generally enclose a small nodule of quartz, around which the fibres interlace, and from which they radiate. Mr. Dean was of opinion that the gold veins were richest, and the other veins likewise, at the points of intersection; that the rich gold veins dip towards the north, and that veins dipping towards the south are poor in the vein and at the points of intersection.

The gold veins, he says, are very numerous, sometimes occurring singly, at others, in considerable numbers, within a few feet of each other.

A well known geologist states, that the country or prevailing rocks consists of certain beds of the Lower'Silurian system, interrupted by, or alternating with, greenstone porphyry, considerably developed towards the east, but thinly towards the west. The porphyry range runs nearly north and soutli through Merionethshire, and the chief mineral district is on its borders.

Another describer states, that a peculiarity in the structure of the strata of this district, is the frequent alternation of parallel beds of the so called igneous and sedimentary deposits, observing the same strike and dip, and following every modification of form and inclination to which the sedimentary beds have been subjected. These are again occasionally traversed by dykes or veins of trap or elvan, and other injected rocks, and by numerous mineral veins. Sometimes a stratum of sedimentary rock, not more than one foot thick, is interposed between two beds of igneous rock, but in no degree disturbed by them. At other times, the igneous rocks themselves are divided by floors perfectly parallel to the upper and lower surfaces, lying on each other with no other substances between them; and in this manner vast thicknesses of these rocks have been built up, floor upon floor, presenting the tranquil appearance of sedimentary deposits, having perfectly smooth beds, both upper and lower, in many cases smooth and curved, as if moulded by human labour, having none of the rough and rolling surfaces observable in all great masses of molten earthy matter, which has been poured out from some vast furnace and subjected to a refrigerating process in its onward course. Professor Sedgwick considers these rocks as deposited cotemporaneously. Many of these strata vary from one foot to three hundred and four hundred feet in thickness, extending miles in length, and are of such frequent occurrence that Mr. Dean says he counted upwards of fifty alternations of parallel beds of igneous and sedimentary rocks within the short space of one mile.
, The trap dykes are stated, in almost all instances, to be accompanied by mineral veins, either of the first or second series, running parallel with them and lying immediately Arthur Dean's Memoir, read before the British Association. upon them, the trap vein forming invariably the under wall of the lode, and following exactly all the sinuosities of the mineral vein; in fact, partaking of its nature. The dip is always to the north, and the veins are always on the north side of the trap. The same remark as to the parallelism of the mineral veins has been made by another observer.

Professor Ansted and Mr. Dean are of opinion that gold veins are to be found over a considerable district, but Professor Ansted says, " The exact position of the gold bearing rocks has, however, still to be determined in this district."

The veins in the district are described as being of three classes. Those of the first class are for the most part filled with quartz, containing ores of argentiferous galena, copper, blende, &c. The prevailing direction of these veins is south-east and north-west, and they dip generally towards the north.

The second series of veins is indicated by their always passing through the first, when an intersection takes place of veins belonging to the two series, and also by a striking change in the contents being generally filled with carbonates and sulphates of barytes, &c, which enclose galena and blende ores, and but seldom carry any copper. The general bearing of this series is north-east and south-west, with a dip towards the north.

The third series of veins is the gold bearing series already referred to.

Mr. Arthur Dean further states, that the quartz veins are frequently accompanied by a channel of clay slate, several yards in width, which also follows the vein and with it traverses the igneous and sedimentary beds, precisely as the veins do the lamination of the clay slate, being thin, and having the same vertical inclination as the quartz veins.f Arthur Dean's Memoir, read before the British Association,
t Supplementary Remarks on ditto.

The Snowdon range forms the north western boundary of a large mountainous track, and contains the highest summits in England. Its.direction lies from N.N.E. to S.S.W. Swindon itself rises to the height of three thousand five hundred and seventy-one feet. The whole length of the range is about thirty-six miles following its windings, but only twenty-four miles between its extreme points. Its breadth varies from five to seven miles. The loftier summits are of the crystalline formations. These are flanked on both sides by immense beds of slate, and this slate supports strata of limestone upon the Menai Strait. Copper ore is found in many places.

There are specimens from Merionethshire in the Museum of Practical Geology in Jermyn Street.

The lodes and mines in which the gold is found, are in and near the Mowdach Valley, about eight miles north of the town of Dolgelly, and having access to the port of Barmouth.

a. Cwmheisian Mine.—Of this mine I have seen no account, but it produces argentiferous galena, copper, and iron pyrites, and the galena is said to be very rich in gold, f *b. Cwmheisian Issa Mine.* — Argentiferous lodes cross the Mowdach stream from the Tydden Gwladus Mine. A porphyritic or elvan dyke, three fathoms wide, crosses the stream in the same or nearly the same direction as the lead lodes. A level was driven on a lode running into the hill in an east southeast direction about twelve fathoms and cut the lode, where it consisted of argentiferous galena with blende, and occasionally a little copper pyrites. The country is much mineralized with iron pyrites. A specimen of this lode yielded one and a half pennyweights of Useful Knowledge Geography of Great Britain, by G. Long, G. R. Porter, and Hyde Clarke, p. *64.* t One assay of oxide of iron produced eighteen pennyweights three grains of gold per ton of ore, and another of iron pyrites and lead the same quantity. gold per ton. On this mine is a small feeder cropping out at the stream, and bearing south-east. The veins in this mine comprise ten quartzose silver lead veins of the first series, which intersect each other nearly at the same spot, and are again crossed at a few fathoms from the former intersection by two veins of the second series, producing iron pyrites, lead ores, and oxide of iron, &c. These two systems of veins are again crossed very obliquely by numerous goldbearing veins or joints, varying from one inch to one-eighth of an inch in width.

The assays from this mine have proved very rich in gold. Arthur Dean, in his Memoir, speaks of lead ores producing from two to twenty ounces of gold in a ton of washed ore, and of some of the ores yielding from twelve to fourteen ounces of gold per ton as broken.

The following are the results of various assays:— GOLD PEE TON. Oz. DWT. GR.

1. Clean lead ore; lead 67 oz.; silver 10 oz. 5 dwt. 8 gr 115 0 *2.* Earthy matter, pyrites, and blende; silver, 16 dwts. 8 gr 1 *12* 5 3. Galena ore 0 1 *12*

At first the process of working was to break down the whole body of the lodes and pulverize the stuff in a crushing mill. The gold being mixed with the heavy lead ore, was supposed to be protected by it while being washed, and Mr. Dean thought the loss of gold by washing did not amount to more than eight per cent.; but that is very questionable, and it is observed by one of the assayers that a very slight blow flattens the atoms of gold, and they swim on the water. Indeed many rich gold mines prove unproductive from bad stamping and illtreatment of the ores.

On the Cwmheisian lode meeting a large flookan, the country changes, and the lode becomes highly auriferous. *c. Moll Gwyn Cynydd.*—These seem to be. old workings, and are on a hill. They include a set of quartz lodes. The principal vein runs N. N. W. and E.S.E., hanging slightly to the north, and parallel at about a hundred yards is another like vein with a west branch. A third vein converges towards these, and is supposed to cross them. The general appearance of the veins is much the same, and they all contain in some parts a quantity of iron pyrites scattered throughout in small cubes. They have likewise minute specks of gold, visible sometimes to the naked eye, with a sprinkling of goldcoloured mica, supposed to be auriferous. There is likewise a peculiar arrangement of the pyrites. The breadth of these gold quartz veins is considerable. In one of them the upper side contained the pyrites, in another the lower side or hanging side. The quartz is represented to be usually massive and tough, but in some cases was observed to be perfectly crystalline, and a mass of crystals was remarked almost detached. Gold has been found by assay in this vein; but two specimens were found to contain only a trace of gold, but a distinct trace.

d. Dolfrwynog.—These mines are stated to be in and near the eastern edge of the mass of porphyritic greenstone. The top of the ridge on the left bank of the Mowddach is marked by a trace of bog, and this has been found to contain a large quantity of copper, indeed, to such an extent as to be worth burning for the metal. A little beyond, to the east, the country is highly mineralized, and several bunches of copper ore have proved very productive. Above a dozen levels have been driven into these mines at different times, and have cut lodes in them. One of these levels cut into a large flookan, or crevice, filled with fine clay, and this being very soft and unsatisfactory, paused a suspension of the works for a time.

The flookan, which has been mentioned, runs nearly north and south, and is supposed to occur exactly at the contact of the greenstone and the Silurian schists, underlying about one in one towards the east, and has been proved to have a width of seventeen fathoms at one spot, but narrower towards the north.

The main lode, in some parts, is regular, with clean walls, but has a number of branches, and ranges a little to the east of north, coming into the flookan near a shaft. The whole of the ground where this shaft and level are cut, is a kind of gravel of considerable thickness.

The Fownog level consists of a level running for some distance to a lode in a very pale and highly mineralized schist, loaded in some parts with sulphate of baryta, and spotted with carbonate and phosphate of copper. The principal lode consists of quartz, with at least one branch of sulphate of baryta, containing on each surface a seam of very rich gold, bearing galena, in contact with the schist. The lode and the branch appear to underlie with the schist, and at an angle of nearly 45. The thickness of the branch is from one to three inches, and it yielded about two to three cwt. of ore per fathom, with from £40 to £50 per ton for gold. The galena is associated with copper pyrites, but not in large proportions. This working does not appear rich for silver, but the yield of gold is very large.

The following are assays of some of these ores:— *e. Tyddyglwdus.*—The Tyddy or Tydden gwladus mines have a great resemblance to the Cwmheisian. Tyddyglwdus is mostly known for silverbearing galena, but is reported as likewise rich in gold. It contains much copper and iron pyrites. The lodes from Tyddyglwdus extend into Cwmheisian Issa mine, crossing from the right or western bank of the Mowddach stream, and are supposed to be continued into North Dolfrwynog. The gold is found in quartz, with mica and pyrites.

A few assays, made in 1851, gave the following results:— GOLD PER TON.

Oz. Dwt. Gr.

1. Quartz, (silver, 7 dwts. 7 gr.).. 0 7 10 *2.* Micaceous quartz, (silver, 10 dwt. 6 gr.) 0 6 10 3. Quartz, with pyrites, (silver, 18 dwt. 3 gr.) a trace. 4. Slag, (silver, 3 dwt. 6 oz.)... a trace. The district around Tyddyglwdus is reported as auriferous, but, as yet, has been surpassed by the Dolfrwynog mines, in the production of gold.

Careful investigation would doubtless show many other and perhaps richer gold localities, but, except by Mr. James Harvey, and the company founded by him, little has been done to explore the district for gold, as yet the profits have not proved sufficient to induce others to engage in the same branch of enterprize. */. North Dolfrwynog.* This is on the western side of the Mowddach valley, and opposite the Fownog level on the Dolfrwynog mines. It is traversed by large quartz lodes, running towards the north-west, which crop out on the hill side and have been opened in several places. These lodes are supposed to be continuous with those of Tyddengwladus, and were reported as very promising for copper, besides looking well for gold. The country is a white schistose rock, like that of the Fownog level. *g. h. Berthlhoyd* and *Caequernog* Mines are situated about four miles from the Cwmheisian Mines. Berthllwyd is on crown land. Several rich specimens of gold have been found where the auriferous veins intersect a large quartzose vein of the first series, containing silver lead ores. Blende ore, in one instance, the produce of several fiundred pounds weight of ore, as broken, was found by assay to contain, besides sixteen ounces fifteen pennyweights of silver, as much as fifty-nine ounces five pennyweights of gold. In another place the produce of gold was one ounce, and in another eight pennyweights per ton of ore as broken. Berthllwyd was included with the other mines in the operations of the North Wales Mining Company. II. Carnarvonshire.— I obtained from near Snowdon, in this county, a specimen of gold ore, containing three hundred and thirty ounces of gold to the ton, but this was of course a picked specimen. Mr. St. Pierre Foley has ascertained the existence of gold at Hafod y Morfa, in the Prince of Wales Mines.f The Snowdonian range extends through the county north of Merionethshire. Professor Ansted and Mr. Dean both state that they have ascertained gold in this range within the county. Arthur Dean's Memoirs. t Mining Journal for 1853, p. 46'4. III. Flintshire.—Gold was discovered in this county by Mr. Standish Motte, who likewise possessed, some years ago, a sett of gold slate in an adjoining county. A specimen of gold ore, belonging to this gentleman, contains three hundred ounces of gold to the ton of ore. Mr. Maugham, the chemist, assayed for him some rich gold quartz. IV. Cardiganshire.—Cardiganshire is a gold district, according to Moses Stringer, as already stated in the general history of gold working in Wales, at the beginning of this chapter. He states, that Mr. Thomas Bushell extracted much silver and gold from the Mines Royal Mines in Cardiganshire, which included Consomblock and some others, but the particular mine is not designated by Bushell.

V. Caermarthenshire.—In the Museum of Economic Geology is a specimen of gold ore from Oogafau near Caio, a Roman mine. Mr. Stutchbury, in one of his reports, says, that gold is there found in quartz lodes.

VI. Pembrokeshire.—The authority for the existence of gold in Pembrokeshire, is Sir John Pettus, who includes it in a list of counties having copper mines, containing some gold and silver.--This is the only Welsh county so distinguished by him, but no locality is stated. It is, however, reported in the adjoining county of Caermarthen. Opera Mineralia Explicata, p. 245.

t Pettus' Fodinae Regales, p. 6.

CHAPTER VII. GOLD FIELDS OF SCOTLAND. *Caledonians.—David I.—James I.—James III.—James IV. —Mary Queen of Scots.—James VI.—Queen Elizabeth. — British Museum Manuscripts as to Clydesdale Diggings. —Localities.*

Scotland has proved one of the richest gold workings in these islands as yet, but the history of them is very incomplete. The only early reference is a very vague one in the address of Agricola to his soldiers, in leading them to the attack of the Caledonians under Galgacus, stationed in the Grampians:—" *Fert Britannia aurum et argentum et alia metalla pretium victories.*" " Britain produces gold, silver, and other metals, the booty of victory."

If we consider that this referred to the gold production of Scotland, we might conclude that some of the large deposits were then worked. It is possible, from the gold ornaments found in Scotland, that native gold was worked by the local chiefs. There is no evidence as yet that the Iberians penetrated there, and it is uncertain whether the Romans worked the southern diggings. The Romans held quite sufficient possession of the South Lowlands to have worked the Clydesdale diggings, as is proved by the researches of Sir Tacitus Vita Agricola.

Robert Sibbald and the other local antiquaries as to the relics of Roman power.

The earliest allusion we have to the actual finding of gold in Scotland is about the close of the thirteenth century. David I. made a grant of a mine of gold in Fifeshire.f

In the Parliament of James I. of Scotland, held at Perth, in May, 1424, it was provided, that wherever gold or silver mines were discovered within the lands of any lord or baron, if it can be proved that three halfpennies of silver can be produced out of the pound of lead, the mine should, according to the established practice of other realms, belong to the king.J

From this time till the reign of James IV. there is no further allusion to gold in Scotland. Then the Clydesdale diggings seem to have been discovered, and a gold mania began. Hector Boethius says: " In Clydesdale are the gold mines and diamonds, rubies and hyacinths, discovered in the time of James IV."§ Lesley, Bishop of Ross, confirms this. In the accounts of the treasurer are a number of payments under the head of 1511, 1512, and 1513, made to Sir James Pettigrew and the men employed by him in working the mine at Crawford Moor. If In 1512, a lead mine was worked at Wanlockhead, in Nithsdale, by some of the royal workmen, but operations were suspended by the defeat of Flodden and the death of the king. The Queen Regent, however, early directed her attention to these sources of income. About 1515 is the following entry in the account of James, Bishop of Murray, the treasurer:— " Item, deliverit to my Lord Postulate of the Ylis, for to pas Sibbald's Historical Inquiries,

t P. Fraser Tytler's Hist, of Scotland, vol. 3, p. 201. *X* P. F. Tytler's Hist, of Scotland, vol. 3, p. 63; Gentleman's Magazine, May, 1853, p. 462.

§ Boethius' Hist, of Scotland, p. 6.

Lesley's Descriptio Regionum et Insularum Scotiae. *%* Gentleman's Magazine, p. 462; Chalmers' Caledonia, vol. 3, p. 732.

K to Crawfurd Mure, and thare to set workmen and mak ordinances for the gold myne, to gud compt in ane hundredth crownes of wecht xxxxli." From the correspondence of Wharton, the Lord Warden of the English Marches, in the State Papers, we learn that these mining operations were successfully continued by the Regent, Albany. In July, 1526, when the King was under the power of the Earl of Angus, a lease of the mines was granted to certain High Dutchmen for a period of forty-three years, with very extensive privileges. Although the laws forbade the exportation of bullion, they were allowed by a bribe to carry some of the ore to their own country to be refined.f A very interesting chapter of history, as yet unwritten, are the enterprizes of the capitalists and miners of the High Dutch free towns in working the gold, silver, and other mines of England, Scotland, and Spain. The annals of Nuremburg and other towns would afford many interesting particulars.

It is stated that as much as £300,000 of gold was got from these mines, and that three hundred men were employed. The High Dutch adventurers did not hold the works long, but they were resumed and worked for the benefit of the crown. At the marriage of James V. with Magdalene of France, covered cups filled with native gold were presented, as specimens of Scotch fruit. This incident, however, like others, is related in different ways.

According to one account, James was jeered by the French ambassadors on the barren appearance of the country; that he instantly wagered with them that it could produce better fruits than their own, and won, by introducing at their repast covered bowls filled with gold coins.§ The Gold Mynes in Scotland, by G. L. Meason, Bannatyne Club, containing Atkinson's MSS. p. 4; Gentleman's Magazine, p. 452.

t Gentleman's Magazine, p. 452; Pennant's Scotland. *X* General Dirom, quoted in Jameson's Mineralogical Description of the County of Dumfries; Cottonian MSS. Otho E x.

§ Gentleman's Magazine, p. 462.

second marriage of the king, with Mary of Lorraine, led to the introduction of a number of Lorraine miners, who are supposed greatly to have increased the produce of the mines. Many returns appear in the records supporting this view. A curious entry is the issue of Scotch gold to form the regalia, thirty-five ounces being devoted to the queen's crown, and forty-six to the king's. In James V.'s time a gold mine was found in Leamington burn.f

On the death of the king, and in the regency of the Earl of Arran, the mines seem to have been neglected, but were resumed by the queen dowager. In one of the accounts is the entry, " For a copper kettle sent to the English miners at Crawford Moor, *£3 Is.,* and also seven stones of lead to fine gold with."

On the return of Queen Mary, from France to Scotland, there were grants of the lead mines, one dated 23rd January, 1562, is to John Achison and John Aslowan, burgesses of Edinburgh, to work the lead mines of Glengonnar and Wanlock, and transport the lead ore to Flanders, so that the silver may be refined. J The second grant was to John, Earl of Athol, dated 26th August, 1565.§ A third was to James Carmichael and others.

In 1564, a license was granted to John Stewart, of Yarlair, to search for gold and other metals, between the Tay and the Sheriffdom of Orkney.*"%*

On the removal of Mary, the Regent Murray was applied to by several English adventurers.

The first who resumed the working of the gold mines of Scotland seems to have been that great schemer, Cornelius De Voz, or Devosse, a High Dutchman. He was, among other pursuits, an artist and painter to Queen Elizabeth, Gentleman's Magazine, p. 463.

t Gold Mines in Scotland, p. 86. *% Ibid.* pp. 87, 463.

§ Gentleman's Magazine, p. 463; Gold Mynes, p. 88.

Gold Mynes, p. 89. t *Ibid.* p. 90.

Walpole's Anecdotes of Painting, vol. 1, p. 148.

likewise a lapidary. In the early part of Queen Elizabeth's reign, he obtained from her a grant, or patent, for mining and digging in the realm of England for alum and copperas, and for divers ores of metals to be found in digging for the same metals.f This patent he disposed of to the Mines Royal Corporation. He early turned his attention to gold in Scotland, and engaged in it Nicholas Hilliard, a wealthy goldsmith.

From the Regent, Murray, Cornelius obtained a license, and went to Leadhills and found gold. He then formed a company, but as the law prohibiting the exportation of precious metals, interfered with remittances to the English shareholders, he was obliged to take in a greater number of Scotchmen, and the company was thus divided. The Earl of Morton ten shares; Mr. Robert Ballantine, Secretary of State, ten shares: Abraham Paterson, a High Dutchman, of Edinburgh, ten shares; James Reade, a burgess of Edinburgh, five shares; and Cornelius and his London friends, ten shares. The latter chiefly found the capital.J The company proved profitable.

The writer in the " Gentleman's Magazine" conjectures that Abraham Paterson is the same as Abraham Gray, or Graybeard, of whom is the legend that he lived some time in London, and got a good quantity of natural gold. " He paid his workmen weekly, and lent to divers men beforehand, as it is written in that parchment book, saying with this natural gold, gotten in Great Beard's time (for so he was called, because of his great long beard, which he could have bound about his middle), was made a very fair deep basin, without any addition of any other gold, at Edinburgh, in Canongate Street. It was made by a Scotchman, and contained, by estimation within the brims thereof, an English gallon of liquor. The same basin was of clean natural gold.

MSS. of Colonel Borthwick. *X* Opera Mineralia Explicata, p. 26, and elsewhere. *X* Gentleman's Magazine, p. 463.

It was then filled up to the brim with coined pieces of gold, called unicorns, which appear to have been only coined in James III. and I Vs. time."

The first authentic records are some documents of Queen Elizabeth's time. That adventurous princess, among other schemes that she countenanced, patronized an undertaking for working the Clydesdale diggings, under grants obtained from the infant king of Scotland, James VI. Several persons had proposed this project, on account of notice having been drawn to the great produce from the Scotch gold district. Mr. Secretary Davison, when ambassador in Scotland, had made himself acquainted with many facts as to the gold workings.-- The Earl of Cassilis, Scotch ambassador in London, who was himself a proprietor of mines, had endeavoured to obtain miners from Germany, and likewise applied to Gawyn Smith and offered to make him mine master of all Scotland, if he could obtain the consent of the English government. This we learn from Smith's letter, addressed in 1578 to Lord Burleigh. J It seems, however, that Smith had some idea of working the mines on Queen Elizabeth's account. It so happened that Smith was employed by neither government, for Mr. (afterwards Sir Bevis) Bulmer was charged with the mission to the Clydesdale mines and the working of them. Gawyn Smith gives a list of mines known in Scotland, including the Clydesdale and Nithsdale gold mines, and seems to have wished the English government to employ him in further operations. In his letter, he says—" His Honor Secretary Davison said it is a general report that in times past the kings of Scotland did quoyne (coin) in their mint gould and silver from their own mynes. And for that the workmen had but small skill, it could not MSS. of Colonel Borthwick and others, quoting " Anderson's Diplomats et Numismata Scottica," but founded upon Mr. Atkinson's statement hereafter given.

t Gawyn Smith's Letter. *X* Lansdown MSS. British Museum; Burleigh Collection, vol. 26. be gotten in any great quantity." This latter version is at variance with the statement of other records, and it is more probable that the workings were suspended on account of the disturbed state of the country. The suspension did not take place on account of the unproductiveness of the district, for soon after Gawyn Smith wrote, Bulmer succeeded in getting large returns from it.

Secretary Davison's account of the coinage seems to be correct, for a large gold coinage did take place in the reigns of James IV. and James V., but of Mary's reign there was only a coinage of the early year. These coins were popularly known as bonnet pieces, and were always reputed to be the produce of Crawford Moor gold, nor does there seem to be any reason to discredit the legend.

It is worthy of observation that Gawyn Smith states that he intended, had he been employed in Scotland, to resort to amalgamation with quicksilver, as done by the Spaniards. This is the first proposition of the kind in Britain; but, unless carried out by Sir Bevis Bulmer, there has been no amalgamation of gold ores in Britain.

The most remarkable document as to the Crawford Moor mines is unfortunately only a fragment, and causes us to regret the want of the whole document, which is evidently drawn up with great minuteness. Who is the author is not stated; but, from internal evidence, he must be one of the parties connected with Sir Bevis Bulmer's enterprise, and most probably that gentleman, unless it was one of Cornelius De Vos's colleagues. The date is perhaps from 1578 to 1600. It is in the Cottonian MSS. and marked Otho Ex., being the burnt remains of a manuscript on the Crawford Moor mines. It is seemingly headed 12, as if part of a longer treatise; and another part is numbered 13.

" First. I have been informed in King James IV.'s Archbishop Nicholson's Historical Collections for Scotland, p. 300.

time Scottishmen did begin to washe gold, and in King James V.'s time, in some summers, there was three hundred persons which did maintain themselves by getting gold; but for this forty last years there hath been little washing, but in the foresaid eighty years many gills, waters, and valleys have yielded gold therein, of greater value than an hundred thousand pounds; yet by the people working for gold no veins of gold have been known to be found.

" Secondly. Gold hath been gotten by washing by the L: of Markesdale, distant from Leadhill House, in Crawford Moor, 28 miles; and hath been gotten in Langham

Water, 14 miles, and Megget Water and Phin land, 16 miles distant from Leadhill House, and in many other, places by testimony of sundry, reputed honest; which gold, to have been gotten in places so far distant one from another, doth show there are either many —or that the gold so found is generally dispersed, and doth but lie in the surface? and not in solid and knit veins.

" Thirdly. There hath been adits or drifts driven in the works for conveying water from the lead mines about 120 fathoms in Glengonner Water, as also other drifts, as in Glanggres Gill, near Wenlock Water, for conveying water from a ... gold having been plentifully gotten, and at a lower level, within several former drifts, yet not any veins of gold have been known to be found in levels or drifts.

" Fourthly. The gills—many of them being in ascent from the level of the 4 ... in the valley above 120 (feet or fathom) and the little springs running down the said gills disturbed sundry leaders and some veins of copper and lead, yet in that way the workmen have not found any known veins of gold.

" Fifthly. Although gold have been founde in more than 40 several gills falling into the greater waters of Alroyn, Words inserted to connect the meaning between .

Glangoner, Wanlock, and Mannock, and along the sides, and in the channels of the said great waters, yet the same gold may be seen dispersed in certain black rocks of chiver next the heads of the gills, such as I have found in Clanclough and Tempie Clough, having seen many times iron pyrites, marcasites, and lead ore to be growing in like black chiver rocks, but have never found the said rocks to contain any solid or .. containing veins of any of the former metals, conceiving the said rocks as unnatural vessels for veins of metal."

This concludes one folio of the manuscript, and which seems to have been headed, " These reasons make me think there are no veins of gold, but rather lying dispersed on the surface of the ground." The heading of the next folio has suffered still more from fire, but refers to " veins of gold in sundry parts of Crawford Moor." The beginning of this part is so mutilated, that it cannot be satisfactorily made out. It is a long clause, describing the views of the gold washers and lead miners as to certain veins or indications, which they called *leaders, hingetts* and *liggetts,* or *husband* and *wife,* leading to the mother ore. These leaders he considered to be tinged by the *metalline fumes* of the main lodes, and to be infallible leaders to them, if followed up; and he introduces a comparison with the chimneys of a house. " As through a chimney, the smoke will show the nature of the fire below, so the said leaders or metalline fumes give divers tinctures and colours to both sides of the rocks along which the same doth pass, which tinctures, colours, or metalline fumes, an expert miner will thereby discern whether the vein at a depth be apt for iron, lead tin, copper, or silver. And I have observed in two several places in which I have found .... together between two rocks, spar, keele, and brimstone, all which are found wherever gold is gotten by So called, when I was at Leadhills, by the miners, being a local name for an earthy oxide of iron.

washing, and therefore called by the gold washers the ... of gold. The like of which foresaid leaders I have not seen in colour and quality either in Cornewall, Devonshire, Somersetshire, ... wheresoever I have travelled, but only in those places where gold is found in Scotland, which, together with the bluish and yellow coloured mothers, I am persuaded are leaders to veins of gold either at a depth or in their ..., and may be best tried by damming, driving, and shafts, sinking so far and so deep as the directors shall think fit.

" Secondly. By report of sundry workmen, some whereof affirm that at Pontshields and Wanlock Water, and in sundry other places, they have found gold in bigness of cherrystones, and some greater pieces, lying between two rocks, in a yellow or blewish mother or leader, which they have followed about five foot deeper than the water would pass from their work but by casting; at which time they did not know the use of shafts and buckets, and therefore were enforced, by influence of waters and thickness of the earth, to desist from working of such gold works, which places may be tried in some few months, and if answerable to their report, the veins of gold will be soon discovered.

" Thirdly. By testimony and voluntary oaths of such as have found pieces of gold and have seen found by others, one piece of 30 ounces, and some of greater weight, which were flat and mixed with spar, and some with keel, and some with brimstone, and the Lord of Markestone Merchistoun, did shew me a piece of three quarters of an ounce, and some lesser ... those pieces were torn by the force of water ... of the waters since that time, whereby I do conclude that spar, keel, and brimstone are leaders to the veins of gold...

13

" Fourthly. Wheresoever gold is found by washing, there are... found therewith which are not flat beds lying about the ... smoother as though torn from the veins and tossed by the water and made smooth, like to those stones which being carried by violence of brooks and rivers do grow smooth and are not so rough as the same quarries which grow or remain in their beds.

" Fifthly. The gold washers ignorance hath been such, as they did not seek where were any veins of lead or copper, neither of keel, brimstone or spar which have been known to them, within these last ten years that though descending into the depth between two rocks, which they constantly have seen gold growing in the former metals in sundry places and conceiving that there be sundry veins of the same metals they ... to find the veins of gold growing therein.

" Sixthly. I find the great works for gold to have been along the sides of the great waters in the valleys between the mountains and along the waters and gills and as the inhabitants report, having made many trials in the sides of the hills and gills, though but 200 yards from the former workings in the waters, in the valleys and gills they found not gold, and by ... his works he affirmeth the like, and I having made two days trials on the tops and sides of the hills did likewise not find gold; so as if not thoroughly dispersed, but lying in some places as the said workmen affirmed in a manner of being drawn together into lesser room and straiter the same are ... shows that there are veins of gold; and the rather that there hath been plenty of gold gotten in the said cloughs and gills 80 fathoms above the foresaid waters in the valleys, which gold being ponderous and bulky must by common reason descend, was consequently whereas some pieces of gold of above 30 ounces weight have been found in the said gills, the same must either grow thereabouts or by violent waters be driven out of higher places where they did grow within the circumference of those place where the gold is found."

This document, which I believe is now for the first time published, is very interesting, and gives a most faithful description of a gold region, familiar to many an Australian explorer, as to me, and which I recognized on my visit to Scotland for the purposes of this work. It likewise gives a curious view of the mining knowledge and theories of the times. The author states his experience in the western districts of England. The whole of the original document must have referred to Crawford Moor, and must have described the mode of working proposed. It alludes to a company of adventurers.

It will be observed that the nuggetty character of the diggings is distinctly affirmed, and here we get an account of the largest nuggets from actual observers. The author had the usual prepossessions as to the mother of gold, and his plan of operations is in some degree sketched out. The supposed growth of gold was a favourite subject with the early writers on minerals, and any arborescent specimen of gold or silver was considered a proof of the growth of gold. These writers were, however, aware of the testimony among miners, that metals are found reproduced in old workings.

Soon after the Earl of Morton became Regent, in 1572, Cornelius returned to London, and assigned his privileges to Arnold Bronchorst, or, according to one account, employed him as his agent. This Bronchorst was likewise a painter, and settled in Scotland. The Regent, Earl of Morton, however, refused any relaxation of the bullion laws, and Devos's company fell to the ground, unless it became the basis of Bulmer's company; f but Bronchorst's Aldrovandus, Agricola, Boyle.

t Pennant's Wales, vol. l,p. 90; Jacob's History of the Precious Metals, vol. 1, p. 291; Abbot on Mines, p. 216; Gentleman's Magazine, p. 464. patent had a lingering existence, as it is referred to in 1592, in an Act of James VI., for promoting the mines.

The date of Bulmer's operations does not appear; the writer in the "Gentleman's Magazine" supposes them to have been subsequent to Foulis's lease, in the year 1592. Now Gawyn Smith's letter, before referred to, and dated 1578, states that Bulmer was then employed. Sir Bevis Bulmer was one of the great speculators of that era. Leadhills seems to have been his first venture. He then engaged in working the silver-lead mines at Chewton Minery, in the Mendips, where queen Elizabeth lost £10,000. He was more successful in the reworking of the Combe Martin silver-lead mines. The waterworks at Broken Wharf caused, most properly, a heavy investment of capital without an adequate return. He had the good fortune to obtain the farming of the duty on seaborne coals at £6,200 a year, but having too many irons in the fire, he suffered it to be mismanaged by his agents, and at length lost it from nonpayment of the Crown rent. About 1605, James I. (6th of Scotland) took him under his patronage, but the scheme of the Knights of the Golden Mines failed; nor was he more successful in the silver mine at Hilderstone,f but he remained governor of the king's mines until his death, in 1613. He was, during this time, largely engaged in the plantation of Ulster and other Irish schemes, by which he became greatly embarrassed.J

In 1593, James VI. had granted the mines in the Crawford Moor district to Thomas Foulis, goldsmith of Edinburgh, for twenty-one years, he then being indebted to Foulis £14,594. In 1597 he appears to have been at work on the lead mines.§

In 1591, eighty stone weight, or five hundred and sixty pounds of gold, worth £28,000 were ordered to be coined; and again, in the same year, two hundred weight, say two hundred pounds only, would be worth £10,000. This sum of £38,000 in one year confirms the productiveness of the mines.

Although the foregoing account gives a tolerable idea of the history of the Scotch gold mines in the sixteenth century, several points are left unsettled. Besides the manuscripts already referred to, there is a very long account of the transactions in Clydesdale, by Stephen Atkinson, one of Bulmer's copartners and managers, who was a refiner in the Mint of the Tower of London, in 1586, and afterwards employed in Devonshire in refining silver-lead ore from Ireland. He was subsequently engaged in Bulmer's Irish adventures, and in 1616 became his successor at Crawford Moor, on condition of paying a royalty of one-tenth. Atkinson was not successful, and in 1621 a lease was granted for twenty-one years to John Hendlie, a physician. Atkinson is stated to have spent £3,000 of the king's money, and to have got only three ounces of gold. One result we have of Atkinson's labours is a long manuscript treatise, which is the chief authority, but is very loosely written. One copy of this was printed by the Bannatyne Club, in 1825. For the use of this, and some other information, I have been indebted to George Vere Irving, Esq. Another copy is in the Harleian MSS. of the British Museum. An imperfect copy, but one seemingly nearer to the original English, was lent to me at Leadhills. I have used this and the Bannatyne edition in giving the following account on Atkinson's authority. The Bannatyne edition, for some not very good reason, retains the spelling and errors of the ignorant Scotch transcriber, which I have endeavoured to avoid.

At an early part of his work, Atkinson says that there are, within England, Scotland and Ireland many who term Gold Mynes of Scotland, p. 6. themselves assayers who indeed prove no proficients. He likewise objects to the artists who profess the making of the philosopher's stone at the expence of their employers. He complains too of the current prejudices as to gold workings. " Others who would fain catch their own shadows, may not, nor will not, be persuaded that any goodness can be produced out of Scotch ground, and are doubtful whether the sun, moon, and stars shine there or not; for, say they, gold and silver engender with the heat of the sun and moon, and also where such riches are, the people cannot be poor nor beggarly as the Scotch are. And others dare presume to swear, that never yet was found within Christendom any solid beds or veins and sears? of gold or silver, but that all gold and silver is reduced out of lead ore, copper, tin, iron or steel ore, for they have travelled over and over the most part of Christendom, and neither saw the like to Scotch natural gold gotten in the ground by me, nor have heard thereof otherwise than is before related." One curious argument of Atkinson against the objectors is, that " twenty fathoms under ground within the entrails of the earth, it is as hot even in the coldest country or nation, under the whole scope of heaven, as in the hottest."

After stating the chief places for gold in the south of Scotland, he proceeds to make some remarks on native or natural gold. " The vulgar sort of Scotchmen usually sought for it upon those moors, after a great rain and after the splits (spouts?) of rains had run his course; and this rain or force of water, brought down no other gold than gold which before had been removed by the force of waves flood, and that gold was and is called superficial (surface) gold to this day." "At the flood," he says, "natural gold and silver (which now are found in combes and valleys) were forced and torn from his bed or vein; and thither even our Scotch gold, which is now found in sterns (stars?) or in grains and pieces, did descend, or was washed down; "in which valleys, combes, skirts of hills or cloughs, even until this present day, it hath lain still and not removed, except after a great split (spill?) of rain, the force whereof doth break and wear the superficies of the earth, but not the solid earth; after which the Scotch men and women and children run to seek for it, and do find it still, even unto this day; and thereby they find with it also the laxer stones in great abundance, and also much of the calamineer stones; but in the salineer stones it is as small as mustard seed, and some like meal; and in the sappar in lumps, and like unto the fowls or birds' eggs. And the strongest of all is this: there is found natural gold linked fast unto the sappar stone, even as veins of lead ore and white spar do grow together, &c. But their usual manner is, when they seek for gold in combes and valleys, to frame or make a long sough or scouring place, into which they bring the streamwater to scour away the light earth from the heavy sandy earth, and to cull away the great stones from the heavy sand, which sand or heavy earth they scrape into their troughs or trays, and by stirring it and by washing the same often, there is found both rain gold, flat gold scale gold?, pale gold and black gold, yet all these be natural gold. "

Atkinson alludes to Brunswick or Hartz miners, in Scotland. He says, " and the Brunswickers confessed, when they were in Scotland, that under the Duke there was both gold, silver, copper and tin."

Of De Vos's adventure, Atkinson gives a long account: " I happened on a book of records at Crawford John wherein were registered the labours of many employed by Mr. Cornelius, a lapidary in London, sent thither to discover the gold vein or bed, at the charge of merchants of London, who procured queen Elizabeth's signet to the Scotch king, on account of which he was admitted, and got This is Cornelius De Voz.
some gold on the mountains of Clydesdale and Nithsdale, some of it like bird's eyes and eggs, whereby he persuaded friends at Edinburgh to adventure with him, and procured a new grant to him and his co-partners in Edinburgh and London, of all the gold and silver mines in Scotland; each according to his disbursement was to have his part. Some bought corn, meal, malt, and victuals, besides five thousand pounds Scotch money. Cornelius was chosen to govern and direct both artists and workmen; but they never sought gold in solid places, but in combs or valleys, where it had been washed down since the general deluge.

" Cornelius was called the superior of his Majesty's mines, and had authority to punish offenders, and to take workmen from England. He was obliged to bring all the gold and silver they got into the king's mint house at Edinburgh, to be coined, whereinto in thirty days' time they conveyed half a stone weightf of natural gold, worth four hundred and fifty pounds sterling. The workmen sometimes got gold at their own charges, by toleration of the superior, which they sold at a mark sterling per ounce, or eight pounds Scotch. At the highest rate they had but twenty shillings sterling per ounce.

" Cornelius had six score men at work in valleys and dales. He employed both men and women, lads and lasses, who before begged. He profited by their work, and they lived contented and well. He bought their gold which they washed, for a mark sterling, which was worth five marks sterling per ounce.

" The Earl of Murray, deceased, and Cornelius had a new grant from the Earl of Morton, next Regent, who also obliged him to bring all the gold into the mint house which he got, and where it was coined into three pound pieces, each an ounce in weight. Much gold was there bought of the workmen at twenty shillings per ounce.
Nuggets and coarse dust. t Eight pounds.

" The same book mentions one Abraham Gray, a Dutchman from London, who brought artists from England, and others of his own country, into Scotland, on the good report of the gold there. He sold much of his effects and procured his countrymen to adventure with him. He went with authority. He hired many inhabitants at four-pence per day, which contented them as well as twelve-pence did the English at that time. He had plenty of victuals in his Storehouse at Wanlockhead, now in decay, and was supplied with all necessary tools. His workmen washed in the valley. He never sought on high hills or solid places for a bed or vein of gold. In valleys at Wanlockhead he got a good quantity of solid gold. He paid his workmen weekly, and lent money to divers before hand. With this natural gold got in Graybeard's time, for so he was called because of his great long beard, was made a basin by a Scotchman in Edinburgh, which contained an English gallon, and was filled with coined pieces called unicorns, and presented the French king by the Earl of Morton, saying, ' Behold! all that is therein is natural gold of this kingdom, got by Abraham Gray, a Dutchman.' Which Abraham Gray, standing by, affirmed upon oath, and said he thought it did engender, and more ore within the earth, and that he observed it to be so, by the influence of the heavens, that it grew not by the power of the sun, moon, or stars, but by the omnipotent power of God. The Earl of Morton said, ' I also believe it engendereth in the earth of water and earth, and that it was made perfect and malleable gold from the beginning by God the Creator.'"

Another adventurer was Mr. George Bowes. Atkinson says, " Mr. George Bowes, an English gentleman, 'procured a commission into Scotland unto the gold mines, and I happened also on a book of his making in England. I carried it with me in Scotland, and compared the same with the report of the country, and the countrymen at Wanlockhead *h* said, ' It is so, and most true that Mr. Bowes discerned a small vein of gold, which had much small gold in it, upon Wanlockhead.'"

It is possible that the book of Mr. Bowes may be the MSS. Otho Ex. already given, and which is certainly a very vivid account of the gold regions.

Atkinson says of the vein, " Mr. Bowes swore all his workmen to keep it secret, and never discover it to the Scotch king nor his council, for so he had promised to do to the Queen of England, on whose letter he had a warrant from the Scotch lords to dig and delve where he would, so that it was after another fashion than Mr. Bulmer before did.

" Mr. Bowes digged several shafts in solid places on the mountains in Robertsmoor, in Wanlockhead, and often found large pieces and much small gold. He gave ten or twelve ounces thereof to make the owners of the ground his friends, and gave the merchants in England as much more.

" He did keep many workmen, and paid them with the same gold. He built houses to himself and people, but none for his Scotsmen, who sought their victuals and lodgings far from the works, which was a great hindrance. When they had fillled their purses, Mr. Bowes caused the said shafts to be filled up, and swore his agents and workmen not to discover the same, which was confessed by some of his chief servants since he died. He returned and told the Queen of England that he had performed and concealed his trust, that he had found a small vein of gold, and shewed a long purse full of it, which was admired and valued at seven score pounds sterling, without melting, but he had given much thereof away privily, and this had much of the salmoneer stones in it. He said,' I have hidden it till my going thither, for which she thanked him, and promised to reward this gift trebly, and that he should go again next spring at her charges, to seek for a greater vein.' He was killed by the breaking of a ladder in a copper work at Keswick, in Cumberland."

It seems that Hochstetter, another great speculator, nearly lost his life by the same accident, as he afterwards told Atkinson, when the latter was in his employment. " I travelling further into the north parts had certain intelligence of the vein; hoping to have discovered that small vein again, it moved me, at my own adventure to go and see if I could find out the same, which before Mr. Bowes had hidden up. And I sought it diligently, but I could not get any of Mr. Bowes' men that there wrought before."

Atkinson states that his specimens of Scotch gold from Shortcleugh were mostly put into the. hands of Mr. John Murray, of the king's bedchamber, to keep, by his Majesty's command, and that he could neither obtain value for them nor the use of them, and that thus not being able to show them to the capitalists interested, he failed in getting up a company.

Atkinson says of Arthur or Arnold Van Bronchorst, that Mr. Hilliard and Cornelius De Vos made an assignment to him of their patent, who, after that, powerful, set sundry workmen to work without any trouble or molestation. He marked sundry moors and found gold in sundry places, but he was forced to leave it all at the minthouse in Scotland. This he vainly endeavoured to have set aside.

Of Bulmer he says: " Mr. Bulmer had a patent from the Queen of England and King of Scotland, to seek for the gold and silver mines in any places of that kingdom, especially within these five moors or forests. On Mannock Moor, in Nithsdale, his workmen got some natural gold, but built no houses there, which was a hindrance. On Wanlock Water, in Roberts Moor, he caused search diligently for natural gold, of which he got a pretty good quantity, and made watercourses to wash it; neither builded he houses there, but went to Thomas Flood's house in Leadhills, and repaired not Mr. Bowes' house at Wanlockhead, which might have sufficed him. Some say he found out the vein of gold Mr. Bowes had discovered. In Frier Moor, in Glengonnar Water, in Clydesdale, Mr. Bulmer got store of gold; and there he built a very fair country house, where he kept great hospitality. He purchased grounds about it for cattle. By help of a watercourse, he got much straggling gold on the skirts of the hills and in the valleys, but none in solid places, which kept him in great pomp, keeping open house for all comers, as is reported.

" On Short Cleuch Water, in Crawford Moor, he brought another goodly watercourse, and intended to make several dams there, to contain water for the buddies and scourers, and for washing gold, of which he found store, and purposed to have built there another dwelling-house, and cut his purse bottom by the extravagant entertainment with which he used strangers. Thus he wasted what he got in gold, which was very much. He got as much gold at Long Cleuch as would have maintained three times as many men as he kept royally. From Short Cleuch he removed up the great hill to Long Cleuch Head, to seek gold in solid places; whereof he discovered a small spring, but there he wanted a watercourse to help him. This vein had the sappar stone plentifully in it, which sometimes held natural gold, but the salmoneer stones in that vein at Long Cleuch Head held much silver, and may prove a rich mine, if followed by such as know the nature of minerals. It is said that vein was powdered with gold, called small powdered gold. It was a vein, and not a bed. They removed from Short Cleuch Trial to Long Cleuch Head, because the workmen found two pieces of gold there, within two feet of the moss. The one piece was reported to weigh six ounces, and the other better than five, which was thought to descend from the gold bed. None ever saw natural gold more perfect of God's own han

See the next page.

dywork. It never was made by the art of man, but by the Great Philosopher of Heaven, who makes the true philosopher's stone of nothing to be discovered in the bowels of the earth, called God's Treasure House. At Long Cleuch Head, as I heard it reported, and saw a piece of the same, was found a piece of brown spar, somewhat like sugar-candy, which, after it was broken, had in it an ounce of pure gold, which spar, as I suppose, is called the sappar stone in foreign nations. This brown spar stone weighed two pounds troy.

" At Long Cleuch Head Mr. Bulmer made a stamping mill, called, abroad, anacanago. Such are used in the West Indies, and in Cornwall, where it is sometimes called a plash mill, to dress tin out of stones, in which the eye can discern little or nothing. By the same means Mr. Bulmer used to get much small meally gold at Long Cleuch.

" On Glengaber Water, in Inderland, in the Forest of Ettrick, he got the greatest gold in Scotland, like Indian wheat or pearl, and black-eyed, like beins. He did not mind to settle there till a fitter time, being driven away by force of weather. Mr. Bulmer presented Queen Elizabeth with as much gold as made a porringer.

" After Mr. Bulmer had lost his former living ortune, he recalled himself, and wrote a book of all his works and devices, which he named ' Bulmer's Skill.' It was not printed. Among his many memorable deeds, a great part of his book was how the silver mines and mineral stones might be effected, and how his tin and coal mines and salt works in Wales were followed, and how his lead mines in Mendip were most profitable, of all others, to him.

" I had his speech to the king concerning his gold mines in Scotland, whereupon the king resolved to set them on anew. The king proposed to erect a company of Twenty Four Gentlemen of sufficient estates, and each was to lay out three hundred pounds sterling on these gold mines, for James I. and VI.

which each was to have the honour of knighthood, and to be called the Knights of the Golden Mines, or the Golden Knights. The money or victuals so collected to be committed to an English or Scotch Treasurer, in a storehouse. That Mr. Bulmer be Chief Governor during his life. That the workmen be weekly paid. That mills, dams, sluices, watercourses, &c. be made by Mr. Bulmer and his agents. Lastly, to erect a chapel, where the workmen may make their prayers to God for their souls' health, and then their work would be blessed, and come to a good end, as in other nations."

" The next time Mr.Bulmer came from court he grew sick, and confessed that the Earl of Salisbury had crossed all his expected fortune; then he called himself and family to remembrance, and said, " Well, God giveth and God taketh away, and blessed be the name of the Lord for ever!" More he said, " Methinks it is strange that the King should make a grant, and a nobleman should cut it off."

" Mr. Bulmer, in his book, mentions how the rich silver mines of Hilderstone, in Scotland, were found and lost; how Sandy Maund found a heavy piece of red metal, descended from a vein when it engendered with spar called cacilla. He found this under the silver Burnat Kingapple Hill. It proved wonderful rich when tried in the assay furnace by Mr. Bulmer, and that the great quantity of silver got in the pit called God's Blessing, was fined out of the red metal. The purest contained twenty-four ounces of fine silver, in each one hundred weight,f valued at *£120* sterling per ton. It remains good till twelve fathoms deep, and from that till thirty it proved nought. Its ore grew like hair or grass. The pit called God's Blessing was so In the same way as the haronets were created for the colonization of Ulster, and the haronets of Nova Scotia, for the colonization of Nova Scotia, t Four hundred and eighty ounces per ton. called by Mr. Bulmer because of the wonderful works of God he had seen there, the like never known before in these kingdoms!"

Atkinson says, when he refined the red metal three days a week, that he made one hundred pounds sterling each day, but that when this mine fell to the king it was not so rich.

In another place, Atkinson mentions that the red metal called bell metal in Scotland, was both plentiful and rich a long time, and that, on a sudden, God took his blessing from it, and then none could reduce any silver out of it, countervaluable to the charge thereof.

Mr. Bulmer offers to discover the like near Hilderstone, saying, at the same time, " how long it will continue is known unto God, for mines are as uncertain as the life is to man, which is like a bubble on the waters to-day, tomorrow none!"

From an old parchment, the author says, " that in the time of Henry VII. the silver mines of Combe Martin and Beerferris gave yearly forty-four thousand pounds sterling in bullion and in lead for five years, which lead was sold at four pounds sterling per ton. It yielded, above all charges, twenty thousand pounds sterling, and above one thousand men were employed at it in the year one thousand five hundred and eighty-seven."

" A new silver mine was discovered at Combe Martin, by Adrian Gilbert and John Poppler, a lapidary, with whom Mr. Bulmer bargained for one half of the whole, he bearing charges for two years. This mine yielded to each of the partners ten thousand pounds sterling. It continued four years reasonable good. The last cake of silver Mr. Bulmer gave to the city of London, which Mr. Middley made into a cup and cover, with Mr. Bulmer's picture, and these verses thereon:— Four, that is 1487.

" When Waterworks at Broken Wharf
At first erected were,
And Bevis Bulmer by his art
The waters 'gan to rear,
Dispersed, I in the earth did lie
From all beginning old.
In place call'd Comb where Martin long
Had hid me in his mould,
I did no service on the earth,
Nor no man set me free,
Till Bulmer by his art and skill
Did frame me thus to be."

Atkinson says, " Mr. Bulmer writeth of the variety of stones and metals found by him in Scotland: 1st. Natural gold, great and small. 2nd. Natural silver, the like he never saw. 3rd. Copper stones of the richest sort. 4th. Lead ore, great store at Leadhills. 5th. Iron stones in abundance. 6th. Beds of alabaster. 7th. Marble stones.f 8th. Amethyst stones, very amiable, for he had a man that wrought them, one of which the king wore. 9th. Natural pearl in the sea sand in Galloway. 10th. Infinite other riches are there also. The author saith of Mr. Bulmer that he gave gold several times to unthankful persons, and sold much of it for half-price, and such as he was most liberal to were readiest to cut his throat. He continued still liberal in hospitality. None like him in that time, as is reported through all Crawford Moor, &c. That he had many irons in the fire, and often intricate matters to decide, and too many waiters prodigal hanging on each shoulder. He wasted much himself, and gave liberally to many to be honoured, or else he might have been rich. By such means he was impoverished and followed other venial vices not allowable, so once down, aye down, and at last he died three This was one of Bulmer's undertakings. Sir Bevis erected here, in the year 1595, an engine of vast height, for the purpose of forcing and conveying water to serve the middle and western parts of the metropolis, as the London Bridge water works had been erected to supply the city.
t In my copy of the MSS. some one has interlined—Stone coal. hundred and forty pounds sterling" in my debt, and left me in Ireland in much debt for him, and God forgive us all our sins, but if he had lived till now he might have paid all men."
Now, a little concerning some chief points that I observed from Mr. Bulmer, within these thirty years. He said, " a mineral man should be a hazard adventurer, not much esteeming whether he hit or miss. If he happen to win he must esteem as nothing. If he lose all, yet he must think he has got something. If he find a rich vein, let him not esteem it, for it is like a man stung with a nettle. If he seek in hopes to find out proof of it, yet he must believe that he hath or shall have what he really hath not."

Atkinson, the author, saith, " when mines' hit it is the best got gear in the world, it is so profitable to all and hurts none, and when they hit not, though it be lost for a time, God is hereby honoured in searching his hidden treasures out of the depths of the earth. I read of a godly man's opinion on the first digging the earth for gold and silver, &c."

" Wo to the man that first did dig the ground

To find the mines of silver and of gold,

For when it lay hid, and unto us unknown

Of strife and dehate the seed was unsown.

Then liv'd men well and held themselves content,

With food and cloth and payed then no rent."

The author saith, " there is power given unto minerals to engender in the earth, or to couple with other stones, which are their feeders, as he saith. I have seen natural gold engender with sundry stones in Scotland; *2nd,* Natural silver malleable; 3rd, Natural quicksilver among the sea sands; 4th, Red malleable copper in stones; 5th, Tin, black, brown, and grey; 6th, A white heavy spar, holding malleable lead; 7th, Iron, in several coloured stones, malleable."

Atkinson runs a parallel betwixt the four rivers of Eden and the four waters wherein he got the gold, viz. Glengonnar, Short Cleuch, Wanlock, and Mannock, which ground may be called a garden, though not pleasant and fruitful, yet richer under than above ground, which waters descending from mountains, are divided by God's omnipotent power into four heads. " One Glengonnar, in Clydesdale, in Friar Moor, of which the Marquis of Hamilton is superior, is much natural gold, commonly found near the river sides, washed from the veins or bed in mountains. It looketh pale or wan. The second is Short Cleuch Water, in Crawford Moor, of which the Earl of Lothian is superior, where is red gold. Here gold was got by me and brought to the king, and tried to be worth seventy-six thousand pounds per ton. These brows or braes are likely to turn rich, if diligently sought, and the vein or bed is not far from the gold gotten in the valleys. The water courses there are in great decay for want of reparation. The third river is Wanlock, in Robertsmoor, in Nithsdale, of which the Lord Sanquhar is superior, under the king and Lord of Closeburn, and is fewer thereof, wherein is gold. The fourth is Mannock Water, in Mannock Moor, of which Lord Drumlanrig is superior, under the king. The gold found there is rough, and not smooth like the rest found on other moors. If these moors may be wrought to effect, then God's treasure house in Scotland may be discovered. He allegeth that it is the present time that the two philosophers mentioned in king Josina's time, one hundred and sixty years before Christ, who were sailing from Portugal to Athens, and by tempest they were driven to Scotland, and arriving in Ross, each sitting on the end of a board, after their ship and crew were lost, who, being brought to the Scotch king, Josina, asserted the Scotch climate was more inclined to mineral and stones of wonderful properties under the earth, than it is to products above the earth, which they found by the influence of the heavens, and therefore advised the king and his people to worship the Lord God, the first former of the whole world, and I sis and Apis, the gpds of the Egyptians; and that the king hereon convened his rulers, who consulted and embraced these sayings, that thenceforth God blessed them and the people. He citeth Job 28th and 1st, where he saith, it is said that gold hath its settled place in the earth, out of which it is to be taken as out of its vein or lode. He saith silver hath a beginning like as it were out of a rod, like free. He saith gold and silver engendereth in the earth from their first creation, and thereof I make no doubt saith he the story of the two philosophers he hath from the abridgment of the Scotch Chronicles.

" From Cataia I have seen brought natural gold and silver to London, and when queen Elizabeth sent a ship to be loaded therewith, they found not the like gold as before, but found a vein or bed of mineral stones like to the black saxcers found in Scotland, with another bright black saxcer stone reddish, which in Scotland engendereth gold. Captain Frobisher caused try it, and both gold and silver were reduced from these black stones. He caused dig deeper, and at twenty-nine fathoms these stones were turned into a glittering stuff, spotted with red like gold or silver or copper, from which time, when a discord happened, wherein six men were slain, God took his blessing from it, so that they never could find after that either gold or silver in these stones as before.

" The author prays that God may be his guide in his business of mining, for religion was a special cause in this enterprize to discover the secret works of God. Art, skill, fame, and hopes of everlasting life, led him to these worthy attempts to discovery of minerals within the earth. If it hit it must be a renown to all Christendom, and registrate the names of the undertakers in the kalendar of never-dying memory. He resumes the two philosophers and Josina, and says he always thought this blessed time of discovery of the gold mines of Scotland is now come, or else will never come in his time, which he had pronounced thrice and was not seconded. He asserts that artists can turn malleable gold and silver into coarse, which will abide the toucher, cutter, hammer, forging, nailing, and melting, but cannot stand the assays, masters, strong waters or furnaces. Then the true gold and silver compared to God's word is made known from the compound, and as the righteous shall inherit Heaven and the infidel his torment, so the good gold and silver are prepared to abide all the forcible sorts of fire and water. Compounds mixed with the best gold and silver shall be turned into smoke or vapour, or by the refiner's art made into their own body again."

Atkinson gives a curious account of the introduction of improvements in gold refining. He says of the king of Spain's fleets, " Sometimes the English pirates meet therewithal, knowing the time when they are to be laden, and strip them quite of all such gold and silver. I have sometimes seen of the same brought into Devon and Cornwall, so as Londoners have ridden thither and purchased much thereof. For about the year 1585 there came a fleet from the W. Indies to Seville with eleven millions of pieces of eight. Much of the same silver was conveyed into London before it came to Seville, for good fellows met with them and forced them to share, for which they gave the Spaniards store of victuals, and therewith must of force be content. I was then an apprentice at the Appletree in Red Cross Street, without Cripplegate, and was admitted to be refiner or finer at the Tower of London, instead of my master, Francis Tiver, a gold refiner, where I refined three days in the week round Indian cakes of silver (plata pina?) for Sir Richard Martyn, knight and master of the mint; and one Wm. Clarke was a chief agent therein, and saw it all done.

Besides this many times there came of such like cakes to be done in Red Cross Street, and Anthony Martyn was agent for Sir Richard Martyn, and I did refine thereof some days looolbs. weight, and on some days 5001bs. weight or '600 lbs. weight. And sometimes I have had round cakes of silver brought to be refined, in great batches, which we before sent out for plumbers sweepers by cart loads, because the common sort of people should not perceive it from tin or lead. And it was commonly refined by night, and afterwards melted and cast into ingots of fine silver of 40lbs. weight each ingot, and so returned by night always to Sir Richard Martyn's house in Cheapside by laborers and porters, which blew the bellows for me; and so thence to be conveyed into the Tower of London, to be coined by his own servants; and thus it was weekly turned into money.

" I have seen lead before the silver was extracted, make good tavern pots, bowl pots, member pots and saucers, much like unto pewter, but was none. Now again some men demand how I first knew these things, and of whom, saying, ' I knew his master with whom he was an apprentice, and himself, and his master never knew any such art.' I answer, ' Neither knew you the names of those who first discovered the art of extraction in England, nor who taught the same, to whom nor why. To discover the art thereof cost my master, Tiver, £50 sterling, besides other charges, meat and drink.' They also taught the art of the true searing furnaces, and for drying furnaces, and semeteering furnaces, and sundry other furnaces to melt by flame, &c. And lastly, how gold and silver might, by the easiest means, be drawn out of dry minerals and mineral stones, and how verditer might be made without the use of strong water, which painters do use to paint with.

" About this time Sir Frances Drake brought into England great store of gold and silver and copper in abundance, especially of the copper mines from St. Domingo.. A great quantity thereof he brought into London, and much thereof was sold for red copper in price, whereof was made both kettles and pans, and great caldrons to boil in, ordnance, and other cast pieces, before the worth thereof was known. At last these foreign travellers, who had taught the art of extraction out of dry minerals and mineral stones, having travelled throughout far countries and behaving themselves like artists and workmen, were much accounted of in London, for their experience. First showing how the silver may be extracted out of the copper mines, and most of the copper saved, for which they were well paid by Mr. Tiver. And at that time they taught him to make aqua regis, to eat up gold into it, and leave the silver, as aquafortis did silver, and leave the gold like sand. And lastly, how to make blue verditer and green verditer without the help of strong waters, or green waters; and-Mr. Tiver paid them well for it. The name of one and the principal was:—

" Jacob Yaughall, a Jew.

"Henrique Guarro, a Portingal.

" Don Francisco, andl two travellers come from the West

This is further curious as furnishing an instance of Jewish intercourse with England, for it is probable that England was never altogether without Jews.

" Now concerning their acts and what they have seen in foreign provinces. Jacob Yaughall saith he saw natural gold and silver extracted out of dry minerals or mineral stones, and they were called as followeth: the sappar, the callamineer, the saxer, and the salaneer stones, the cacella, the ticano, the centeno, and the menduta stones. Besides he hath seen both copper, tin, lead, and iron to contain in each of it silver; and several other minerals and mineral stones to hold both gold and silver. And he hath seen

Don Ferdinando, quicksilver issue out of the rock or crag, and out of a flint stone, which if any wise man can believe it, then will I believe it also, but I am like Didymus, before I see it I cannot believe it. And they also said that they had seen copper hold perfect gold, and tin perfect gold, and lead to hold perfect silver, in foreign countries, and iron to hold both gold and silver, and many of these to hold-neither gold nor silver, but to be perfect of themselves."

Although Mr. Atkinson doubted this account of native quicksilver, it is nevertheless true, like the rest of Yaughall's description; but Mr. Atkinson, although he professes to have learned much from the foreign travellers, seems to have learned little that was practical.

"Now to return to the four travellers: namely, Jacob Yaughall, the Jew, Henrique, Francisco, and Ferdinando, how they tried themselves severally to be expert artists and great travellers, and to have travelled over the greatest part of the West Indies. They came to London in Anno Domini 1572, where they taught the art of extraction at Mr. Tiver's house unto him, in the year of our Lord God, 1585? and was paid therefore; for at that time few men understood the art thereof and the profit that ensued thereby. First, what a charge of fire, in wood and coals, is to be saved in trying of dry minerals and stones. Secondly, they showed the proof thereof by some minerals and dry stones wherein nothing could be discerned; which they brought with them from Potosi Mines, in the West Indies; and they said they were there when one bed or vein of silver was newly discovered, which was very small, and therefore small accounted of, and that it was a long time in discovering. And third, that the superiors and governors thereof had been twelve years and upwards before they found the depth thereof, not countervailing the tenth part I have often seen native quicksilver in Australia ooze out by the heat of the sun.

of the charge, which thereunto belonged. And this was in Anno Domini 1545; for in that year they washed and scoured much earth, which before had been turned, digged, and gathered together near unto the river sides within valleys and combes, where oftentimes they found out perfect hops of gold and pieces of silver, black eyed, like unto Indian peas, which they called straggling gold and silver, and some like unto pompion seeds or to pippin seeds pepites.

" And there was a book written of their travels called the ' Jews' Travels. '"

In 1609, Bulmer made a search for gold in the Highlands.

Sir Bevis Bulmer presented to Queen Elizabeth a gold porringer, upon which were engraven the following lines:—

" I dare not give, nor yet present, But render part of that's thy own;
My mind and heart shall still invent
To seek out treasures yet unknown."

The scheme of the Knights of the Golden Mines was only carried out so far as the creation of Sir Bevis Bulmer and Sir John Claypool.

Over the lintel of Sir Bevis Bulmer's house at Glengonnar was till lately the following inscription:—'

" In Wanlock, Elwand, and Glengonnar,
I wan my riches and my honour."-)-

In 1620, the gold and silver mines of Lesmahago were bestowed on the Marquess of Hamilton, and in thirty days afterwards eight pounds of native gold were brought to the mint, besides what the workmen got. J

Since James I.'s time nothing effective has been done as to the gold mines, but new localities have been discovered, and nuggets have been constantly obtained.

Gold Mynes of Scotland, p. 94. t Simson's History of Sanquhar, p. 160. *X* Atkinson's MSS. as quoted in Abbot on Miues, p. 21o'. It will be observed this same story is told of Cornelius De Vos. The discovery of gold became known throughout Europe, and the subject has never been lost sight of.

In the seventeenth century the gold mines were spoken of by every writer, f but nothing was done for working them. Charles I. had coronation medals struck of this gold.J Several of the museums, which then began to be formed, contained specimens from Clydesdale; among others, the Edinburgh museum of Sir Robert Sibbald, which had a small nuggett.§ Sir Hans Sloane had a medal of this gold. Boyle had seen a nuggett from Scotland weighing eight pennyweights nine grains, and others of three pennyweights twenty-one grains, and three pennyweights three grain's. The largest nugget found in Scotland weighed three pounds, another thirty ounces, or two pounds and a half; others of six ounces and five ounces. The next largest, one ounce and a half. Two of these are mentioned from Sutherlandshire and Clydesdale, ff

In the last century some gold was obtained from Sir John Erskine's estate, near Stirling. J J About the year 1740, Sir John Erskine, with four others, formed a plan for working the Clydesdale mines again.§§ Some other gold fields were likewise discovered. Nuggets were still occasionally picked up in Clydesdale, mi but the produce fell off.K Aldrovandus on Minerals, vol. 1, chap. 2; Boterus, quoted by ditto; Hector Boethius' History of Scotland, p. 6; Camden's Britannia; Gerard Malyne's Lex Mercatoria, p. 183.

t Opera Mineralia Explicata, p. 9; Pettus' Fodinse Regales; Touchstone, by W. B.; Boyle's Hydrostatic Way of Examining Ores, p. 182; Sibbald's Natural History of Scotland, lib. 4, p. 52.

J Cramer's Assaying, p. 157. § Catalogue, p. 70.

Cramer's Assaying, p. 157. Boyle's Works, vol. 5, p. 30. Cottonian MSS.; Pennant's Wales, vol. 1, p. 90. tt *Ibid.* p. 90; Mining Journal, 1849, p. 290. *XX* Pennant's Wales, p. 66.

§§ Reise von J. C. Fabricius in Jacobs' Hist. vol. 1, p. 293.

lll Pennant's Scotland, vol. 3, p. 416.

IfH Camden's Britannia, 1769.

M

In the present century the working of the Clydesdale gold was attempted to be resumed under the superintendence of the manager of the lead mines at Wanlockhead, but the price of labour was considered too high to induce the continuance of the working. At the present time there is no gold mine at work in Scotland, nor has there been for some years, but many new gold localities have been discovered, principally in Aberdeenshire.

There is probably gold all over Scotland, but from records or actual inspection of specimens, I am only able to enumerate the following counties:—

I. Sutherlandshire.

II. Aberdeenshire. III. Fifeshire. IV. Perthshire.

V. Stirlingshire.

VI. Linlithgowshire. VII. Lanarkshire. VIII. Dumfriesshire. IX. Ayrshire.

X. Selkirkshire.

XI. Kirkcudbrightshire.

The Scotch rivers which contain gold are:—

The Clyde.

The Nith.

The Tweed, in the Ettrick and Yarrow.

The Forth.

The Don.

The Tay.

Williams' History of the Mineral Kingdom, vol. 2, p. 364; Jacobs' History of the Precious Metals, vol. 1, p. 292.

CHAPTER VIII. GOLD FIELDS OF SCOTLAND. *Sutherlandshire.—Aberdeenshire. —Fifeshire. —Perthshire. Stirlingshire. —Linlithgowshire. —Lanarkshire.—Clydesdale Gold Field.—Dumfriesshire.—Ayrshire.—Selkirkshire.—Kirkcudbrightshire.*

I. Sutherlandshire.—The earliest mention we have of gold in Sutherlandshire, is in the last century, in Gough's edition of Camden's Britannia. It is there stated that gold is found in Durness. In 1840, a nugget was found there weighing one ounce and a half, in the bed of the Kildonan, a mountain stream.

II. Aberdeenshire, seems to be a considerable gold region, as several localities are named; but there is no reference to its auriferous qualities in any of the older writers. The localities named are:—

Dunidar, near Aberdeen,f Menzies, Foveran (1).

New Leslie bogs, Drumgavan, near Aberdeen *(2).*

Overhill, Bechelvie (3).

Glenclought, near Kirkhill (4).

The Breadalbane estate (5). The gold at Overhill is said to be very rich. It was found in the parish of Bechelvie, on the property of Lord Glammis, fourteen fathoms below the kiln.

Mining Journal for 1849, p. 290; Year Book of Facts, edited by John Timbs, 1841, p. 248. t (1). Col. Borthwick's MSS.; *(2.) Ibid.* This is two miles from Dunidar. (3.) *Ibid.* (4.) *Ibid.* I am not sure whether this is rightly placed. (5.) From the statement of the Marquess made to me, and from Prof. Tennant. III. Fifeshire.—The gold of Fife was known as early as the time of David I. of Scotland, for, according to Mr. P. Fraser Tytler, he alludes to it in the Cartulary of Dunfermline.

On the statement of mineralogists gold is now found in the Fifeshire mountains.

IV. Perthshire.—The localities stated in Perthshire are Glenturret and Glencoich. Gold is reported at the mouth of tbe Tay, at Long Forglan Moor, near Dundee.

V. Stirlingshire.—Gold was found and worked in this county in the beginning of the eighteenth century, on Sir John Erskine's estate.-f VI. Linlithgowshire. —This county is one of the chief gold regions of Scotland. It has been already stated, that as early as the reign of Queen Mary I. of Scotland, in the sixteenth century, the mines were worked here, said to be near Linlithgow, (but which is not certain,) and that one of the partners in these mines gave to the Regent, Earl of Morton, a bowl made of gold, capable of containing a gallon, and which was filled with coins, likewise of gold, the produce of the mine. J

A gold locality lately identified in Linlithgowshire, is in the Bathgate hills, on the borders of Edinburghshire.§ VII. Lanarkshire is the most productive gold region as yet known in these islands. The vales of the Clyde and the Nith constitute a gold field reaching so far as is yet known into Lanarkshire, Dumfriesshire, Ayrshire, and Selkirkshire.

If the allusion of Tacitus be really applicable to Scot History of Scotland, vol. 2, p. 201, quoting John of Hexham, p. 280; Cartulary of Dunfermline, fol. 7; DalzePs Tract on Monastic Antiquities, p. 30.

t Pennant's Wales, p. 66. *X* Atkinson's MSS. quoted in Abbot on Mines, p. 216; Dr. Nicholson, in Scott's Historical Library.

§ Mining Journal, 1849, p. 15. Tacit. Agric. Vita.

land, this must be the locality-of the Caledonian gold regions; but unless worked by the Romans, it was not until the reign of James IV. of Scotland, that, so far as we know, this gold region was worked, and the working was continued in that of James V. In the reign of James VI. it was resumed by Devoz, Bowes, and Sir Bevis Bulmer, as fully stated in the previous chapter.

Gold continued to be picked up here in greater or smaller quantities till towards the end of the last century, when it began to fall off.

About 1740, Sir John Erskine, with four partners, formed a company, to resume the Clydesdale workings, but it is not supposed with success.

The last account we have of the working of the Clydesdale mines is in the reign of George III., when they were resumed under the superintendance of the manager of the lead mines at Wanlochhead, but the price of labour was found too high to induce the continuance of the workings.f

Gold is found here to this day, but scantily, though many of the miners have some.

The following is an estimate of the amount obtained from this gold field:—

Early periods £ 50,000

James IV. and V. DeVos, Bowes.. 300,000

James VI. Sir Bevis Bulmer... 100,000 „ „ Lesmahagow.... 1,000 1580 to 1780, at £300 per annum.. 60,000 1780 to 1853 4,000

Total produce.. £515,000 The extent of this gold field is about twenty-five miles from north to south, and about ten miles across, so far as is J. C. Fabricius Reise, in Jacobs' History of the Precious Metals, vol. 6, p. 292.

t Williams's History of the Mineral Kingdom, vol. 2, p. 365. yet known, but this does not include the extension to the eastward.

The gold localities known in Lanarkshire are the fol

Lesmahago, (1).

Leadhills, (2).

Frier Moor, or Glengonnar Water, Clydesdale, (3).

Tempie Cleuch, (5).

The following places belonging to the gold region can likewise be named, but a local observerf says there are forty gills or brooks in which gold has been worked:—

Mannoch Moor, Nithsdale, (6).

Wanlochhead, (7).

Wanlochwater, or Glangersgil on Robertmoor, (8).

Langham Water. (9).

Meggott Water, (10).

(1). Atkinson's MSS. quoted in Abbot on Mines, p. 216; (2). Pennant's Scotland, vol. 3, p. 416; Leakes' Coins, p. 287; (3). Cottonian MSS. Otho E. x.; Pennant's Scotland, vol. 3, p. 416; (4). Camden Britannia; Cottonian MSS. Otho Ex.; Gawyn Smith; Lansdown MSS. British Museum, 26— 11; Hector Boethius, p. 6; Aldrovandus on Minerals, vol. 1, ch. 2; Boterus; Gerard Malynes Lex Mercatoria, p. 183; Opera Mineralia Explicata, p. 9; New Touchstone, by W. B. 1679, p. 5; Boyle, Hydrostatic Way of Examining Ores, p. 182; Ditto Works, vol. 5, p. 30; Sibbald's Museum, p. 70; Ditto Natural History of Scotland, lib. 4, p. 52; Pennant's Wales, vol. 1, p. 90; Pennant's Scotland, vol.3, p. 416; Gen. Dirom's Dumfriesshire; Jameson's Mineralogical Description of Dumfriesshire, p. 119; Williams, Mineral Kingdom, vol. 2, p. 365; Abbot on Mines, p. 216; Watson's Compendium; Wyld's Gold Notes; Jacobs' History of the Precious Metals, vol. 1, p. 293; Reise Von J. C. Fabricius in ditto; Leake on Coins, p. 287; Cramer's Mineralogy, p. 157; Cramer Assaying, p. 157; (5). Cottonian MSS. Otho E 10; (6). Cottonian MSS.; Lansdown MSS.; Pennant's Scotland, vol. 3, p. 416; (7). Pennant's Scotland, vol. 3, p. 416; (8). Pennant's Scotland, vol.3, p. 416; (9). Cottonian MSS.; (10). Cottonian MSS.; (11). Cottonian MSS.; (12). Cottonian MSS.; (13). Cottonian MSS.; (14). Jameson's Mineralogy, vol. 3, p. 58; (15). Williams, History Mineral Kingdom, vol. 2, p. 365; (16). Cottonian MSS. Otho.; (17). Lansdown MSS. , p. 26; Gawyn Smith.

t Cottonian MSS. Otho E x. lowing:—

Phinland, (11).

Alroyn, (12).

Pontshields, (13).

Cumberhead, (14).

Gold Scour, or Elvansfoot, (15).

Marksdale, (16).

Cramyll, (17).

Glen Cleuch, (18).

Thiefslack Harse.

Glen Capel Burn.

Elvan Water.

In Clydesdale I found the clay-slates genérally running north and south, and intruded by porphyry and whinstone. I recognized here sands of magnetic or titaniferous iron, in company with the gold. The chief indications of gold looked for by the native miners are the same as three hundred years ago, keele and spar. Keele is an earthy oxide of iron.

When in the district, I examined the old works of Sir Bevis Bulmer, more particularly at Gold Scours, in the Longcleugh valley.

At Long Cleuch Head, running into Elvan Water, some miners, two years ago, got out as much gold as sold at Glasgow for £42. I was told this, on account of its purity, was used for glass and porcelain gilding. Gold digging is followed only as a holiday amusement by the miners, and the washing is very rudely performed. The gold is chiefly sold as specimens, at double price.

Gerard Malynes says, writing in 1622, that the Crawford Moor gold was above twenty-two carats fine, so that it is to be presumed he had access to some assay.

Of individual specimens from this district, one is mentioned as weighing thirty ounces, or two pounds and a half.

f The Malynes' Lex Mercatoria, p. 183.

t Pennant's Wales, vol. *I,* p. 90; Cottonian MSS. E 10.

Earl of Hopetoun had one weighing an ounce and a half, or two ounces. Boyle mentions nuggets severally of eight pennyweights nine grains, three pennyweights twenty-one grains,'and three pennyweights three grains.f Mr. Atkinson, however, mentions six ounces and five ounces. The largest nuggets now got weigh about two sovereigns, but they are rare.

Hector Boethius, it will be already observed, speaks not only of gold mines in Clydesdale, but likewise of diamonds, rubies, and hyacinths. The only other mention made of these gems is by Gawyn Smithy but I am not inclined to discredit the author. They are found in the gold regions of the Brazils and East Indies, and I have myself found them in the gold regions of Australia. In one of my collections, which was exhibited at the Great Globe, and in another which was open to the public in the Strand for a short period, I have specimens of diamond, ruby, sapphire, hyacinth, beryl, chrysoberyl, chrysolite, opal, and others. It was while looking for hyacinths in Mount Remarkable, in South Australia, that I found scale gold.

VI11. Dumfriesshire includes part of the great southern gold region, and its history extends as far back as the sixteenth century. In the earliest authentic description we have several localities in Nithsdale enumerated.§ Gold is likewise found in Annandale.

The district has been already described under Lanarkshire.

In the early part of this century the gentry, with great public spirit, raised a public subscription to obtain a geological survey, which was executed by General Dirom, but he says little about gold. Professor Jameson was to have been Pennant's Wales, vol. 1, p. 90; Scotland Delineated, 1791. t Boyle's works, vol. 5, p. 30.

X Gawyn Smith's Letter to Lord Burleigh, Lansdowne MSS., British Museum, p. 26.

§ Cottonian MSS. Otho E x.

charged with this mission, but was compelled to decline, having an engagement in Germany. On his return, he investigated the geology of the district, but was more occupied with the general features than the gold features of the Nith, of which he made a personal inspection. He states, however, that the gold is found in Dumfriesshire in alluvial land, as in some other gold regions.-

The localities which may be specified in Dumfriesshire are:—

Mannoch Moor and Glen Cleuch Burn.

Wanloch Head.

Wanloch Water. I found gold at Wanloch Head, in the middle of the town, and a small specimen in quartz in Wanloch Head mine.

IX. Ayrshire.—This county includes the source of the Nith, passing downwards to Dumfriesshire, and though few gold localities are enumerated in it, it must be considered as belonging to the southern gold region.

X. Selkirkshire.—It is mentioned in Mr. Atkinson's MSS. that gold was found by Sir Bevis Bulmer at Glengaber Water, in Ettrickdale, in Selkirkshire. The Ettrick is one of the feeders of the Tweed. It was also found in the Yarrow, another feeder of the Tweed.

XI. Kirkcudbrightshire.—Captain Andrew Livingston, of Liverpool, informs me by letter that gold is stated by tradition to have been found in the beginning of the last century in the hills of Cairnsmuir, of Carsphairn, or rather in the brooks running from those hills. Miueralogical Description of Dumfriesshire. t *Ibid.* p. 119. CHAPTER IX. GOLD FIELDS OF IRELAND. *History. — Iberians. — Gold Ornaments.— Tighernmas.— Norman Tribute.—Middle Ages.—Mayola.— Wicklow.— Nuggets.— Gold Localities.— Ulster. —Londonderry.— Antrimshire. — Connaught. — Leinster.—Dublinshire. — Wicklowshire. — Croghan.—Kinshela.— Wexfordshire.— Kildare.*

In the general chapter on gold in these islands will be found some remarks on the intercourse of the Iberian or Phenician nations, in which reference is made to the probable descent from them of part of the west Irish, in conformity with some of the Irish traditions.

The theory that Ireland was sought for gold by the Phenicians is also alluded to.

Sir R. Kane considers one of the strongest proofs of the finding of gold, by the ancient nations, in Ireland, is the very great number of gold ornaments and weapons found there, and now preserved in the Irish museums. Specimens, seemingly from native gold, may be seen in the Dublin Exhibition and the Museum of Practical Geology. These relics are in much greater proportion than in this island or in other European countries. Such ornaments were found by Columbus and his followers among the natives of the West India Islands, the description of whom affords, perhaps, the best picture of what the Homeric ages must have presented, or the early chiefs of the world of Britain.f Kane's Industrial Resources of Ireland, p. 221. t See note p. 179.

Another circumstance, which he considers is not without weight, is the relative proportion of gold required to be furnished by Ireland to the exchequer of Normandy. When treasure was exacted for that exchequer by the Norman princes of these islands, the demand was as follows:—

England...23,730 marcs of silver.

Ireland 400 marcs of silver and 400 marcs of gold.

England was not required to supply gold, and when the Irish gold is reduced to its equivalent in silver, the demand upon Ireland, the resources of which were narrow, appears very large.

Moore, following the legends of the early writers, says: During the reign of Tighernmas, gold is said to have been, for the first time, worked in Ireland; a mine of that metal having been discovered in the woods to the east of the river Liffey.

The statement of the Four Masters, under the date A.m. 3656, is: " In this year gold was first wrought by Tighernmas, king of Ireland, in the woods eastward of the Liffey; Uchadan, of the men of Cualan, was the artificer who first worked it, and by him were ornaments of gold and silver first made." O'Flaherty, in his " Ogygia," says that this was in that part of Cualan called Fothart, and on the eastern bank of the Liffey. Some suppose that Ballymore Eustace, now included within Kildare, is the golden locality.

Simon says, at Fothart, near the river Liffey, in the county of Wicklow, gold, silver, copper, lead, and iron have of late years been found out.f

The silver mines of Ireland are referred to in 1276, 1289, and 1303; and in 1360, Edward III. issued a commission to search for gold and silver mines in Ireland, " because it is given to us to understand that many mines of gold and silver exist in that our dominion. " In 1543, under the authority Thos. Moore's History of Ireland, vol. 1, p. 109.

t Simon on Irish Coins.

of the Lord Deputy, St. Leger, a very active search was made for Irish mines.

In queen Elizabeth's time, Ireland does not seem to have been in much estimation as a gold country, for Houghsetter, who for his patent selected the best known gold districts, preferred Wales; and the Mines Royal Corporation only obtained their claim to a monopoly in Ireland by a second grant of those districts not taken by Houghsetter. The Mines Royal claims extend, however, only to the pale, though some affirm that it would include the greater part of Ireland.

The first modern notice we have of the discovery of gold in Ireland, is towards the middle of the seventeenth century. Boate, in his Natural History of Ireland, says: " I have grounds to believe that there are gold fields in Ireland. I believe many will think it very unlikely that there should be any gold mines in Ireland, but a credible person hath given me to understand that one of his acquaintance had several times assured him that out of a certain rivulet, in the county of Nether Tyrone, called Miola (the which rising in the mountains of Slieve Galen, and passing by the village Maharry, falleth into the north-west corner of Lough Neagh, close by the place where the river Bann cometh out of it), he had gathered about one dram of pure gold, concluding thereby, that in the aforesaid mountains rich gold mines do lie hidden." Boate's work was written in 1645, and is dedicated to Cromwell by Samuel Hartlib.

There must, however, have been other contemporary evidence; for Moses Stringer, writing in 1713, says, "gold, silver, and quicksilver have been largely produced in Great Britain and Ireland;" and further, that in Ireland "good gold" may be found, "in perfect form, like to the Arabian gold, and collected the same way after hasty rains."+ Boate's Natural History of Ireland, Dublin, 1652, chap. 16, sect. 2. Repeated in edition of 1726. t Opera Mineralia Explicata, p. 9.

This account of Stringer's cannot be supposed to have any reference to Boate's, and is very explicit in its details. It may, perhaps, refer to the Wicklow or Antrimshire diggings, and seems to describe river diggings. Stringer, perhaps, meant to imply that gold was found in rivers in Ireland; for the words before are: " Gold hath been, and now may be found in the hills of Mendip, in Somersetshire, called the Golden Rake; in certain rivers in Scotland; and in Ireland good gold, in perfect form, like to the Arabian gold," &c. By good gold, Stringer most probably means gold of good or high quality, as good as standard, or better.

The Irish newspapers, in 1759, announced that gold had been found at Inchmore, in the Shannon.

In the middle of the last century some silver gold was worked on a small scale at Cronebane.f

In 1796, the great Irish gold mania took place, the nature of the Wicklow gold diggings having become known, although they had been worked quietly for some time before. The history of this district will be fully detailed further on. It is enough here to state, that the workings were taken possession of by the government, and worked. for some time, but the operations were stopped by the rebels in 1798.

The gold of the Wicklow district has continued to be worked by the peasantry, and a considerable amount has been raised for the use of the Dublin goldsmiths,:; who work it up into ornaments with Irish bog oak and pearls. Some specimens of this work were exhibited at the Great Exhibition in 1851, and others are now exhibited in the Dublin Crystal Palace.

In 1825, a company was brought forward in London, under the name of the Glenarm and Antrim Mining Asso Kane's Industrial Resources of Ireland.

t Weaver's Memoir on the Geology of the East of Ireland.

J Mining Journal, vol. 19, p. 15.

ciation, which proposed, among other objects, to work the gold said to exist in the Aura mountains.

In 1839, a crown permission was obtained, and in 1840 an attempt was made to work the Wicklow district. About fifty men were employed, and in four months £1,800 worth of gold was obtained; but the workings were suspended, in consequence, it is stated, of disputes with the Woods and Forests. f Another attempt was made in 1849 to get up a Wicklow company by Mr. Collett, who had been concerned in the Brazils with the National Brazilian Mining Association, but it was unsuccessful. J

At the present time there is no gold mining company at work in Ireland. Attention has usually been concentrated on the Wicklow district, and that with a view to gold streaming or gold mining; and as the works have been generally unproductive, there has been but little encouragement for other enterprizes. It is strange that, although many companies have at different times been brought out for streaming gold in South America, there has been none for streamworking in Ireland. Measures are now in progress for re-working Wicklow.

The gold obtained from Ireland is, like most native gold, of very good quality, being as high as twenty-two and a half carats. There are specimens in the Museum of Economic Geology, in Jermyn Street, of native gold from Wicklow.

The largest nugget picked up at Wicklow weighed twentytwo ounces, or nearly two pounds, and another five ounces. The former was erroneously supposed to be the largest nugget obtained in these islands, or in Europe,§ but the great Crawford nugget, found in the sixteenth century, weighed thirty ounces, or two pounds and a half. Ireland has, how Prospectus in Collection of Mr. Hyde Clarke.

t Mining Journal, vol. 10, p. 30; vol. 11, pp. 47,213, 326; vol. 19, p. IS; Kane's Industrial Resources, p. 221. *X* Mining Journal, vol 19, p. IS. § Fraser's Wicklow, p. 19. ever, obtained the honour claimed for her, as, in 1844, the Mining Company of Ireland sent to the exhibition of the Royal Dublin Society, a nugget weighing forty ounces, but from what locality is not stated. There is a loose report of a nugget of seven pounds from Wicklow.

In 1851, Irish gold was exhibited at the Crystal Palace, from Wicklow only; No. 180, Class I., by the Royal Dublin Society, and No. 472, Class I., by J. Lentaigne, Esq. of Tallaght House, Dublin.

Gold is known to exist in three provinces of Ireland. The following is a list of the known gold districts tj—

Province. Shire.

A. Ulster,.. Londonderry.

Antrim.

B. Connaught,

C. Leinster,.. Dublin.

Wicklow.

Wexford.

Kildare.

A 1. Londonderyshire.—The authority for the gold locality in this district is Boate's Natural History in the passage already cited, according to which gold had been several times obtained towards the close of the seventeenth century, from the Miola or Mayola rivulet, running into Lough Neagh.-f-The gold is described as pure or native gold. This discovery is confirmed by the circumstance of gold being found on the other side of the Bann.

The Mayola is a considerable rivulet flowing through the heart of Tyrone, for the lower part of its course in clayslate. Colonel Pollock says nothing of the production of gold, nor of Boate's description, which he does not appear Mining Journal, 1844, p. 199.

t Boate's Natural History, ch. 16, sec. 2; Mining Almanack, vol. 2, p. 1822. to have seen. Several ores found in gold districts are here met with.

A *2.* Antrimshire.—The prospectus before quoted of the Glenarm and Antrim Mining Association, in 1825, asserts that there is gold in the Aura Mountain, and relies upon the circumstance that *auru* means gold in Irish, as testimony that the existence of this metal must have been formerly known. If so, an ancient date may be assigned to it previous to the settlement of Ulster by the English race. The prospectus states, " Gold has actually been, from time to time,.collected by the peasantry in grains, from thesands flowing down from the mountain."f

B. There are no particulars given as to the finding of gold at Inchmore, on the Shannon. Sir R. Kane refers only to the Irish newspapers of 1759. *%*

C 1. Dublinshire.—The only authority we have for including Dublin is the tradition of the Four Masters already referred to, and the supposed auriferous character of the Liffey.§

C *2.* Wicklowshire.—This shire is supposed to be a gold locality, in the north and south, in the north in the basin of the Liffey, and in the south in that of the Ovoca.

Of the former, Simon says, " at Fothart, near the river Liffey, in the county of Wicklow, gold, silver, copper, lead, and iron, have of late years been found.

The gold localities enumerated in Wicklow, are:—

Croghan Kinshela.

At Ballinvalley, Ballytemple, Killahurlen.

Croghan Moira.

Ballycreen.

Report on the Geology of the County of Londonderry, 1843. t Glenarm and Antrim Mining Association, p. 18. *X* Kane's Industrial Resources, 2nd edition, p. 175; Gentleman's Magazine, 184?9, D'Alton.

§ Moore's History of Ireland, vol. 1, p. 109. Simon on Irish coins.

Ballynacapogue.

Cronebane.

The native gold was found in South Wicklow, in the clay-slate. The metallic substances there found are gold, silver, copper, iron, magnetic ironstone, iron pyrites, lead, zinc, tin, tungsten, manganese, arsenic, and antimony.

The clay slate extends in length about ten miles, with very narrow breadth, from Croghan Kinshela, on the south, through the townlands of Knocknamohila towards the West Aston range.

It was in 1796 that the discovery of gold was promulgated, and the peasantry flocked to the spot. The digging went on for about six weeks, when the government took possession. An act of the Irish Parliament was passed constituting directors for the prosecution of the works. Regular stream works were established, and paid the expenses of working up to the period of the rebellion, in May 1798, when the works were destroyed by the Irish rebels. In 1801 the operations were resumed, with a view to the discovery of gold bearing veins. Numerous trials were made by driving and sinking, and specimens collected, but in no instance was gold obtained from them by any process of analysis. Hence the works were abandoned.

The gold was found in massy lumps, and smaller pieces, down to the minutest grain. One piece weighed twentytwo ounces, another eighteen ounces, a third nine ounces, and a fourth seven ounces. The gold was found, accompanied by other metallic substances, dispersed through a kind of stratum composed of clay, sand, gravel, and fragments of rock, and covered by soil, which sometimes attained to a very considerable depth, from twenty to fifty feet, in the bed and banks of the different streams. In the Ballinvalley district, the gold was constantly found attended by magnetic ironstone, sometimes in masses of half a hundred weight; magnetic iron sand; cubical and dode

N cahedral iron pyrites; and in small pieces and grains by specular iron ore, brown and red ironstone, iron ochre, fragments of tinstone crystals, wolfram, grey ore of manganese, pieces of quartz and chlorite, and sometimes fragments of quartz crystals. Mr. Weaver collected specimens, showing that gold, magnetic ironstone, and wolfram were frequently intermingled with quartz, and some specimens not only incorporated with iron ochre, but ramifying in slight threads through wolfram. Some of the gold, though very rarely, occurred crystallized in octahedrons, and also in the elongated garnet dodecahedron.

The principal deposit of the Ballinvalley gold extended about twelve hundred yards down the stream below the ford. In other quarters the gold obtained was comparatively of small amount. The largest piece found in any of the other streams was on the Coolbawn side, and weighed two and a half ounces.

In the Ballinvalley trench, twenty-seven veins of quartz were found, varying from nine inches to four feet wide, in a distance of one thousand four hundred yards; and in the same manner in the Ballingore trench, eighteen quartz veins were discovered in a distance of one thousand two hundred yards.

Besides Croghan Kinshela, the directors tried Croghan Moira, about seven miles distant from it. Gold was obtained there, though in small quantities, the largest piece not exceeding two and a half pennyweights in weight. One trial was made on Ballycreen, in the stream at the eastern foot of the mountain, and minute particles of gold were found accompanied by magnetic iron-stone, magnetic iron sand, compact brown iron-stone, cubical iron pyrites, and numerous small garnets. Another trial was made on the western side of the mountains in Ballynacapogue brook, and small particles of gold were obtained, with magnetic ironstone, magnetic iron sand, and fragments of tin-stone crystals.

In the higher grounds of Cronebane, a brown indurated oxide of iron, which formed the upper part of a metalliferous bed was found to contain native silver, which yielded about thirty grains of gold in the ounce. The silver sold for about half a guinea an ounce. This silver was worked about the middle of the last century.

The extent of these diggings has never been ascertained, nor is the amount of produce well known. About £10,000 was obtained previous to the rebellion, and probably about £100,000 since. The produce seems to be about £2,000 yearly.

C *3*. Wexfordshire.— Croghan Kinshela is on the watershed, between the heads of the Avoca and the Bann, which latter runs into Wexfordshire, and deserves examination.

C 4. Kildare. — According to the opinion of some writers, Ballymore, on the eastern bank of the Liffey, is the site of the gold discoveries in Cualan, reported by the Four Masters.

Weaver's Memoir on the Geology of the East of Ireland.

Note On Page 170.—The Athenaeum, describing the Dublin Exhibition, observes, that the department of Irish Antiquities includes gold torques, bracelets, brooches, rings, bullae, boxes, discs, and other ornaments. " The native gold of which these ornaments are composed is very rich in colour, and must have been found, in early times, in great quantity—one of the torques weighing as much as twenty-seven ounces and a half, and of the bracelets, nearly seventeen ounces. The great antiquity of these golden ornaments is proved by the fact, that the style of ornamentation employed in the decoration of such of them as are ornamented, is very simple, like that of the earthen vases found in early graves, and quite unlike the ornamentation adopted in metal, stone, and manuscript work of the early Christian period." (1853, p. 1257, Oct. 22.) CHAPTER X.

NATIVE GOLD OF BRITAIN. *Dust.—Scales.—Nuggets.—Largest Nuggets in the World. —Crystals of Gold.—Assays.*

Gold is found in Britain in most of the forms in which it is obtained in other gold regions. I have already had the opportunity of seeing here most of the varieties of gold with which I had become acquainted in my explorations for that metal in Australia and elsewhere.

Gold specimens may be divided into two classes:—

Native gold.

Gold combined with other materials as an ore.

Native gold consists of two kinds:—

A. Gold in *situ.*

B. Gold that has been removed.

A. Gold in *situ* is chiefly gold in the clay-slates, and in clays resting on the clay-slates, in the neighbourhood of quartz strings and dykes, which seem to be the principal conductors into the clays. Gold is sometimes found as a surface incrustation on these quartz dykes. " Gold resulting from the decomposition of granite at the bottom or bed of creeks and rivers will likewise come under this class. This gold will not be found waterworn.

B. Gold that has been removed consjsts of the gold of the classes already described, subjected to the action of water, which has carried it away from the site. This will be more or less waterworn. Deposits, strata, or layers of gold may be found high and dry in consequence of alterations of river beds and accumulations of banks. Several layers of gold may be found in a river basin as the result of successive depositions. The strata above the bedrock may, perhaps, consist of alternations of loose beds and clay. More commonly the heaviest gold is found in the lower strata.

The abrasion, weathering and decomposition of surface goldbearing rocks afford a supply of gold, which is carried by the violent action of water to the nearest river basins. The schistose rocks, for instance, being more easily acted upon by rain and other atmospheric agencies, disintegration constantly taking place, leaves the harder rocks, such as quartz dykes, &c., standing. These being unsupported, roll down in large blocks, and by degrees gradually find their way into the bottoms of creeks and gulleys. They then come under the powerful action of floods, when they become broken up and torn to pieces in the rapids and torrents through which they are propelled. The gold, however tenacious it may be when in the quartz as a block, is now let free in large and small pieces, and on account of its gravity, rests wherever alluvium accumulates or banks are formed, which would not be the case on a small scale, until it had travelled into some larger water course, where there was room for deposits of various matter to accumulate. The smaller watercourses only stay the progress of the few grains and pieces that would be held with the soil accumulated in the vertical slates. It often happens, as a brook gradually deepens, it leaves many patches of accumulated debris, high and dry, above the present level. These, again, may be cut through by small watercourses, and the ancient deposits of metal again may be disturbed and washed down in the torrent, gaining nothing by the friction with harder substances in the pebbles and gravels, with which it is accompanied. The scale gold generally proves that it has travelled far, and been much beaten by pebbles and boulders, with which it has come in contact. Gold will always be accumulating in valleys below wasting mountains of gold-bearing rocks.

Scale gold, gold dust, or gold in small particles, is called by Boyle sand gold, and is obtained by washing sands in wet or dry diggings. This is one of the earliest forms of gold recorded, though that of nuggets must have been first known. The book of Job says, " Surely there is a vein for the silver and a place for the gold where they fine it;" and again, " the earth has dust of gold."f Jacob remarks, that Job, though living in a country which yields none of the precious metals, was thus familiarly acquainted with the fact that silver is found in veins, and gold commonly in small particles.J

Gold dust has been obtained, to some extent, from the diggings in Clydesdale and Wicklow, and to less extent from Antrim. I found it in Lanarkshire, Dumfriesshire, Cumberland, Westmoreland, and Devonshire. The gold is of several shades of colour dependent on the locality and neighbouring mineral character. The Westmoreland gold was particularly rich in colour, and all the English gold I have seen is very pure, with the exception of that from some of the ores.

The nugget is a more noticeable form of gold, and being often found in river beds and dry diggings, is that most commonly found in these islands. Among the localities enumerated for nuggets, are

Cornwall, in many rivers and streams.

Derbyshire.

Cumberland.

The great gold region of the south of Scotland.

Boyle's "Works, vol. 5, p. 30. t Job, chap. 23, verses 1, 6, 15, 17, 18, 19, 20. *X* Jacob's History of the Precious Metals, vol. 1, p. 5.

Aberdeenshire.

Sutherlandshire.

Wicklowshire.

According to the size of the nugget it has received various names, and it receives different designations in the several mining dialects. Very small lumps of gold are called by the earliest English writers, " hops," or " corns." Larger lumps have been called lumps, *pepites,* and latterly, in English, " nuggets," having received that name in California and Australia. In the Guinea trade they used to be called 'rock gold. These forms of gold were well known to the ancients, and Pliny gives Greek, Iberian and Roman names for them.f It was from the Spanish discoverers of America that they received the name of *pepites,* pippins, or pomegranate seeds,J a term which has been much used by naturalists. Specimens of gold were engraved in the sixteenth century in the great work of Aldrovandus.

Woodward, in his works, although he speaks of foreign nuggets,§ says nothing of English; but Webster and Boyle had seen such.

The nugget has always attracted attention from the public and the gold diggers. With the former it is an object of curiosity. In the gold regions of Siberia, California, and Australia, enormous nuggets have been obtained; but as yet the known nuggets of these islands are of only moderate size. More active working of the gold fields may produce more remarkable specimens.

The following is an account of some of the nuggets obtained in these islands:—

Nugget of forty ounces, or three pounds four ounces, Carew's Cornwall, 1602. Pliny's Hist. Nat.

J Acosta, c. 4, pp. 212, 213; Peter Martyr, Dec. 1, lib. 22, p. 16; lib. *3,* p. 19.

§ Woodward's Nat. Hist, of Fossils; Ditto Method of Fossils.

Webster's Metallographia, p. 132. Boyle's Works, v. 30; Ditto Scept. Chym. p. 372. from Ireland, exhibited at the Exhibition of the Royal Dublin Society, in 1844. The Crawford Moor nuggets are supposed to have reached the same size.f

Specimens containing forty-one ounces of gold, the mass weighing fifty-seven ounces, found by myself in Westmoreland.

Nugget of thirty ounces, or two pounds six ounces, from Crawford Moor, in the Clydesdale diggings.:

Nugget of twenty-two ounces, or one pound ten ounces, from Wicklow.§

Nugget of eighteen ounces, or one and a half pounds, from Wicklow.

Nugget of nine ounces from Wicklow.If

Nugget of seven ounces from Wicklow.

Nugget of six ounces from Clydesdale.ff

Nugget of upwards of five ounces from Clydesdale.JJ

Nugget of five ounces from Wicklow.§§

Nugget of four ounces from Wicklow.

Nugget of two ounces from a stream working in Cornwall, in 1808, of the size of a lady's little finger.H This is the largest Cornish nugget.

Nugget of two ounces, or one ounce and a half, from Clydesdale gold field, in the collection of the Earl of Hopetoun.

Nugget of one ounce and a half from Sutherlandshire.fff

Nugget of one ounce and upwards from Creed, in Corn Mining Journal, 1844, p. 199. t Cottonian MSS. Otho Ex. *X* Pennant's Wales, vol. 1, p. 90; Cottonian MSS. § Fraser's Wicklow, p. 19. Weaver's Report; Ansted's Manual, p. 5. If *Ibid. Ibid.* tt Atkinson's MSS. *Xl Ibid.* §§ Frazer's Wicklow, p. 19. 1ll Mining Journal, vol. 10, p. 326.

Annual Register, vol. 50, p. 8. Pennant's Wales, vol. 1, p. 90; Scotland Delineated, 1791. ttt Mining Journal, 1849, p. 290.

wall, of the size of a walnut, producing

nearly an ounce of gold.

Nugget of fifteen pennyweights sixteen grains from Creed, in Cornwall.f

Nugget of fifteen pennyweights from Clydesdale.J

Specimen of ten pennyweights in quartz, in the Museum of the Royal Geological Society of Cornwall, in Penzance.§

Nugget of eight pennyweights nine grains from Clydesdale diggings.

Nugget of five pennyweights from Wicklow.f Nugget of three pennyweights twenty one grains, and another of three pennyweights three grains from the Clydesdale diggings.

Nugget two pennyweights twelve grains found at Ballycreen.ff

There is a statement in the " Annual Register," that a shepherd in Northumberland had picked up a lump of gold weighing eighteen pounds; but this is unauthenticated.

There is likewise a statement of a nugget of seven pounds from Wicklow.

The nuggets of other gold regions weigh more pounds than our Cornish nuggets do grains. The following is an account of some of the most remarkable specimens, given, as far as possible, in pounds Troy, but some discrepancies will be found:—

Peter Martyr gives an account of a nugget three thousand Borlase's Natural History of Cornwall, p. 214; Lewis's Commercium Philosophico-Technicum, p. 187.

t Borlase's Natural History of Cornwall, p. 215; Lewis's Commercium Philosophico-Technicum, p. 187. *X* Cottonian MSS. Otho.

§ Frederick Burr in the Mining Review, vol. 5, p. 17.

Boyle's Works, vol. 5, p. 30.

If Mining Journal, vol. 10, p. 326.

Boyle's Works, vol. 5, p. 30.

tt Weaver's Geological Report on the East of Ireland.

XX Annual Register, vol. 12, p. 96.

three hundred and ten pounds weight, found in the West Indies, which was shipped to be carried to Spain, but was unfortunately cast away.

Peter Martyr likewise gives an account of a lump of three hundred pounds weight, found in the West Indies.f

What is called Dr. Kerr's hundred weight of gold was a large mass standing upon the surface, close to the vein to which it appears to have belonged, and the quantity of gold obtained was about one hundred and six pounds from about two hundred weight of quartz.

The nugget exhibited at the Great Globe was found in the early part of the year in Victoria, and brought to England. It weighed between eighty and ninety pounds, and was altogether, in the matrix, one hundred and thirty-four pounds. I doubt whether any of these lumps enumerated are any more to be called a nugget than the three hundred weight of quartz I chipped off in New South Wales in 1852, and which yielded me seventy-eight pounds of gold.

Having named these most considerable lumps, I shall say nothing further as to Australian or Californian nuggets and lumps, which are found of all sizes and weights, beneath those already stated.

The largest nugget from the Ural weighed ninety-five pounds, or ninety-six pounds and a half,J and it was found in 1842.

A nugget found in 1843, at Zarevo Alexandrofsk, weighed seventy-eight pounds.§

A nugget from Miask, in the Ural, weighed twenty-seven pounds. ll

Other Russian nuggets have weighed twenty-six pounds, twenty-three pounds, sixteen pounds, thirteen pounds.

Peter Martyr, Decad. 10, lib. 10, p. 56. t *I X* Mining Journal, 1842, p. 414; 1849, p. 266; Brande's Chemistry. § Murchison's Russia, pp. 489, 490. Mining Journal, 1849, p. 266. If Brande's Chemistry. Murchison's Russia, pp. 489, 490.

The largest nugget from the United States weighed thirtythree pounds, and was found in 1821; another from Carolina weighed twenty-eight pounds, and was found in 1810. f

A nugget from Hayti, found in 1502, weighed thirty-seven pounds. *% A* nugget at Gongo Soco, weighing twenty-one pounds, was found, in 1832, in the mines of the Imperial Brazilian Mining Association.

A nugget weighing forty-five pounds, was found at La Paz, in Peru, in 1730, and one in Choco was found, weighing twenty-five pounds. §

The largest nugget found in Europe seems to have been a nugget of ten pounds from Spain.

No large African nugget is enumerated. Woodward, in 1728, says, that the largest African nugget he had seen weighed four one-eighth ounces, and he mentions another of three ounces. If

Gold has sometimes, but very rarely, been found in the crystalline form; but the only record of such a specimen from these islands is that of octahedral aud dodecahedral gold from Ireland.

The native gold found in these islands, so far as assayed, is found, as usual, in gold regions of very good quality, above standard.

The gold of the ancient ornaments is evidently of this class, f-j

Of Clydesdale gold we have only one assay, that mentioned Mining Journal, 1849, p. 266.

t Dictionaire des Sciences Naturelles. *X* Mining Journal, 1849, p. 266; Lewis's Commercium PhilosophicoTechnicum, p. 182. Mining Journal, 1849, p. 266.

§ Jameson's Mineralogy, vol. 3, p. 62. Jonstone's History of the Wonderful Things in Nature, London, 1657, p. 117. If Method of Fossils, p. 46. Weaver's Memoir on the East of Ireland, tt Athenaeum, 1853, p. 1257 by Gawyn Smith, who says it was twenty-two and a half carats, and who seems to have been a competent authority. The same is repeated by Gerard Malynes.f

Of Wicklow gold, an assay by Mr. Weaver, gave twentytwo, fifty-eight,:: and by Mr. Alchorn, twenty-one six-eighth, carats.

Lansdowne MSS. vol. 26. t Malynes' Lex Mercatoria.

J Weaver's Memoir on the East of Ireland.

CHAPTER XL GOLD ORES OF BRITAIN.

Gold Ores.—Gossan.—Goldfrom other Metals.—Tin.—Gold from Copper.—History.—Localities.— Gold from Lead

Ores.—History.—Localities.—Assays.—Gold from Silver Ores.—Localities.—Assays.— Gold from Iron Ores.—Localities.—Assays.— Gold from Zinc Ores.—Assays.— Richest Gold Ores of Britain.

The public draw a distinction, though not a well-founded one, between gold in river-beds and gold in rocks, but, for mining purposes, certainly a great difference exists. A classification may be thus made:— Gold secreted in rocks.

Gold precipitated in metals, or amalgamated with them.

Of the gold secreted in rocks, quartz and granite afford examples, under certain conditions, to which I shall hereafter allude. The gold only becomes visible on natural or artificial decomposition taking place under certain favourable conditions, which would in some instances happen where creeks run through the portions of those granitic formations containing gold in that present unknown state.

Of the gold precipitated in metals, or amalgamated with them, a very extensive class of combinations exists, as will be hereafter shown.

What are commonly called gold ores are chiefly gold with iron pyrites, or gossan. Of this class are the ores of Exmoor. The average yield is good, but not extraordinarily rich.

A recent specimen from the Poltimore mine, on Exmoor, gave seventeen pennyweights to the ton, which is more than twice as much as the St. John del Rey ore, and another gave eighteen pennyweights. A cargo of sixty-one tons yielded one hundred and two ounces five pennyweights, at 84s. per ounce (£429 9s.), being sixteen pennyweights to the ton.

In St. Just, gold is reported in granite,f and I found it in the granite of Dartmoor and Roach Hill.

Gold is found with quartz in Cornwall,:): North Wales, Leadhills, and Wicklow.§ Some of these ores, assayed by myself and Mr. Marsham, have proved very rich.

Gold is found with slate in North Wales.

Gold has long been known in this island as existing with other metals. It is found among tinstones, though not united with the tin, but it is so united with other metals.

As the connection of gold with tin is matter of interest, it may be as well to refer to it. Pliny is the first author who mentions it. It is likewise alluded to by many other writers, as Carew, Boyle, Stringer,*ff* and Dacosta.JJ Merrett seems to say that gold is got from tin in small quantity.§§

Tinstone is found in the gold regions of Cornwall, Devon, Lanarkshire, and Wicklow associated with gold.

In other countries it is found in the German gold districts, in Spain, in Malacca, in Chili, and by myself in Australia.

Assay of Messrs. Rawlins and Watson, of St. Helen's, 16th Aug. 1853. t Mr. Stutchbury's Report. *X* Frederick Burr in the Mining Review, vol. 5, p. 17,

§ Weaver's Memoir on the Geology of Ireland.

Plin. Hist. Nat. lib. 35, c. 16.

If Carew Survey of Cornwall, 1602. Boyle Works, vol. 5, pp. 30, 196. tt Opera Mineralia Explicata, p. 20. J J Dacosta on Fossils.

§§Merrett's Pinax,1667,p. 208. Cramer's Mineralogy, p. 158. f f *Ibid.* Gold has been obtained by the Germans from tin.

In 1670, Sir John Pettusf stated that all the gold and silver obtained in England was got by extraction from other metals, and not from mines of perfect gold and silver. This seems to have been the case.

The metals or ores of metals from which gold is obtained in Britain are:—

A. Copper.
B. Lead.
C. Silver.
D. Iron.
E. Zinc.

A. *Gold from Copper.*—Gold appears to have been obtained from copper ores at an early period in England. The first mention is of a mine in Shropshire, in the 7th Edward III., containing copper mixed with gold and lead.J

In the 2nd of Richard II., is a general grant of mines in Cornwall, &c., bearing gold and silver, in the 6th, 21st, and. '38th of Henry VI., and in the 1st Edward IV.

In the 31st of Henry VI., Bottwright, the comptroller, had charge among other mines of the mines of copper in Devon and Cornwall containing gold and silver.§ In the 27th Henry VI. was a like grant. Edward IV. granted to Gallias Lynn, &c., in the twelfth year of his reign, a prospecting license for mines of copper holding silver or gold in the counties of Somerset and Gloucester; and in the seventh year to Goderswick, &c., of like mines in Northumberland and Westmoreland.

It was most likely, on account of the existence of gold in the copper ores, that copper mines were classed among mines royal.

On the continent the extraction of gold from copper was Dacosta's Fossils; Cramer's Mineralogy, p. 158.

j Pettus' Fodinse Regales, p. 18.

X Plowden's Reports, p. 322.

§ Plowden's Reports, pp. 324, 325; Pettus' Fodinoe Regales, pp. 39, 40, well understood, and is alluded to by the writers on the subject of mining.

In the sixteenth century the mine of Keswick, in Cumberland, is enumerated as yielding gold and silver with the copper, and was therefore seized by Elizabeth.-

In the seventeenth century Sir John Pettus states as follows: " Copper mines containing some gold and silver are in Cornwall, Devonshire, Somersetshire, Gloucestershire, Derbyshire, Shropshire, Cheshire, Northumberland, Cumberland, and Pembrokeshire.":!;

Stringer says that there is " no mine of copper void of gold or silver."§ The judges in Queen Elizabeth's time had likewise expressed this. They say " the smelters and refiners make it evident that there is in copper naturally gold and silver.

Boyle in his " Useful Philosophy," says: " A friend of mine found in his own land a parcel of ore, which seemed to be copper. After fusion it yielded very good copper, but the person to whom he committed the examination being extraordinary skilful, found besides the copper a considerable quantity of silver, and in that silver a good portion of gold."

At the present no gold is parted from the copper ores in England. So far as the evidence of practical men goes, a great deal of copper is produced and sent into consumption containing gold largely. Examples of this have been already stated. Were more attention paid by mining companies to assaying, a considerable quantity of gold would be obtained from copper.

Gold is found in France, at Allevard, in grey copper Agricola de Re Metallica, lib. 10, cap 1.

t Plowden's Reports, pp. 310, 323.

X Pettus' Fodinae Regales, 1670, p. 6.

§ Opera Mineralia Explicata, p. 182.

Ibid, p. 100; Plowden's Reports,

f J. Mitchell, Mining Journal.

ore, and at Cochette, Theys, and Chalanches, in copper pyrites.

The reported localities in which gold is found with copper are:—

Cornwall, (a).

Devon, (a). North Molton.f

Somerset, (a).

Gloucestershire, *(a).*

Shropshire, (a).

Pembrokeshire, (a).

Merionethshire, Dolfrwynog.

Cheshire, (a).

Derbyshire, (a).

Cumberland, *(a).* Newlands in Derwent Falls.J

Northumberland, *(a).* Alston Moor, §.

Most of these counties are now known to produce both copper and lead. A copper ore from Dolfrwynog yielded thirteen grains of gold per ton.

B. *Gold from Lead.*—The extraction of gold from lead ores is as ancient as from copper, and with copper ore was among the chief supplies of gold during the middle ages. It is during this period we find the earliest mention of such ores in the frequent records and writs.

In the 7th and 34th Edward III., mention is made of the discovery of a mine in Shropshire, of copper and lead mixed with gold.If This prince is said to have worked the Mendip mines for gold.

In the 2nd Richard II. is a general giant of mines hold Dictiotinaire des Sciences Naturelles.

. (a) Sir John Pettus' Fodinae Regales, p. 6.

t Polwhele's Devon, p. 69.

X Plowden's Reports, pp. 310, 323; Mining Almanack.

§ Hodgson's History of Northumberland.

Pettus' Fodinas Regales, pp. 13, 16, 18.

If Plowden's Reports, p. 322; Pettus' Fodinas Regales, p. 34; Opera Mineralia Explicata, p. 17.

ing gold and silver, in the 6th, 21st, 27th, and 34th Henry VI., and 1st of Edward IV

Henry VI. in the 17th year of his reign, granted to John Sollers, all mines of lead holding silver or gold in the counties of Devon and Cornwall;-f-in the 31st year of his reign, the lead mines of Devon and Cornwall holding gold and silver, were put under Bottwright, as provost and comptroller. J

Edward IV. in the 8th year of his reign, granted all mines of lead bearing gold and silver on the north of the Trent, to the Earl of Warwick and others. § In the 12th of his reign, he granted license to Gallias Lynn and others, to search for lead ore holding silver and gold in the counties of Somerset and Gloster.

The act of Henry IV. against multiplying gold and silver, operated at times as a discouragement to the refiners; and the monopoly of the Mines Royal created by Elizabeth, likewise discouraged persons from attempting to part gold or silver from copper or lead ores. The seizing of the Earl of Northumberland's copper mines at Keswick, and the resumption of the Mendip and Cardiganshire mines, and placing them under the Mines Royal, were measures well calculated to deter any one from attempting to part the precious metals from ores they might find on their property. So long as they appeared to produce lead only, they were safe from the clutches of the Mines Royal, and might work under the local mining laws; but if the lead or copper had been reputed to contain gold or silver, it would have been seized by the corporation, which was long supported by the crown lawyers on the grounds of prerogative, in a high pre

Cottonian MSS. Otho E x.

t Plowden's Reports, p. 324; Pettus' Fodinae Regales, p. 39. *X* Plowden's Reports, p. 325; Pettus' Fodinae Regales, p. 40. § Plowden's Reports, p. 326; Pettus' Fodinae Regales, p. 42. Plowden's Reports, p. 326; Pettus' Fodinae Regales, p. 42. rogative age. The case of the Earl of Northumberland in Queen Elizabeth's time, and the opinions of the judges, exemplified this. They declared that the king hath the mines of copper containing or holding gold or silver, although the gold or silver be less. In the reign of Charles I., many leading lawyers gave a like opinion.f According to this doctrine, if gold or silver more than sufficient to pay the charge of refining were found in a lead or copper mine, then not only the gold or silver belonged to the crown, but the whole of the base metal likewise; acting as a penalty against discovering or working gold and silver bearing copper or lead ores.

In the reign of Charles I. Bushell is said to have obtained silver and gold from the lead ores of Cardiganshire and Somersetshire.J

In the reign of William III. the acts were passed for enabling lead and copper mines to be worked which contained gold or silver, allowing the ores to be exported, and removing all obstacles to parting. This has not, however, produced any effect, so far as gold is concerned.

Although many lead mines in England are now worked for silver, none are worked for gold.

Gold is found in galena, at Portrant, in France. §

The districts reported as containing lead and gold are:—

Cornwall.

Devonshire.

Somersetshire, Mendip Hills.

Shropshire.

Cardiganshire.

Merionethshire, Cwmheisian, Cwmheisian Issa, Dolfrwynog, &c.

Plowden's Reports, p. 210. Opera Mineralia Explicata, p. 148. + *Ibid.* p. 245.

§ Dictionnaire des Sciences Naturelles.

A lead ore from Cwmheisian Issa

yielded one ounce fifteen pennyweights of gold per ton; another from the same mine, one pennyweight and a half per ton.

Lead ores from Cwmheisian Issa, from two to twenty ounces of gold in a ton of washed ore; and from twelve to fourteen ounces of gold in a ton of broken ore."

A lead ore from Dolfrwynog yielded from fifty to sixty ounces of gold per ton.

Other ores from that mine gave, respectively, thirteen grains per ton; four ounces eighteen pennyweights per ton; five ounces, thirteen pennyweights, two grains per ton; six ounces, twelve pennyweights, two grains per ton; thirteen ounces per ton; fifty-one ounces per ton; and one hundred and thirty ounces per ton, and when dressed, two hundred and forty-six ounces per ton. These are remarkably rich ores.

It is probable that, if other lead ores were assayed for gold, that metal would be found.

C. *Gold in Silver.*—Of proper silver ores we have, perhaps, few in the island, but where silver is found with other ores, gold is commonly present; and so, likewise, where gold is found native, it has commonly a proportion of silver. Much of the gold of California and Australia is so alloyed, and requires refining.

At Cronebane, in Wicklowshire, an indurated oxide of iron has been worked, which contains native silver, yielding gold.f

The union of gold with silver was known to the older writers,J and to one alloy the name of electrum was given.

They are found to be so united in some of our copper ores and some of our lead ores.

Memoir of Arthur Dean, read before the British Association, 1844. t Weaver's Memoir of the Geology of the East of Ireland. *X* Plin. Hist. Nat. lib. 32, cap. 22; Agricola de Re Metallica, lib. 1, cap. 2; Boyle's works, vol. 2, p. 515.

The reported localities of gold and silver in combination with other metals are:— Somersetshire, Mendip. Cardiganshire.

Merionethshire, Dolfrwynog, &c.

Ireland, Cronebane. The following analyses will show the relative proportions of gold and silver in various ores from these islands:— GOLD. SILVER.

The assays of our ores give, so far as they have been published generally, a larger proportion and larger value of gold than of silver.

D. *Gold with Iron.*—The existence of gold in iron ores and more particularly in pyrites, has been long remarked. It did not escape the notice of Boyle.J It does not, how Scoffern's Chemistry of Gold. t Weaver's Memoir.

X Boyle's Works, vol. 1, p. 196. ever, seem that gold was obtained from this source in the middle ages.

Most of the iron ores from which gold is obtained in this island, are in. the form of oxides, and called gossans, and from pyrites. These are likewise found rich ores for gold on the continent, and are worked at Marcugnaga in Savoy, Gardette, in France, in Hungary.f and at Beresof, in Russia, j

The localities reported for auriferous iron ores are:—

Cornwall.

Devon, North and South Molton.

Merionethshire, Dolfrwynog, &c.

Westmoreland.

Some of the Cornish pyrites are very rich, and so are those of Devon, nor do the Merionethshire ores fall behind.

The following are some assays for gold of auriferous iron ores:— GOLD PER TON.

Oz. Dwt. Gr.

Cornish pyrites§

Cwmheisian. .

„... Dolfrwynog

„... Poltimore.

„... „... Keswick „ Devon, Poltimore, Gossan » »» Jj

»»)» »

Gold is said to be found in the bog iron ore near Paris J. Mitchell, on Assaying, p. 376; Weale's Rudimentary Mineralogy, p. 104.

t Lewis's Commercium Philosophico Technicum, p. 187. *X* Weale's Rudimentary Mineralogy, p. 104. 5 Dr. Barham, Mining Review and Mining Journal, 1841, p. Ob'. 0 18 3 1 *12 5* 6 *2 12* 130 0 0 8 19 14 1 6 0 1 17 0 0 19 0 0 17 0 0 18 0 0 16 0 and Pontoise, but no assay has been made of English bog iron ores or iron sands, though there have been reports ol gold mines in some of the south-eastern counties.

E. *Gold in Zinc.*—Gold has lately been discovered in the ores of blende, in Wales, as it is in Columbia, and has long been known to be at Schemnitz, in Hungary.

The only localities as yet reported are in Merionethshire, at Cwmheisian Issa, and Berthllwyd.

The assays are as follows:— GOLD PER TON.

Oz. Dwt. Gr.

Cwmheisian Issa, raw ore... 1 *12 5* Berthllwydf dressed ore... 59 5 0 „ broken ore... 10 0 „...080

Platinum, palladium, and rhodium are metals often found alloyed with gold, but they are not yet reported as having been found in our gold by the English refiners.

The richest specimens of gold ores reported from our gold regions are the following:—

Specimen from Wales belonging to Mr. Standish Motte, three hundred ounces to the ton.

Specimen from Dolfrwynog, three hundred and thirty ounces to the ton, which I examined.

Specimen from Dolfrwynog, one hundred and thirty ounces to the ton, in slaty pyrites, with galena (two assays).

Specimen from Cornwall, eighty-nine ounces to the ton, in pyrites. J

Specimen from Fwynog level, Dolfrwynog, sixty ounces to the ton, in galena and carbonate of manganese.

Specimen from Dolfrwynog, fifty to sixty ounces to the ton.

Dictionnaire des Sciences Naturelles. t Arthur Dean's Memoir, British Association. *X* Dr. Barham in Mining Keview and Journal, 1841, p. *96.*

Specimen from Dolfrwynog, fifty-one ounces to the ton, in galena.

I have seen abundance of specimens quite rich enough to pay for working. The Marcugnaga pyrites, extensively worked, contains only eight pennyweights per ton, or less than half an ounce. I would observe that I should look for good-paying ores in England among what would be termed the poorer ores.

CHAPTER XII. GOLD REGIONS OF EUROPE. *France.—Rivers.—Localities.—Rhine Sands.— Total of Gold.—Spain and Portugal.—Rivers. — Switzerland. — Holland.—Italy.—Macugnaga.—Localities.—Rivers.— Greece and Turkey.— Germany and Austria.—Transylvannia.—Hungary.—Bohemia—Hartz.—Gold Rivers of Germany.—Sweden and Norway.—Finland.—Lapland.*

The subject of gold mining and working on the continent, and in other countries, will only be referred to as illustrative of our own gold regions, and for the purpose of giving a more copious list of the gold localities in Europe than has yet been published.

A. France.—The Romans only worked gold in the Pyrenees, or rather the Salassi did for them; nor has France, in any historical period, been esteemed a gold region.

Charlemagne caused searches to be made for gold and silver in 786.f

In 1548, there was a gold mania in France, and Dr. Belon found six thousand persons at work, in the department of the Gard, searching for gold.

Henry IV. caused a search to be made for gold mines, Strabo, lib. 4, cap. 6.

t Jacobs' History of the Precious Metals, vol. 1, p. 258. but unsuccessfully. In 1640, an impostor pretended to discover a number of gold mines. In 1710, Reaumur read a report on the gold of France before the Academy of Sciences. Since that period, few gold localities have been discovered.

The gold of France is principally in river washings, and the following are enumerated:—

Arriege, near Mirepoix, rising in the Pyrenees f(1).

Ferriet,) Rivulets of the above (1). Benagues, *)*

Gardon, in the Cevennes *(2).*

Seze, or Ceze, ditto (3).

Herault, near Montpellier (4).

Ardeche (5).

Isere, near Gardette (6).

Rhone, in the Pays de Gex (7).

Arve, at its junction with the Rhone (7).

Salat, at St. Giron, in the Pyrenees (8).

Garonne, near Toulouse (9).

Rhine, between Brisac, Strasburg, and Philipsburg (10). Of these localities the most remarkable are the following: The Isere.—The mines at Gardette have been worked at several periods.J In 1781 a quartz vein was discovered in gneiss, containing iron pyrites with native gold.§

The Rhine.—This river is auriferous from its source to its mouth. In Switzerland its two feeders, the Aar and Jacobs' History of the Precious Metals, vol. 1, pp. 262, 264.

t (1). Reaumur's Memoir; Dictionnaire des Sciences Naturelles; (2). Reaumur's Memoir; Dictionnaire des Sciences Naturelles; Jacobs, vol. 1, p. 261; Agricola de re Metallica; (3). Reaumur's Memoir; Dictionnaire des Sciences; Jacobs, vol. 1, p. 261; (4). Dictionnaire des Sciences Naturelles; Jacobs, vol. 1, p. 261; (5). Jacobs, vol. 1, p. 261; (6). See references afterwards; (7). Reaumur's Memoir; Dictionnaire des Sciences; (8). Reaumur's Memoirs; Dictionnaire des Sciences; (9). Reaumur's Memoir; Dictionnaire des Sciences; (10). See references afterwards. *X* Reaumur's Memoir; Dictionnaire des Sciences Naturelles; Nicholson's Journal, vol. 22, pp. 124, 234; Mining Almanack, 1849, p. 328.

§ Dictionnaire des Sciences Naturelles, 1825, Art. Or.

the Reuss are so reported. Within the French bounds gold is found in its sands as low down as Philipsburg.f Gold is reported to have been found in the river sands in Holland.

The gold of the Rhine sands has long been worked. Near Strasburg it was the perquisite of the magistrates of that city, who farmed out the right of gold washing, but in 1718 they received only four or five ounces yearly at preemption prices, but it is supposed the quantity obtained was more considerable. J Of late years the produce is estimated at £1,800 net yearly or probably £2,500.§

In the middle of the seventeenth century there were several proposals for working the gold sands of the Rhine and of the sea shore in Holland. The most noted was that of J. J. Becher, already detailed. This was a failure.

In 1846, M. Daubree made his proposition to the French Academy of Sciences, in which he estimates the bed of the Rhine to contain thirty-six thousand tons of gold in its sands, which he valued at £3,600,000,000. He proposed a plan for working these sands.If

The gravel most usually worked is that deposited below a bar, sandbank, or gravel island, which the current has eaten away. M. Daubree states that the gold is only found concentrated in the midst of the larger gravel on the edge of the bar nearest the head of the stream, and seldom for more than a thickness of half an inch. The gold is in small scales or dust, and is always accompanied by tetaniferous iron. The quantity of this iron varies from 0.00002 to 0.000#, and is always in proportion to the richness of the Dictionnaire des Sciences Naturelles; Ure's Dictionary, t Reaumur's Memoir; Dictionnaire des Sciences Naturelles; Boyle's Works, v. 5, p. 34. *X* Lewis' Commercium Philosophico Technicum, p. 185. § Mining Journal, 1846, p. 264. See page 25. H See page 26.

sand in gold. The scales are always very small and thin, the number required to make a grain being from eleven to fourteen hundred. These scales are dispersed throughout the stuff, and the French calculator estimates that in a cubic yard there are from five thousand to forty thousand scales.

Besides the gold in the river, there are dry diggings, consisting of the ancient deposits of the river, and extending for about three miles in breadth. M. Daubree says that there is no trace of gold in the sand deposited by the Rhine in the delta, nor in the diluvial clay known as loess.

On M. Daubree's estimate the gold stuff of the Rhine yields only one fifth of the Siberian sands, and only one tenth of those of Chile.

Other localities enumerated in France

are:—
Doux in Franche Comte, (1).
Portrant. The gold is found in galena, *(2).*
Auris. The gold is found in sulphuretted anti-
mony, (3).
Puy de Dome, (4).
Theys,

Cochette, near Allemont, in copper pyrites, (5).

Allevard, in grey copper ore, (6). Paris and Pontoise, in bog-iron ore and iron-sand, (7). St. Santin, Cantal, in galena mines, twenty-seven grains of gold per ton, (8). The whole produce of gold in France was at one time estimated at one hundred pounds weight yearly.

B. Spain And Portugal.—Gold was worked in Spain by the Phenicians, Carthaginians, Romans, and Moors, but very scantily in latter ages.

(1). Reaumur's Memoir; (2). Dictionnaire des Sciences Naturelles Article Or; (3). *Ibid.;* (4). Mining Journal, 1846, p. 389; (5). Dictionnaire des Sciences Naturelles; (6). *Ibid.;* (7). *Ibid.* ; (8). Timbs' Year Book of Facts, 1841, pp. 154-156.

The localities enumerated are the

Pyrenean provinces, (1).
Catalonia, *(2).*
Asturias, (3).
Galicia, (4).
Lusitania, (5).
Leon, (6).
Castille, (7).
Granada, (8).

Andalusia, (9). Individual mines mentioned are in the mountains of Guadarama, near St. Ildefonso, never worked; a mine near Talavera, worked by Donna Isabella;f a mine at Adissa, near St. Ubes, in Portugal,;: worked in this century, and which produced as much as forty-one pounds weight in 1815. A mine at Domingo Flores, in Leon, was worked from 1639 to 1749.§ At Culera, in Gerona, is gold quartz.

The gold rivers of the Spanish Peninsula are,

The Tagus, (10).
The Douro, (11).
The Ebro, (12).'
The Mondego, (13).
The Minho, (14).

The SO, in Galicia, (15). In Dr. Grew's book, in the Museum of the Royal Society, mention is made of specimens of gold sands from the Tagus and the Mondego.

(1). Plin. Hist. Nat. lib. 33, ch. 21; (2). Wyld's Gold Notes, p. 25; (3). Plin. Hist. Nat. lib. 3, ch. 34; (4). *Ibid.* lib. 33, ch. 21; (5). *Ibid.* (6). Wyld's Gold Notes, p. 25; (7). Wyld's Gold Notes; (8). *Ibid.* p. 25; (9). *Ibid.*; (10). Plin. Hist. Nat. lib. 33, ch. 21; Grew, Museum Royal Society, p. 322; Ovid, Metamorph. 2, v. 251; (11). Sil. Italicus; Aldrovandus 1, ch. 2; (12). *Ibid.;* (13). Grew, Museum Royal Society, c. 323; (14). Aldrovandus 1, ch. 2; (15). *Ibid.* t Jacobs' History of the Precious Metals, vol. 1, p. 272. *X Ibid.* p. 283. § Wyld's Gold Notes, p. 25. *Ibid.*

C. Switzerland.—The gold localities named in Switzerland are the Reuss and Aar, two of the heads of the Rhine, which is auriferous lower down, and the Rhone in the Pays de Gex,f affording a probability that the central region is auriferous as the southern range of the Alps is known to be. The Tessin, in the Canton of Ticino, is likewise gold-bearing.

D. Holland.—Holland was the scene of experiments for finding gold in the sea and river sands in the seventeenth century.J The Rhine discharges through it; but we have no account of gold below Philipsburgh,§ though M. Daubree supposes gold is found lower down. Gold was reported to be found in red sand between Arnheim and Sulvensteen.If

E. Italy.—Several gold sites in Italy were known to the ancients. The Salassi, in Upper Italy, near Aosta, in Piedmont, produced gold of very pure quality by washing the sands of the river Po, whose streams were divided into various branches, and after that tribe was conquered by the Romans, the several rivulets were let at a yearly rent by the imperial farmer-general of the finances.

The country round Aquileia and the whole district of the Noric Alps (now Illyria), was rich in gold, which was found partly in large grains on the surface and partly in mines so pure that an eighth part only was supposed to be lost in the processes of refining. At one period this gold was worked so extensively that its great quantity caused a decrease of one third in the prices through all Italy, and induced the Dictionnaire des Sciences Naturelles. Or. t Reaumur's Memoirs, *X* Becher's Minera Arenaria, several editions; Lewis' Commercium Philosophico Technicum. § Reaumur's Memoir.

Mining Journal, 1846, pp. 202, 264, 388.

% Becher's Minera Arenaria Perpetua, London, 1C80, p. 81.

Jacobs' History of the Precious Metals, vol. 1, p. 87.

proprietors to employ fewer workmen, in order to raise the value.

Other ancient localities for gold were Dalmatia,f the Po,J the territories of the Ictimuli, a tribe near Vercelli,§ and Pithecusa, opposite Cuma.

In the middle ages several gold localities were found in Italy, but not worked from want of persons understanding the business. Such were a vein of gold pyrites, near Bologna, Caravisia in Tuscany, Ischia, (discovered in 1465) and Messina, in Sicily

The most considerable gold region in Italy, of later years, has been that of Piedmont and Savoy, though gold is known in many streams of the Po.

The chief works are at Macugnaga, at the foot of Monte Rosar and head of the Sesia, where gold is found in the valleys of Anzasca. Toppa, and Antrona to a considerable value and to a less extent in those of Alagna, Sesia and Novara. ff The chief mines in Anzasca are at Peschiera and Minera di Sotto. The ore is an auriferous pyrites, yielding only two hundred grains, or about eight pennyweights of gold per ton,JJ but these mines have long been worked, and at one time employed one thousand workmen.§§ English auriferous pyrites are thrown away which yield eighty-nine ounces to the ton, or two hundred times as much as the Alpine ores.

In 1844, the yield was as follows:—

Strabo, lib. 4, cap. 6; Jacobs' History,

vol. 1, p. 88.
t Plin. Hist. Nat. 33, 21. I *Ibid.* § *Ibid.* Strabo.
H Aldrovandus, lib. 1, ch. 2.
Boyle's Works, vol. 5, p. 34. tt Mining Journal, 1845, p. 610. *XX* Dictionnaire des Sciences Naturelles, 1825; Weale's Rudimentary Mineralogy, p. 104.
§§ *Ibid.*; Mitchell's Assaying, p. 376. lll Mining Journal, 1845, p. 610.

Kilograms. Value.

Valley of Anzasca... 153 £16,092 Toppa... 19 2,032 Antrona... 20 2,150 The yield of Alagna, Sesia and Novara, in that year, was only two hundred and eighty pounds sterling.

At Pallanzana is a vein of auriferous pyrites, and in a mountain near Challand, gold is found in quartz veins.f The following is a list of the gold localities in Italy:— Aosta,J (1). Vercelli, (2). Macugnaga, (3). Alagna, (4). Sesia, (4). Novara, (4). Pallanzana, (5). Challand, (6).

Chivasso, in the hills near, (7).

Aquileia, (8).

Caravisia, (9).

Bologna, (10).

Ischia, (11).

Cuma, (12).

Dalmatia, (13).

Illyria, (14).

The following are the rivers in which gold is found:—

Po, (15).

Oglia, (16).

Tesin, above Lago Maggiore, (17).

Mining Journal, 1845, p. 610. t Dictionnaire des Sciences Naturelles. *X* (1). Jacobs, vol. 1, p. 87; (2). Pliny, 33, 21; (3). Boyle, vol. 5, p. 34; Mining Journal, 1846, p. 610; (4). *Ibid.;* (5). *Ibid.;* (6). Dictionnaire des Sciences Naturelles; (7). *Ibid.;* (8). Strabo, vol. 4, p. 6; (9), Aldrovaudus, 3, 2; (10). *Ibid.;* (11). *Ibid.;* (12). Strabo; (13). Pliny, 33, 21; (14). Strabo, vol.4, p. 6; (15). Pliny, 83, 21; (16). Bonardo Minera, 1589, 112; (17.) Dictionnaire des Sciences; (18). *Ibid.;* (19). *Ibid.*; (20). Pliny, 33, 21; (21). Mining Journal, 1846, p. 610; (22). Reaumur's Memoir.

Avanson, or Evenson, (18).

Oreo, (19).

Doire, (20).

Gogna, (21).

Arve, (22).

Gold is reported at Messina, in Sicily, and is supposed to be found in Sardinia. f

F. Gold In Greece, Turkey, &c.— Gold was worked by the ancients at Mount Pangaeus, in Thrace;J at Thasus, or Scaptesyle;§ in Thessaly; the islands of SiphnosIf and Cyprus; and in the river Hebro, in Thrace.f f

The workings in this district are now inconsiderable. About 1546, Dr. Belon visited the mines at Siderocapso, near Salonica, and found them worked by Spanish and German Jews.JJ The produce was then about £100,000 yearly.

Gold is now found in Macedonia, but the best known deposit is that of the river washings in Bosnia, where gold is found among sand and pebbles, but through the disordered state of the country, is not worked.§§

G. Germany And Austria.—The Austrian empire has many gold producing districts. Of these, the chief is Transylvannia. Gold is found there in ores at Kapnik, Iffl Stanisha,f1T Boiza, Vereshpatak, Abrudbanya, Santa Barbara, Offenbanya,Fatzebaya, Toplitza, Treshtyan, Zalathna,1ffl and Nagy Ag, Iflf near Deva.

The gold pyrites, in which no gold can be discovered by Aldrovandus, lib. 1, cap. 2. t Jacobs', vol. 1.
X Diodorus Siculus, lib. 16, cap. 8; Herodotus, lib. 7, cap. 112.
§ Herodotus, lib. 6, cap. 46, 47.
Jacobs on the Precious Metals, vol. 1, p. 72.

Tf Pausanias, lib. 10, cap. 11.
Jacobs on the Precious Metals, vol. 1, p. 69. tt PHny, Nat. Hist. lib. 33, cap. 21.
H Jacobs, vol. 1, p. 69. §§ Wyld's Gold Notes, p. 26.
Rces' Cyclopedia. Tit Dictionnaire des Sciences Naturelles.

P the eye, hold from two to four ounces of gold in a ton. Some specimens hold five thousand ounces, but these are rare. The mountain of Faczebaya, near Zalathna, is celebrated. Alabandine, or sulphuret of manganese, is an ore in which gold is found. Graphic tellurium, or gold, is found at Nagyag and Offenbanya.f This ore contains sixty parts of tellurium, thirty of gold, and ten of silver. The black tellurium contains sometimes fifteen per cent of gold.

Gold is found in the sands of the rivers Nera,J § Araniosh, % Morosh,J OlapianJ and Roshinar,J all feeders of the Danube. The gold washings in the Bannat of Temeswar are performed by gipsies, who display great skill in finding the metal. They dig chiefly on the banks of the river Nera, where it is said more gold is found than at the bottom of the stream; that is to say, they work dry diggings. Gold washing is said not to be a remunerative business.

Transylvania, or Siebengebirgen, is estimated to yield one thousand three hundred and seventy-five pounds of gold yearly, the gold washings of the Bannat yielding sixty pounds.

Gold is worked in Hungary, at Konigsberg, Borsony, Schemnitz, Felsobanya, Telkebanya, Rimezembat,f f Magara,JJ Posing, Magurka, and Chemnitz, in antimony.§§ The yield is about one thousand and fifty pounds of gold yearly. Gold is found in quartz.

In Bohemia, there were gold washings on the Iser, a Cronstedt's Mineralogy, vol. 2, p. 526.
t Weale's Rudimentary Mineralogy, pp. 105, 127. *X* Rees' Cyclopaedia.
§ Jacobs' History of the Precious Metals, vol. 1, p. 245.
Dictionnaire des Sciences Naturelles.

If Jacobs' History of the Precious Metals, vol. 1, p. 245.
Rees' Cyclopaedia. t t Cronstedt's Mineralogy, p. 521. *H Ibid*
§§ Jacobs' History of the Precious Metals, vol. 1, p. 245.
lll Wyld's Gold Notes, p. 25. f f Cronstedt's Mineralogy, p. 521. feeder of the Elbe, within the circles of Bedschow, and Turnau, and in the Moldau,f and at Eule, Neuknin, and Bergreichenstein.

There are gold mines near Salzburg, which have been very productive. They include Altenberg,J Schellgadin,J Rauris, and Rothhausberg. The yield is now only about thirty-five pounds of gold yearly.

In the Tyrol, there are gold washings two miles from Zell, at Schwazen, and at Saltzberg, in arsenical pyrites.f f

In Styria, gold is found in the Ems.

Gold is found in the Danube between Presburg and Comorn.JJ

In Silesia gold is found in arsenious ores in the River Katzbach and at Nikolstadt.If

In Saxony some gold is obtained from the silver mines, and gold was formerly washed in the Mulda and its brooks.§§

In the Hartz, between Hanover, Brunswick, and Prussia, a small quantity of gold has been obtained at Tilkerode, &c. It is found in decomposing iron pyrites.

Gold is found likewise in the Schwarz River in Schwarzburg Rudolstadt, in the Eder River in Waldeck,If in Bavaria, in Baden, and in the Sala(a feeder of the Elbe), at Reichmansdorf, in Saalfeld. The gold of the Schwarz is very rich. A nugget the size of a bean was found.

Jacobs' History of the Precious Metals, vol. 1, p. 245. t Phillips on Gold Mining, p. 4. *X* Jacobs' History of the Precious Metals, vol. 1, p. 245. Wyld's Gold Notes, p. 25. f Woodward's Natural History. Ure's Dictionary. ++, Cronsted's Mineralogy, p. 581. *XX* Wyld's Gold Notes, p. 25; Becher Minera Arenaria; Grew's Museum of the R. Soc, p. 322.

§§ Jacob's History of the Precious Metals, vol. 1. lll Weale's Rudimentary Mineralogy, p. 16,

Tflf Woodward's Natural History of Fossils, Lewis, p. 186; Voight's Kleine Schriften in Jameson's Dumfries, p. 119.

Lewis's Commercium Philosophico Technicum, p. 186.

The rivers of Germany and of Central Europe in which gold is found, are:—

The Rhine, (1).
The Reuss.
The Aar.
The Danube, *(2).*
The Inn, (3).
The Enns, (4).
The Morosh or Maros, (5).
The Nera, (6).
The Araniosh, (7).
The Olapian, (8).
The Roshinar, (9).
The Avanyos, (9a).
The Temes, (10).
The Elbe, (11).
The Iser, (12).
The Sala, (13).
The Schwarz, (14).
The Moldau, (15).
The Oder, (16).
The Katzbach, (17).
The Weser.
The Eder, (18). H. Sweden And Norway.—Gold is found in Sweden, in the copper and silver mines at Fahlun,-f-Helfors,J and elsewhere; at Asheda and Adelfors, in limestone; in Smal (1). See authorities before quoted; (2). P. 210; (3). Rees's Cyclopaedia; (4). Lewis's Commercium Philosophico Technicum, p. 185; (5) Dictionnaire des Sciences Naturelles; (6). *Ibid.;* (7). Rees's Cyclopaedia; (8). *Ibid.;* (9). *Ibid.;* (9a). Cronstedt'sMineralogy,vol. 2,p.523; (10). Jacobs' History of the Precious Metals, vol. 1, p. 245; (11). Lewis's Commercium, p. 185; (12). Jacobs, vol. 1, p. 245; (13). Lewis's Commercium, p. 185; (14). Woodward's Natural History; (15). Phillips on Gold Mining, p. 5; (16). Lewis's Commercium, p. 185; (17). Woodward's Natural History; (18). *Ibid.* t Jacobs' History of the Precious Metals, vol. 1, p. 287. J *Ibid.* and; at Riddarshyttan; in Westmanland, in limestone; at East and West Silver Mountain; in silver ore in Norberk.f The mine at Adelfors formerly yielded fifteen to twenty pounds of gold yearly, but now only from one to two pounds. The Fahlun mines yield two pounds yearly.J At Adelfors is gold pyrites.§

Gold is found in Norway at Edswold, in Rommarge, at Kongsberg, in quartz, and at Westhimmes in Akershuis.If

Gold was found in the last century in Swappawari, above Tornea, in Lapland.

In 1850, it was found in the low, laky, and swampy districts of Lapland and Finland, by M. E. F. de Furuhjelm. It is found in gulleys or creeks, and above sixty of these have been determined. The gold is found in small grains or scales, about two feet below the surface, in sand and clay, fine and coarse together, with rocky boulders, and associated with magnetic iron sand, termed schliech. These soils rest on igneous and transition rocks, mica slate, clay slate, diorite, accompanied with iron and copper pyrites, most probably auriferous.

Cronstedt's Mineralogy, p. 522. t Jacobs' History of the Precious Metals, vol. 1, p. 287. *X* Wyld's Gold Notes, p. 25.

§ Cronstedt's Mineralogy, p. 522.

Ihid. % Mining Journal, 1849, p. 371. Cronstedt's Mineralogy, vol. 2, p. 522.

CHAPTER XIII. GOLD IN RUSSIA, ASIA, AND AFRICA. *Ural.—Siberia.—Asia Minor.—Hindostan.—Assam.—Am. Malacca.—Annam Tibet China.—Japan.—Philippines.*

—Borneo.—Sumatra. — Celebes.—Timor.—Molucca.— Ceylon.—New Guinea.—New Zealand.—New Caledonia. —Africa.—Barbary.— Guinea.—Madagascar.—Canaries.

In Russia in Europe, there are no remarkable gold deposits, though a mine at Olonetz, on the lake Ladoga, was discovered in the time of Peter the Great.

The gold regions are in the Russian provinces of Asia, and may be classed as those of the Ural and of Siberia. Of these districts I purpose only to give briefly the characteristics as illustrative of the general objects of this work, as they are so fully described by the author of the Silurian system, Sir Roderick Murchison, and by Von Humboldt, the author of the Cosmos, in their great works on Russia.

The Ural district extends over a zone of about five or six degrees of latitude north and south of the town of Ekaterinburg; and it is remarked by Murchison, that the gold is only found on the eastern side of the range, and he has pointed out on several occasions, the resemblances between it and the Australian formations to which I shall hereafter refer. The Silurian rocks occupy with the metamorphic rocks and intruded rocks, the axis of the chain for eighteen degrees of latitude. The deposits here consist as usual of dry diggings of sand and gravel on the surface, and of gold Dictionnaire des Sciences Naturelles, Art. Or.

in the rocks. The gravel has been compared to that found near Woolwich, and is found in gulleys,

Berezovsk is the chief mine, the gold being found in iron pyrites f in veins or dykes of quartz, inclosed in talcose and chloritic schists and clayslates.

On the surface, the gold has been found with fragments of quartz attached. Platinum and palladium are associated with the gold and diamonds, and have been found, as I have found them, in similar situations in Australia.

Very large nuggets have been found, of which descriptions have been given elsewhere.

The yield of gold from the sands of the Ural, is only thirty-six grains per ton;*X* but even this is of picked and prepared sands, so that the yield in the rough sand may be taken as still less. Some sands yield, but rarely, seventy grains per ton.

In the Miask district, which has yielded the largest nuggets, there is a remarkable similarity to. what has been observed in New South Wales. The edges of the rocks are found inclined at a great angle to the horizon, and the tops of high hills show fragments of quartz veins. In the hollows of these rocks are found large nuggets, and lumps of gold, sometimes like nests, taking the shape of the rock surface. In this district, the detritus js about ten or twelve feet thick, lying on a bed rock, which is found occasionally hollowed out.

Sir Roderick Murchison thus describes the auriferous alluvia. He says, " they are especially rich along the zone where greenstones, porphyries, and serpentines have traversed ancient lime stones, and have been followed by the Russian miners to the north of Petropavlosk, between which place and Berezovsk, the excavations and works have been numerous. Around the zavods of Nijny Tagilsk and Bla Murchison's Russia.

t Weale's Rudimentary Mineralogy, by D. Varley. *X* Ansted's Geology, vol. 2, p. 267; Gold Digger's Manual, p. 9. godat, and even extending to the western talus of the watershed, these gold alluvia have been considerably worked, and in some instances the ore of platinum is found in the very same masses. In reference to the works depending on Nijny Tagilsk, it may be stated that the zone which ranges close along the western side of the crest of the chain, is poor in gold; the particles of which are associated with chromate of iron and platinum, and are supposed to have been derived from the hornblend and metamorphic rocks, which there rise up to form the axis. The richest band is that which runs from north to south, a little to the east of Leusk; while two other, but poorer zones, occur in the mineralized low ridges still further east, or at forty and sixty versts from Nijny Tagilsk. In this parallel of latitude, therefore, the goldbearing detritus is found at intervals, and in zones extending from north to south over a country near one hundred versts in width, and is everywhere made up of fragments of the metamorphic and eruptive rocks of the region, and most frequently in portions of quartz veins. Varying in thickness and importance, according to the original depression or cavities in which they have been deposited, these materials lie at all levels, the little modern streams having had no-sort of influence in accumulating them."

Some allusion has been made to a remarkable circumstance connected with the Ural mines, a curious affidavit of Walter Basbee, connected with the mint in the Tower of London, who in the reign of James I. went to Russia for the purpose of assisting in the Ural mines, and was taken prisoner by the Tartars.f

It has been remarked by the Russian mining engineers, that the goldbearing sands in several gold regions, rarely repose on granite or syenite, but usually on schistose rocks, near serpentines and hornblend rocks. They are also found, Murchison's Russia, vol. 1, p. 479.

t Pamphlet of Thomas Bushel.

not in the recesses of the mountains, but principally forming plateaux parallel with and terminating the chain, or exhibited in the lower and broader part of the valleys. They are not continuous, and in certain localities the gold is more abundantly distributed than in others.

The Siberian gold regions constitute three districts—the valleys between the Obi and the Tom, those between the Tom and the Yenessei, and those from the Yenessei to the Lena, including the rivers Grande Birussa, Upper Tongooska, Ooderei and Pita, in the Yenessei province, and those of Kholivan, Voskressensk, and Nertchinsk, and extending beyond Lake Baikal.

In these districts, the geological formation, in its general composition, resembles that already described. Granites, metamorphosed schists, and other rocks of like class, are to be recognised along the flanks of the Altai. The chief diggings are in a quartzy sand or gravel, mixed with oxide of iron, and are found on the tops of hills, summits of steep mountains, and in gulleys. The gold is noticed to be most abundant in veins of diorite, or where the diorite appears.

As in Australia and California, the gold-bearing alluvium is often formed under a covering of clay and shingle, and it is necessary to go down to the bed rock.

The proportion of silver in the gold of Siberia is commonly very small, according to Mr. A. Rose, except at Sinarowski, in the Altai, where it reaches 3838 per cent. This is, in fact, an alloy, or electrum.

Gold was found by the ancients in the river Pactolus,f and in Mount Tmolus, near Sardis. The ancients had vague ideas as to the gold of India, J and of Central Asia. §

Gold is found all over our Indian empire, more particularly in the Madras presidency, in Assam, the Indus, and the Ganges.

Ansted's Geology, vol. 2, p. 282. t Pliny's Nat. Hist. lib. 33, cap. 21. *X Ibid.*

§ Humboldt's Cosmos. Wyld's Gold Notes, p. 27.

In the basin of the Indus, between Attock and Kalabagh, are river washings, employing about three hundred people. The gold is found in scales.

Gold is found in the Ganges, Goomty, Ramgunga, and other rivers at the foot of the Himalayas. Gold is likewise found in the gneiss, which is traversed by veins of granite, and distinctly stratified.

In the Dekkan, gold is found in the rivers Poliaur and Poniaur, in Mysore; in the Nolampoor, Kapoor, Srussumjee, Polwye, Tirumpaddy, and other rivers in Calicut and on the Malabar coast; of Malapuram, in Nedingabad; of Kadalaonely and Parpanagady, in Shernaad; of Kahil, Aripanad, and the Tirumaly Hills. In the Ernaad district are twenty river workings, f

The river sands of the Burrampooter, in Assam, yield thirty-eight thousand ounces yearly,J more particularly at the junction with the Dontriri.

In Ava, gold is found in several rivers, particularly the Choe Lien Kioup, or river of golden sand.§

Gold is found in Malacca, at Ophir, Naning, Pahang, Tringanu, Calantan, Battang, Moring, Gamunchi, Chindras, Tabong, Ladang, and Ayer Kuning. The gold at Mount Ophir is in quartz.

Gold is obtained largely from Annam, Tonquin, or Cochin China.

In Thibet, gold is found on the chain of the Cailas Mountains, in river-washings, in the Sutledj and the Sindh, and likewise in quartz veins.If

In China, gold is worked in river sands in Sechuen and Yunan, and is found in Kiansi and Kweichou.

In the islands of the Asiatic seas, gold is extensively found.

Pliny's Nat. Hist. lib. 33, c. 21. t Wyld's Gold Notes, p. 28. J *Ibid.*

§ Jacobs' History of the Precious Metals, vol. 2, p. 330.

Wyld's Gold Notes, p. 28. f Moorcroft's Travels.

All accounts of Japan agree that gold is worked there.

It is found in the Philippines, at Mindanao, and elsewhere.f The yield is said to be about twelve hundred pounds yearly.J

Gold is found in BorneoJ in ores, in river-beds, and in dry diggings. The yield is said to be nine thousand pounds yearly, obtained principally by Chinese. At Mount Trian, in Sarawak are good dry diggings.

Sumatra yields about three thousand pounds of gold.J Celebes, eight hundred pounds.J Timor, eighty pounds. J In the latter it is found in copper ore. Gold is found in nuggets in the Moluccas.§

Gold is reported in Ceylon.

To the south gold is reported in New Guinea, and I found it in New Zealand and in New Caledonia.

The African localities include Barbary, in Morocco, near Tarudant, in mines; in South Morocco dry diggings for dust and nuggets in a glen or gully of alluvial soil near Shiebon; at Luca a gold mine. Gold is washed from the sands near the town of Tripoli and many other places in the government of Tripoli, and likewise near the Fezzan border.

Gold is found in sands and mines in Nubia, in Kordofan, on the Fazangoro, and in the rivers of Abyssinia.

In north Africa gold is reported, likewise in the mountains of Mandara, at Bourra, on the Wassolo, dry diggings, and at Bambook, on the Wankaral.

In the interior, gold is found in Footajalloo; Bambarra; in dry diggings at Bukanti and Kentosoe, in the Bunkatoo country, near Ashantee.

The Bambook diggings are in an alluvial formation of Jacobs' History of the Precious Metals, vol. 2, p. 335. t Aldrovandus' Minerals, lib. 1, cap. 2; Williams' Mineral Kingdom, p. 369.

X Wyld's Notes, p. 28. § Aldrovandus, lib. 1, cap. 2. Williams' Mineral Kingdom, vol. 2, p. 364, 369; Jacobs' History. sand and pulverised emery, with grains of iron ore and gold.

Gold is found in the neighbourhood of Natal. The gold islands are Madagascar and the Canaries,f at Teneriffe.

F. Caoourt's History of Madagascar; Boyle's Works, vol. 1, p. 207. t Boyle's Works, vol. 5, p. 171. CHAPTER XIV. GOLD REGIONS OF AMERICA. *Canada.— Virginia. — Geology.— California.— Geology.— West Indian Islands.—Mexico.— Central America.— Columbia. — Peru. — Brazil. — Geology. — St. John del Rey.*

Unless gold be found in Greenland, the most northern goldfield known in the western world is that of Canada, on La Chaudiere River, where there is stream gold and auriferous quartz. Gold has been found at Sherbrooke, in Canada, at Canaan, New Hampshire, and Albion Maine.

The geological formation of Canada is strongly in favour of its being a great gold region, as I pointed out in my paper before the British association at the Hull this year.

The Virginian gold region includes Virginia, North Carolina, the northern part of South Carolina, Georgia, part of Alabama, and East Tennessee.

In Virginia the chief deposits are in Spotsylvania county, on the Rappahannock, at the United States mines, and at other places to the south west, in Stafford county, at the Rappahannock gold mines, ten miles from Falmouth, in Culpepper county, at the Culpepper mines, in Rapidan river, in Orange county, at the Orange Grove gold mine, described further on, and at the Greenwood gold mines, in Goochland county, at Moss and Bussby's mines, in Louisa county, at Dana's Manual of Mineralogy, p. 313.

Walter's gold mine, in Buckingham county, at Eldridge's mine. In North Carolina the gold region is mostly confined to the three ranges of shires between Frederick and Charlotte, which are situated about in a line running N.E. and S.W. parallel nearly with the coast. The mines at Mecklenburg are principally vein deposits; those of Burke, Lincoln, and Rutherford, are mostly in alluvial soil. The Davidson county silver mine yielded a large quantity of gold. In Georgia the Shelton gold mines have long been worked, others have been opened in Rabun and Hall county and the Cherokee country. In South Carolina the chief gold regions are the Fairforest, in Union district, the Lynch's creek, and Catawba regions in Lancaster and Chesterfield districts, and Picken's county adjoining Georgia.

The chief yield has been from Georgia and North Carolina; very little from Tennessee and Alabama.

The gold rock of the United States is described by Dana as consisting, to a great extent, of micaceous or talcose schist, with veins or beds of quartz. The gold is mostly confined to these veins, though also found to some extent in the rock on either side. The schist is often found half decomposed or rusted. The quartz is usually more or less cellular, or wanting in perfect compactness, and sometimes tabular. Yet it is at times quite solid. Iron pyrites is frequently present, and by decomposition it stains the rocks with iron rust. Other minerals often associated with the gold are copper pyrites, blende, anglesite, galena, and sulphur (in minute yellow crystals, proceeding from the decomposition of pyrites). Heavy spar is sometimes a large constituent of the vein, and fluor spar is now and then present. The peculiar appearance of the quartz, somewhat cellular, more or less rusted, and its position in veins, though an imperfect shale, and generally not firmly attached to the inclosing walls, affords the best indication of the presence of gold, though the absence of all these conditions is not evidence that no gold is to be found. The grains of gold may sometimes be seen in the cavities of the quartz, or it sparkles on a surface of fracture; but very commonly a mass of quartz that shows nothing to the eye yields gold on trial.

The Orange Grove gold mine is in Virginia, and was first worked for dry diggings, and paid well. There are quartzose lodes running N.N.E. and S. S.W., dipping N.E. and traversing talcose and other schists. The width of the lodes varies from four to twenty feet, but sometimes more. The lodes are connected by threads or leaders. The minerals associated with the gold lodes are sulphurets, oxides, and hydrates of iron, which latter, at a depth of seventy to eighty feet, are found incrusting the sulphurets, and both containing gold. The schists are impregnated and coloured with iron. Parallel with the gold lodes are ores of copper, rich in gold, and containing in some places native copper. Lumps of from two to four pennyweights have been found in the lodes. The ores by analysis yield severally sixteen ounces, twelve ounces, six ounces, and two ounces and a half, to the ton.

On the western side are the gold fields of Vancouver's Island, Queen Charlotte Island, Oregon, New and Old California, and thence extending into Mexico. New Mexico has gold near Santa Fe, Cerillos, and Avo.

California has been written upon at length, and as I have little to say regarding it of my own personal knowledge, I shall no further refer than will be sufficient to illustrate the geological features of the gold regions. These are briefly summed up by Professor Blake,/ who has had the opportunity of making a geological survey. He says that, "with the exception of the diluvial strata the whole geological formation of the Sierra Nevuada range consists of igneous

Dana's Manual of Mineralogy, p. 316.

t American Journal of Science and Art.

-;. and metamorphic rocks; the former are mostly porphyritic in the lower hills, whilst higher up trachytic rocks are more frequently met with. The metamorphic rocks consist of micaceous schists, slates both talcose and micaceous, metamorphic sandstones and limestones, with occasional beds of conglomerate. The stratified rocks have been much displaced; it is rare to find them with a dip of less than 70, and they are generally very nearly perpendicular." A conformity with the general structure of the goldbearing regions will be recognized in these descriptions. He proceeds to observe that "the strike of the beds in that section to which my observations have been confined (between the Stanislaus and the Yuba rivers), is extremely uniform, being from 5 to 10 west of north and east of south. The extent of the diluvial deposits is commensurate, or nearly so, with that of the goldbearing region, in that part of the country which I have examined. They are found in a belt of land from thirty to forty miles broad, and running parallel with the axis of the range; and from facts that I have ascertained from others, I have no doubt that they exist throughout all the goldbearing region both north and south. These diluvial deposits are met with as we advance towards the lower hills of the Sierra, extending frequently some miles into the plain. They are often of considerable thickness, and frequently rest on tertiary rock. On approaching the foot of the lower hills, the conglomerate and gravel are found in greater abundance, the pebbles and boulders are larger and contain more of the heavier rock. They are seen also covering extensive valleys or flats of many miles in extent, inclosed by low ridges of porphyry and slate, which rise rather higher than the surface of these beds. On ascending from the lower hills towards the mountains, the diluvial beds no longer occupy the same relative position; occasionally deposits of rounded stones can be found in the valleys and on the sjde& of die hills, but when this is the case their origin can always be traced to the deposits existing on the tops of the surrounding hills, from which they have been brought down by the action of the causes now at work. As we ascend towards the axis of the chain, these deposits become more extensive, and at a distance of twenty or thirty miles from the lower hills, they are found occupying the crests of almost all the highest hills in the country." This has been already described as occurring in the Russian gold regions, and I have seen it in Australia.

Besides being found on the crests of the ridges where their extent frequently does not exceed a few yards in breadth, the Professor observes the deposits " are also met with covering in the extensive flats which exist on the banks between the different watercourses, forming continuous beds of many miles in extent, which are rarely interrupted by the protrusion of any of the older rocks." These conditions have been remarked by the anonymous describer of the Clydesdale gold field, and are likewise found in the Brazils. " Where found in these elevated situations," says Professor Blake, " the lower hills and valleys are entirely free from them; frequently a large section of the country will be enclosed from two high ridges capped by deposits and diverging from a common point; in the intervening space will be seen many secondary ridges, sometimes fifteen or eighteen hundred feet high, formed entirely of the older rocks, no traces of deposits being found on their surface, nor in the ravines that lead from them."

The same observations apply to the depth of the alluvial deposits in California, as in Leadhills, Cornwall, Wicklow, Siberia, or Australia. It is extremely variable. "Sometimes," says Mr. Blake, " nothing more than a trace of them in the presence of a few round pebbles lying on the top of a ridge is found; the valleys and ravines in the neighbourhood containing their disintegrated elements in considerable quantities. In other instances, particularly where

Q spread out over the elevated flats, they are of moderate and pretty uniform thickness for a considerable distance, varying from two to three feet to a few inches, and this, too, in positions where the surface could not have been exposed to any great amount of denudation. They are again found many hundred feet in thickness, composed of superimposed strata of different mineralogical constitution, generally horizontal and conformable with each other."

A very good description is given by this close observer of the elements of these deposits, which differ it seems considerably in different localities, conformably to what might be expected by those having practical experience in gold regions, though there are many points of resemblance in the whole series. In the lower valleys and flats, between the ranges of the lower hills, they appear to consist of beds of gravel, containing occasional boulders of quartz and the harder rocks. On the elevated flats higher up in the mountains, the surface of these deposits is generally covered by a reddish loam, mixed with small gravel; whilst reposing on the bed rock, and a few inches above it, is a stratum containing large boulders and gravel, the boulders being principally quartz. On the top of the hills and the crests of the ridges, where they generally attain their greatest thickness, we find them composed of many distinct strata, lying nearly horizontal, and conformable with each other, and generally also with the surface of the underlying rock. In these situations, the most superficial stratum is composed of a mass of extremely hard conglomerate, containing principally trachytic rocks, embedded in a hard argillaceous cement. It is this hard stratum that has undoubtedly preserved the underlying beds from the destructive influences which have so powerfully acted on the surrounding rocks.

At other points, the whole series consists of conglomerates and soft friable sandstone. In the lower strata, quartzose conglomerates, with an argillaceous cement or loose quartzose gravel always prevails with large boulders of quartz, weighing frequently two or three tons, having their surface worn smooth and the angles rounded. The deposits of these heavier rocks have been formed on spots which were evidently lower than the level of the surrounding rocks; whilst on those parts which were higher at the time the deposits were formed, the higher trachytic rocks are found. As far as my researches have extended, the mere quartzose conglomerates have been invariably found in the erupted rocks, whilst the stratified rocks which they had upheaved were only covered by the trachytic conglomerates. The pebbles of which these conglomerates are composed, present specimens of all the harder rocks. Metamorphic sandstones, clinkstone, trap, porphyries, and quartz make up the larger part of the mass. They are all perfectly rounded, but in the lower deposits are so soft, that, with the exception of the trap and quartz, they generally fall to pieces on exposure to the air. The strata, as before observed, are nearly horizontal and conformable: if they have any dip, it appears to have been owing to the slope of the surface of the rock on which they were deposited; in fact, no displacement seems to have taken place in this country since the period of their formation. They lie perfectly horizontal over the almost vertical edges of the upheaved slate rocks. The characteristic of these deposits is their bearing gold, which is found whereever they exist. " The ravines coming from the ridges on which they are found are generally extremely rich, and always contain gold, even in places where the deposits themselves have been worked without success. In some places where they have been worked, as much as thirty thousand dollars (£7000) have been taken from a claim of fifteen feet square. But few of these rich spots have, up to the present time, been opened. Yet there can be no doubt but that many still remain to be discovered. Where these deposits are found extending over a large surface on the elevated flats, gold is always met with, generally diffused through the gravel immediately above the rock on which they rest. In the valleys on the lower hills, and even on the plains to the west of them, where they are extended over vast tracts of country, these deposits are still auriferous, the gold being very generally diffused, and found in greater quantities the deeper they are worked."

In the West Indian Islands gold has been found in ancient and modern times in San Domingo, Cubaf and Jamaica.J

In Mexico the chief gold regions are in the north, in Sonora and Sinaloo, of which the best known mines are those of Triarte, Rosario, Cerala, Alamos, Hermosillo, and Guadalupe y Calvo. There are rich workings at Quitovac and Sonitac, to the north of Arispe. In Oaxaca§ and Catorce are rich workings, but most of the gold from Guanajuato is from the silver ores, containing only 1-360th of gold. The gold at Oaxaca is in veins in gneiss and mica slate. In Mexico a rhodium gold is found with thirty-four to fortythree per cent, of rhodium.

In Central America gold is worked at Del Aquacato in Costa Rica, and is said to be found at Mineral de Veraguas, Estrella, Chiriqui and Cuna in Darien, and the river Concepcion and its branches.

InColumbia, gold has been worked by English companies' as well as by natives. The gold quartz of Marmato contains only a small portion of metal. Here the gold is found in quartz in sandstone. In December, 1839, eighty-six tons produced at the rate of twelve pennyweights per ton; in January, 1840, at the rate of twelve pennyweights twelve grains; in February, 1840, at the rate often pennyweights four grains. The average produce of the whole of 1839, Peter

Martyn, Decad. 3, cap. 8; Androvandus, lib. 1, cap. 2. t Acosta, History of the Indies, lib. *i,* cap. 4; Aldrovandus, lib. 1, cap. 2; Mining Journal, 1843, p. 405. I Boyle's Works, vol. 5, p. 33. § Dictionnaire des Sciences Naturelles, from five thousand and seventy-nine tons of ore, was ten pennyweights of gold per ton. The gold is obtained from river washings and mines. Among the rivers are the Rio Cauca, Atrato, Zulia, Hacha and Sucio. There are likewise washings in the mountains of Guzmoco, Barbacoa, Antioquiaj and Popayan. Caraccas is a. rich gold district. Gold is worked at Marmato, Santa Rita, Supia, Mariquita, Pamplona, Chaco, Barquisemento, Titiribi and Malpaso.

In Peru gold is found in Huailas, Pataz, Carabaya, Curimaro, near Caxamarca, Oruro, Chayanta, Corico, the rivers Chayanta, Tinquemaya, Sopachuy, and San Juan, and other places.

In Bolivia it is likewise worked.

Gold is obtained in Chile from river washings, from ores, and from the silver mines.

In the independent territory of Araucania gold is worked.

There seems to be gold over a great part of the La Platan Commonwealth, and it is found in Paraguay. There are gold washings in the Rinconada.

The chief Brazilian provinces for gold are Minas Geraes and Matto Grosso. There are river washings and gold ores. The chief localities are Gongo Soco, Morro Velho, St. John del Rey, Mocaubas, Cocaes, Villa Rica, Angaba, Jacobina, Jaragua and the rivers Mando, Rio das Velhas, Parahybuna, Ouro Preto, Francisco, Tocantins, Araguay and Guaporu.

The amount of gold received by the National Brazilian Company from Cuiaba during their existence was £48,172, and from Cocaes, £21,711.

In Brazil a palladium gold has been found, with 9.85 per cent, of palladium, and 4.17 percent, of silver. This is one of the chief sources of palladium. A considerable quantity is obtained by the Imperial Brazilian Mining Company.

The washings in the Minas Geraes, and the average produce in 1812 were as follows:—Villa Rica (£10,000), Barba List of Metals, ch. 26.

Santa Mariana, (£12,000), St. John del Rey, (£1500), St. Joze(£1400), Barbacena (£1100), Sahara (£9,000), Villa Nova da Rainha (£22,000), Peracata (£2,000), Villa do Principe (£2,100), Serra do Frio (£3,200), Campanha da Prina (£6,000), Minas Novas (£250), Pilangui (£7,000).

The Brazilian gold mines are chiefly at the foot of a great mountain chain running parallel to the coast, and occupying a similar situation to the great watershed of Australia; gold is there found in the river beds in wet and dry diggings and in mines. The rock includes granite, inclining to gneiss, with a portion of hornblend and frequently mica; gold is found on both sides of the range. The soil or stuff lying on the bed rock is of some depth, and shows great signs of iron. The gold is commonly found in a stratum of rounded pebbles and gravel called cascalhao. The diggers have to go down about eighteen or twenty feet deep. Iron mica is often found in association with quartz sand. The deposits are commonly found in the gulleys and ravines, but likewise on the hills. It is observed that while the stuff in the cascalhao of the rivers is commonly rounded and worn, in the dry diggings of the mountains it is rough and rounded.

In the rich district of Villa Rica, gold is found in small particles, spread over the country in the clay slate or schist, which rests on a nucleus of intruded granite, sand stone, or gneiss. Here is a very rich gulley in the Rio do Carmo.

Gold is found likewise in true veins in the rocks, sometimes very small, but occasionally forming at their junction rich masses or pockets.

The St. John del Rey mines are remarkable for being very profitably worked with very poor ores. The district is represented as composed of a soft kind of gneiss, full of narrow veins of quartz running through it, in plains nearly perpendicular to the horizon. The gold is found in these veins much like the Australian and Californian gold quartz, traversing the spar in small threads or chains of lumps, more or less rich, filling up as it were the chinks in the spar, like a mould.

The produce of these mines is, it is known, very small per ton; but this is one of the best paying companies. In 1840, the average produce was eight pennyweights fifteen grains per ton; in 1841, seven pennyweights twenty grains; in 1842, nine pennyweights four grains; in 1844, seven pennyweights sixteen grains; in 1845, eight pennyweights sixteen grains; in 1847, nine pennyweights nineteen grains. The produce of the several ore varies. In 1841, ore near the surface was found extremely poor, and in February produced only three pennyweights per ton, though the same ore lower down yielded, in December, seven pennyweights eighteen grains. The Champion ore yielded five pennyweights ten grains; Gamba ore, seven pennyweights twenty grains; Louisa ore, seven pennyweights sixteen grains.

The Gongo Soco mines have likewise been long worked by the English. The rocks of the district consist of quartzose rock, a sandstone with grains of quartz, a talcose schist, and a bluish satiny clay slate. In the sandstone, iron glance and carbonate of manganese are found associated with native gold. In the quartzose rock, it is found near black flakes of iron glance, separating the laminated texture of the rock. In the other rocks, the gold is found, native, in flakes or flat leaves, sometimes as much as ten inches long. The first kind of rock is locally termed *jacontinga,* and is most readily worked.

According to Mr. Henwood, up to 1850, thirty-three thousand pounds weight of gold had been extracted in twenty-four years from the mine of Gongo Soco. The produce from Gongo Soco was from two hundred to two hundred and fifty pounds per month, although the proportion from the ore is only half an ounce per ton. The ore is pyrites.

CHAPTER XV. GOLD REGIONS OF AUSTRALIA. *General Observations.—Estimates of Gold.—List of Metals and Precious Stones.*

The geological structure and physical

condition of Australia have been the engrossing subject of my thoughts for the last eleven years, and I have traversed about twentyone thousand miles of its soil, chiefly on horseback, independent of daily local excursions from my camp, for the purpose of determining the mineral character throughout South Australia, Victoria, and New South Wales. In these expeditions I have carefully investigated the auriferous sands, earths, veins, other metallic formations, &c., and laid them down on maps.

Having, likewise, so many assays and practical notes to refer to, I am enabled to arrive at something like an approximate estimate of the extent, as well as of the richness, of the auriferous soils of these three colonies.

My estimate for the average yield of auriferous earth will appear very low, being only nine-tenths of a grain in the cubic foot; but then the extent I would place at sixty-eight thousand, seven hundred square miles, and which, I would consider, will include all the gold fields worthy of that name in the three colonies, of which only a comparatively small portion is at present worked, a great extent not being even known to contain gold, except from my own investigations. The average depth of these auriferous strata will be about thirty-nine inches, whether on the surface of the nearly bare rocks of the mountain tops, or of the rich alluvial flats and river beds, which are in many instances upwards of two hundred feet in depth. I have taken the mean average, although as a general rule, the deeper the auriferous strata lies covered up, the richer is the produce per ton of washing stuff.

The above average is so low, that even were it three times the quantity of soil estimated, it would cease to have any allurements to the working classes with such rude machinery as they have at their disposal, were it not for the digger taking advantage of the self-evident fact that the heavy metal will always be found in greatest accumulation in the lowest hollows of the bed rock, or wherever the debris has met with a check or bar to its onward progress. There are likewise many other little incidents which he learns by practical observation on the spot, or the chances would be decidedly against him.

Supposing nine-tenths of a grain to a cubic foot, and the average depth of the soil thirty-nine inches over an area of ground comprising sixty-eight thousand, seven hundred square miles, the result would give four hundred and thirty-four thousand, one hundred and ninety tons, two cwt. seventy-six lbs., which, at *£3 19s.* per oz., will be about £46,100,571,660.

The above estimate only includes auriferous earth, alluvial debris, and sands, not any gold ores, quartz veins, and metals containing gold, &c., which, if worked, would yield enormous wealth. I will proceed to enumerate some of them below, with an outline of the mineral treasures of these colonies.

Two hundred and thirty-eight gold quartz veins which, with very few exceptions, have been discovered by myself, producing, upon an average, for twenty fathoms down, two and a half pennyweights to the ton. One of these which I called the Macquarie Vein is an extensive one, or as some might prefer to call it, is a great many small ones forming one great system; I traced it for nearly forty miles across the country, running north and south; in some places it contained a very large percentage of gold, which was generally secreted, appearing of a green colour, in almost imperceptible particles, and sometimes connected with the arseniate of iron, whilst, in other parts, it would be associated with a sulphuret or iron pyrites. This enormous vein will yield some millions sterling, provided the ores were treated properly, though I doubt very much if that be possible with the processes at present adopted. I obtained a large quantity of gold from this vein in 1849.

Another quartz vein, discovered by myself in 1852, although much smaller, is by no means behind hand in importance, as it contains the extraordinary average of from half per cent, to twenty-eight per cent, of gold on the surface. Considering the extent and yield, this is the most wonderful fact relating to gold ever yet recorded in the annals of history. It was from this vein that I broke of! the three cwts. of quartz (as much as my horse could carry away, being about thirty miles from my camp at the time), which yielded seventy-six lbs. weight of pure gold, value £3700.

Oxides and sulphurets of iron, many of which contain gold, and some exceedingly rich. I have made many assays of these ores, but cannot attempt to give any average, they being so various in quality, even in the immediate neighbourhood of each other: the highest assay I made gave at the rate of seven hundred and sixty-three and a half ounces to the ton. Vast masses of granite, some miles in extent, containing gold in cryptothesis, which, as the granite decomposes under certain electric oppositions and other conditions, causes the gold to become precipitated and available, such as at Braidwood and many other places.

I found many lead veins, some rich in gold; many of these lead veins contain flour spar, barytes, and blende, but that chiefly happens in Victoria.

I discovered silver pure and in company with other metals, and occasionally mixed with gold in various proportions. Platina in granite and in company with the gold in stream washings. Quicksilver in many places native, and in certain localities cinnabar of very inviting character to the speculative world.

A vein partly composed of tellurium, associated with lead, containing one hundred and ten ounces of gold to the ton.

Three hundred and seventeen rich copper lodes that will pay to work. Many good tin lodes. Tin ground the extent of which I would lay down at about four thousand six hundred square miles, chiefly rich black oxides, which in Cornwall would be called stream tin, about three thousand square miles associated with gold.

The precious stones I found were, in a few instances, valuable, but the bulk were valueless as gems, and only useful to determine the species. I will enumerate a few of the most important, as many were found in company with gold. Diamond, ruby, sapphire, corundum, emerald, beryl, chrysoberyl, peridot, chrysolite, tourmaline, garnet, hyacinth, opal, amethystine quartz, cairngorm, chrysoprase, mochastone, calcedony, agate, onyx, jasper, &c.

The extensive seams of coal and accumulations of iron, of the very best kind, in such abundance, only cause us to ponder and speculate as to the immense future resources of that wonderful and extensive continent. My discovery of coal to the westward of the Australian Cordillera, and at some distance in the interior, I consider as an important point when looking at the geological features of Australia.

The ranges throughout this continent have one seeming tendency from south to north, as is the case in most parts of the world, and that great mountain-chain the Cordillera of Eastern Australia is the most important of the whole and most extensively developed. Strzelecki followed it from south to north, a course which I have myself adopted, with the additional advantage of having proceeded farther, north and west, and of having better opportunities of studying the interior, I am happy, too, in having this advantage over Count Strzelecki, that I have had the benefit of his labours. This general description must suffice; for thoroughly to depict the whole of that immense region would require a book to itself, and would overshadow the limited account of the English Gold Fields. I shall proceed to give a few notes on the peculiar features of that continent, reserving my own observations for their proper place in another work.

At the last anniversary meeting of the Royal Geographical Society, Sir Roderick Murchison explained his views with regard to Australia, as modified by the last discoveries. He said,—" The coincidence of mineral structure, which I pointed out between the eastern watershed of Australia, as described by Strzelecki, and the Ural mountains, which I had then examined, and now seen to be accompanied by other phenomena common to the two chains, to which it is well to advert. The Ural mountains are notably auriferous on the eastern or Siberian side only, and as far as surveys have gone, it would appear that one flank only of the Australian watersheds exhibits rich accumulations of gold debris; but in this case it is the western or interior side of the range. It is, however, to be observed that in his recent exploration of vast tracts along the southern frontiers of the colony of New South Wales, where they unite with the province of Victoria, the Rev. W. B. Clarke has shown, that whilst no copious deposits of large grained gold (with a partial exception near Araluen) have been found on the banks of those rivers which flow to the east or south, yet still that in many localities, and over a wide area, fine grained gold is disseminated throughout the alluvia. In clearing up the geological structure of that region, the author has also given reasons for supposing that the various affluents of the Snowy river, which descends to the south from the high Alps named Mount Kosciusko, by Strzelecki, may be profitably worked for gold when the richer natural magazines are exhausted. But still the fact remains that it is only on the interior flank of the watershed that the great prizes have been found. Such are the tracts of Victoria, whether around Mount Alexander and along the banks of the Lodden, which flows into the Murray or the Ovens diggings, to the N.W., such are the rich accumulations along the feeders of the Macquarie, to the west of Bathurst; those near Wellington, as described in a report of the Surveyor-general, Sir Thomas Mitchell, and numerous fresh auriferous spots noticed by Mr. Stutchbury, in his successive mineral reports; such again are the numerous creeks which supply the head waters of the Peel river. Another striking similarity to the Ural mountains is that like them the Australian range is in many parts a mere plateau, with a scarcely perceptible dividing ridge, along which, however, eruptive or metamorphic rocks peer out at numerous intervals, rising, though rarely, to altitudes varying from three thousand to six thousand feet. Thus, at the source of the west-flowing Peel river, the Hanging Rock of the Colonists, is an eruptive boss, like the Katch Hanar of the Ural, from which various fissures and chasms are said to radiate, in which minor streams meander through the slaty and quartz ore rocks, which have been the chief sources of the gold ore. In like manner, Mr. Stutchbury describes numerous protrusions of granitic, syenitic, and other igneous rocks through metamorphosed strata of schist, sandstone, and limestone of palaeozoic age around Wellington and in the affluents of the Macquarie."

Sir Roderick Murchison likewise observes that the Rev. Mr. Clarke has discovered true fossils of Silurian age in some of the less metamorphosed limestones of the south west tracts of New South Wales and the adjacent region of Victoria Land. This point was, however, settled beyond doubt by my own investigations.

I should differ in opinion from the Rev. Mr. Clarke.

CHAPTER XVI. LAW AS TO ROYAL MINES AND ROYALTIES IN ENGLAND.

History of Crown Claims.—Invalidity of.— Common Law.— Right to dig for Metals.—Prospecting Licences.—Claim of Mines Royal Corporation.—Privileges of. — Decision of Judges.—Acts of Parliament.—Preemption Rights.

The law as to royal mines and royalties varies in different parts of these islands, not only according to the municipal law of each, but according as it has been modified in its operation by various grants.

It will be considered under these several heads:—

A. England.
B. Wales.
C. Scotland.
D. Ireland, within and without the Pale.
E. Berwick-upon-Tweed.
F. Man.
G. The Channel Islands.
H. Orkneys and Shetlands.
I. Heligoland.

Although England may not prove to be the greatest gold region, yet it is that as to which there are the most authorities, the principles of the law of which more or less influence the other jurisdictions, and the discussion as to which may materially affect the administration of the crown rights or prerogatives in the other jurisdictions.

A. England.—In the earliest periods, the English kings had no claims to royalties or royal metals, as property belonged to the marks or local commonwealths. It is on this account that we have no public records relating to mines before the times of the Plantagenets, and the revenues of the government being derived from the three sources of income, the *niodium necessitas,* miscellaneous revenues, were less looked after. The assumption of such claims dates only from the accession of the Norman princes to the government, and the introduction, by their chancellors and lawyers, of feudal notions. In pursuance of these theories, instead of the unappropriated lands being left to the people, these were claimed by lords of manors or by the crown, and assumptions were put forward that the crown was entitled to everything not specifically granted. In the time of the Edwards, the system of the lawyers was fully developed, and the government, acting upon the doctrines imported from the Continent, and from the pandects, proceeded to put them in force.

Commissions were issued to inquire into the rights exercised by the mining population with the view to limit those rights, which could not be safely refused. The people being steadfastly attached to their ancient constitution, the lawyers carried out their usurpations, not by rejecting old institutions, but by setting up new ones, which gradually superseded them. Thus the judges of the King's Bench and the Exchequer gradually annihilated the ancient jurisdictions and legislative functions of the shire and hundred motes which were allowed to subsist in name. Thus the mining population was left in possession of its local organization, but which, in the present day, has become a nullity.

When we first get a knowledge of the organization, we find that the miners in England carried out constitutionally Kemble's History of the Anglo-Saxon Commonwealth.
the principle of local self-government, legislating and managing their affairs for themselves, as they best thought fit. The legislative and judicial functions vested in a court or moot in which all the miners could attend, under the presidence of a chairman. What has been done for public convenience by the gold miners and diggers in California is a repetition of what existed for centuries in the mining districts of England, and what is yet theoretically the law of those districts. Thus, for instance, in the laws of the Derbyshire mines we find arrangements for mining claims and for water claims, conformable to those of the present day. The mode of claiming new mines or veins in Cornwall or Derbyshire, and of preserving them, was on much the same basis as the Spanish mining law,-f-because the same circumstances produced the same institutions. At this day, the setting up of a pair of tin bounds in Cornwall, or the denouncement of a new silver mine in Mexico, proceed from a similar principle, but what is now the law in the Duchy of Cornwall only, was, in the middle ages, the law in any district where the miners chose to establish it among themselves.

In each valley or district there was a local assembly, as in each mark a local court, so an aggregation of mining communities held a general legislative assembly, similar to the Shiremotes or Witenmotes. Of such mining assemblies, the nominal parliament of tinners or stannary parliament, is tne ghost, reported occasionally to have visited the light.

In the sixteenth of Edward I. a general crusade against the rights of these mines seems to have been carried out. So far from mining then beginning or experiencing a revival, or the mines receiving any privilege from Edward I, it is evident, from the measures at that time taken, that mining Houghton's Complete Miner.
t Mining Law of Spain, by Richard Heathfield, Jun. Esq. was carried on in Cornwall and Devon, Somersetshire, Derbyshire, and Glostershire, if not in other districts, and that there was a regular organization of the mining communities. Edward I. did not in reality give the miners any privileges, but took privileges from them, though in the language of the lawyers of that and the after age, he of his own prerogative and pleasure, granted or suffered them to enjoy privileges which they had theretofore exercised, but which were in contradiction of, and as an exception from, the prerogative doctrines then set up.

One writ, bearing date the 28th day of April, and attested by Edward, Earl of Cornwall, was issued from the exchequer, to inquire into the rights of the lead miners of Derbyshire. The writ ran as follows: " Edward, King, &c., to the Sheriff of Derby, greeting, know ye that we have assigned our faithful and well-beloved Reynold of the Ley, and William of Meinill, to inquire by the oaths of good and lawful men of your shire, by the which the truth may be best known of the liberty which our miners do claim to have in those parts, and which they have hitherto used to have, and by what means, and how, and from what time, and from what warrant: and, therefore, we do command that at a certain day and place which the said Reynold and William shall appoint thee, thou shalt cause to come before them so many and such good and lawful men of thy bailiwick, by the which may those be best known in the premises by the inquiry, and that thou have there the writ. "

This shows very well the whole course of proceedings; the king denominates the miners, his miners; he requires to know " by what means, and how, and from what time and by what warrant" the miners exercise their rights, whereas the question might well be, what right the king himself had, and what constitutional ground for the assumption. The whole claims of the crown to mining rights and royalties are Houghton's Laws of Derbyshire.

R assumptions, and nothing more, they have no constitutional origin, as opposed, to the constitutional rights of the people to minerals, and have no constitutional existence except in erroneous recognitions of such assumed rights by the legislature, and arbitrary recognitions of such assumptions by the crown judges and lawyers.

Whenever these crown rights have been tried on new ground, they have failed to meet with acceptance; and if they were fairly argued, it becomes questionable, notwithstanding all the arguments and precedents, whether they are sustainable at home. The imperial government of England has been beaten on these prerogative claims in South Australia, New South Wales, and Victoria; and the United States government has not thought it prudent to enforce such claims in Virginia or in California, neither has the state of California. In the case of California, the federal government of the United States had a double claim to royalties in gold; first, as succeeding to the royalties stipulated under the Spanish mining law, and second, as succeeding to the prerogative claims of the English crown. Colonel Fremont undoubtedly was subject, on the original tenure of his rancho, to royalties on gold, had he been denounced gold, and been entitled to work it; but the United States government has left him the absolute and unrestricted fee simple to the centre of the earth.

The crown claim to gold and silver, as royal metals and royal mines, is just as good, and just as absurd, as the crown claim to royal whales and royal sturgeon as royal fish; the claim rests on the same absurd hypothesis, the same assumption of right, and the same precedents, though the royal fish are nearly enshrouded in the limbo of oblivion, notwithstanding the Iron Duke and the fishermen of Margate did fight for the carcass of a stranded whale, and the queen's consort is still held, by her attorney-general, to be entitled to the whalebone, to make stays and hoop petticoats for herself and her maids of honour. The claim to royal fish and mines royal as a prerogative of the crown, is not to be confounded with claims to waste land, to the soil of rivers, the soil of the seashore, or other such claims which the crown makes, as representing the community at large in the public interests, for the public convenience, and on grounds of public policy. Royal fish and royal metals are claimed, because the schoolmen of the middle ages imagined there were kings of fishes and of metals, as the lion was the king of beasts and the eagle the king of *birds, jure divino.* Royal mines are further claimed, because the medieval lawyers put in a claim for everything as the prerogative of the crown which the citizen could not show a title for from the crown. Prerogative doctrines are exploded, and the claims to gold and silver should share the fate of the rest.

It is because an epoch may arrive, nay, perhaps, has already arrived, when the claims of the crown may be put forward on the ground of precedent, and because a large revenue may be obtained from them, that it is desirable some attention should be given to the validity of these royalties. Already these royalties have been a great impediment to gold and silver mining, as the evidence brought forward in this work abundantly shows; and whether gold diggings are worked here or not, and whether a digging epoch shall or shall not arrive, it is equally desirable, on the grounds of public policy, that the crown monopolies shall be put an end to, as they prevent the development of gold and silver mining, and because the crown itself has no valid title. In the case of a mining company which has attempted to struggle into existence, the crown has compounded its claims for fifteen per cent.; yet fifteen per cent, may prove more than the whole profit on the venture. No one can even pick up a nugget without running the chance of coro Prynne's Aurum Reginse.

ners, sheriffs, treasury solicitors, and exchequer processes. The crown and duchy claims to tin coinage have been abanboned, other branches of mining enterprise have been facilitated, and in an era of free trade, gold and silver mining should be enfranchised.

In pursuance of the writ issued to the sheriff of Derbyshire, a court of Great Barmoot was assembled, which declared what the miners then claimed. The general assembly of the lead miners of Wirksworth was called the Great Barmoot, and is holden at Wirksworth. The rights of the Barmoot were only tolerated, and not recognized until the reign of Philip and Mary. It is still competent to sue a shareholder, or, as he is called, a groovefellow, for calls on a lead mine in the Barmoot, as it is a shareholder for calls on a tin mine in the Stannaries Court.

A like inquisition was instituted by Edward I. into the rights of the tinners of Cornwall and Devon, and he granted them a charter, which became a charter of rights as against the further usurpation attempted by the kings, his successors. The rights of the miners have, however, been to a great extent overridden and superseded, and the Parliament of the Stannaries exists in phantom shape, as the Convocation of Clergy does, being about equally effective. The Lord Warden of the Stannaries and his judge have appropriated to themselves all remaining vital power.

The lead miners of Mendip, in Somersetshire, and the iron miners of the Forest of Dean, did not fare quite so well, but still they obtained a recognition of some rights.

The tin working was chiefly streaming, and the lead mining only working, the surface pipes or rakes, as the veins were called, a single miner or crew of miners working a claim or groove on a vein of lead ore, as in the gold regions on a quartz vein.

The result of the inquisitions of Edward I. was to Houghton's Laws of Mendip; Laws of the Forest of Dean.

limit the rights of tin working within Devon and Cornwall, of lead mining in Derbyshire and Mendip, and of iron working in the Forest of Dean. All else was claimed for the king; all tin working, lead working, or iron working beyond those bounds. Thus, too, all copper, gold, and silver were claimed for the crown, and all metals bearing gold and silver. All mines not appropriated, all mines not in actual work, and all mines to be discovered, except so far as the miners could enforce their reserved rights, were claimed as part of the newly invented prerogative of the crown, which forthwith proceeded to deal with them.

The reason why few records relating to royal mines are to be met with before the time of Edward III. is perhaps not because such records have been lost, but because they never existed. There is, it is true, a record of the 47th Henry III. , in which the Sheriff of Devon is ordered to look after a gold and copper mine till the government can take measures with respect to it; but the granting of the charters to the miners by Edward I. constitutes the era of the crown encroachments on mining property.

Where we have only a few and unconnected records to guide us, we are obliged to resort to conjecture and inference as to the import of particular members of the series. It is in this way that we must seek the motives of the statute of Edward III., by which, in antagonism to the crown policy and claims, he allowed persons to work gold and silver on their own lands under the inspection of such officers as he should appoint. This is not a direct popular concession, and was perhaps given partly to the great landowners who resisted the new invented prerogative of the crown, already a fertile instrument of abuse. It must not, however, be supposed, that a right to landowners to work on their own property was simply a concession to great barons. We shall judge very erroneously if we imagine that the country Cottonian MSS. Otho. Ex; Prynne's Aurum Reginas.
was in the hand of a few feudal lords, for in many districts as in Kent for instance, there were as many franklins and landowners as now, and a greater part of the country population held their own houses than now, though many usurpations of lords of manors had taken place. It could, however, have been by no means agreeable for a great proprietor, still less for a small one, to find his estate in Devon visited by John Ballanter and Walter Bolbotter with a gang of vagabonds claiming to dig and search except under castles and houses, and in gardens, for gold, silver and copper. In the hands of the enterprizing geniuses of that day, who understood working such a monopoly as a Frenchman does a concession, there could be ample means of extorting black mail, or a wheat field would be delivered over to Messrs. Ballanter's followers to be treated *secundem artem.* Those who had mineral property were liable to be deprived of it, and would unwillingly give gold and silver mines to strangers, or the king himself; but to make it worse, any kind of mine might be appropriated under the plea of containing gold and silver.
With a further view to satisfy those landowners on whose lands gold or silver might be found by the adventurers, it was made a condition in most future grants that a due, but less than that to the king, should be paid to the owner of the soil. The tithes of the church were also scrupulously reserved. In the grant to John, Duke of Bedford, the reservations are the tenth part to Holy Church, to the king one fifteenth, and to the lord of the soil one twentieth. The other limitations were likewise more rigid. At first the patentees could dig everywhere, but under houses or gardens, as in the license, 32nd Edward III., to Ballanter and Bolbotter, afterwards we find in the grant of the 8th Richard II. to Richard Wake, clerk, that the digging is to be on paying damage to the owner of the soil, but in this case no reservation of toll to the latter is to be found. In the grant to John, Duke of Bedford, he is restrained from digging under houses, in arable land, or even in meadow, without license of the owner of the soil, and beyond that is required to make any reasonable amends for any damage. A like clause is to be found in the patent to Richard, Duke of York, in the 34th of Henry VI.

Thus the rights of the crown, of the church, of the owners of the soil and of the tenants, were gradually protected, but thereby the working of mines became more burdensome, and we find a sudden cessation of all such grants from the time of Edward IV. to the grant by Queen Elizabeth of the great monopoly of the Mines Royal.

If, in consequence of the evidence brought together in this book, and the practical experience of myself and others who have been engaged in gold working in Australia, the working of the gold fields of Britain should be resumed, the crown may, as in Australia, claim to grant prospecting licenses, for which they have precedent enough, and it may be therefore useful to refer to the medieval proceedings.

It will be observed that the records of that period are of three classes, grants of mines, prospecting licenses, and mixed grants of existing mines, and the right of prospecting for other mines.

It is not necessary here to refer further to the first class of documents.

The following is the form of a prospecting license:— " King Edward IV. by his letters patent, dated 30th July, in the 12th year of his reign, grants to Gallias Lynn, Wm. Marriner, and Simon Pest, power to dig and search for mines within the counties of Somerset and Gloucester, of lead ore, tin or copper, holding silver or lead, for the term of five years, and to agree with the lord of the soil, paying to the king every eighth bowl or dish of rich ore, with a clause to make their mills to fine and melt, as the owners and they can agree, and all officers, &c. to be aiding and assistant."

The cases of mixed grants and licenses are, however, more common, and the following are examples:—

" King Edward III., by indenture dated the 11th of July, in the 32nd year of his reign, grants unto John Ballanter and Walter Bolbotter all his mines of gold, silver and copper in the county of Devon, for two years, with liberty to dig and search, except in gardens, paying twenty marks as a rent or due the first year, and one fifth part of the produce the second year, and all other persons are excluded from digging there."f

" King Richard II. by letters patent, dated the 11th June, in the eighth year of his reign, grants to Richard Wake, clerk, his mines of gold and silver in the county of Devon, and liberty to dig, paying damage to the owners of the grounds, as well within liberties as without, for ten years, paying a tenth part of the profit unto Holy Church, and to the Exchequer the ninth part, and all other parties to be

excluded, *provt ante.*"% " King Henry VI. by letters patent, dated 24th February, in the fifth year of his reign, grants to John, Duke of Bedford, all mines of gold and silver within his kingdom of England for ten years, paying the tenth part to Holy Church, to the king the fifteenth, and to the lord of the soil the twentieth part, to dig and search, &c., but not under houses, in arable land, or meadow, without license of the lord of the soil, and to make reasonable amends for any damage."§ Pettus' Fodinas Regales, p. 42; Opera Mineralia Explicata, p. 22; Plowden's Reports, p. 326.
t Pettus' Fodinae Regales, p. 34; Plowden's Reports, p. 316. Opera Mineralia, Explicata, p. 17. *X* Pettus' Fodinaa Regales, p. 36; Plowden's Reports, p. 317; Opera Mineralia Explicata, p. 18.
§ Pettus' Fodinae Regales, p. 39; Plowden's Reports, p. 317; Opera Mineralia Explicata, p. 19.

" King Henry VI. by letters patent, granted to John Sollers, in the seventeenth year of his reign, all mines of gold and silver in the counties of Devon and Cornwall, and all mines of lead holding silver or gold, to hold for twenty years, paying the fifteenth part of pure gold and pure silver, but not to dig under any houses or castles."

" King Henry VI. by letters patent, in the thirty-first year of his reign, created John Bottwright provost and governor of all his mines, paying the tenth part of pure gold and silver, copper, tin, and lead, to be fined at his own charge, with power to let and set for twelve years, and to dig without interruption."f

" King Henry VI. by letters patent, in the thirty-fourth year of his reign, grants to Richard, Duke of York, all his mines of gold and silver within the counties of Devon and Cornwall, to hold at the pleasure of the king, for twenty-one years, with a clause not to dig under the houses or meadows of any portion."!

These powers will be more fully exemplified in the case of the Mines Royal grant. It will be seen that, in pursuance of these precedents, the crown can claim to grant licences to—

Individuals or companies.

For two, five, ten, or twenty years, for life, or during pleasure.

For one or more counties, or for a mining district.

The right is given to search for gold in private lands, with limitations as to agricultural lands or buildings.

The toll or due to be given to owner of the soil is claimed to be fixed.
Pettus' Fodinae Regales, p. 39; Plowden's Reports, p. 324; Opera Mineralia Explicata, p. 20. t Pettus's Fodinas Regales, pp. 39, 40; Plowden's Reports, pp. 324,325; Opera Mineralia Explicata, p. 20. *X* Cottonian MSS. Otho E x.; Pettus' Fodinas Regales, p. 40; Plowden's Reports, p. 325; Opera Mineralia Explicata, p. 21.
The dues to be paid to the crown are either by fixed sum or by proportion of the produce raised.

The cost of refining the gold is imposed on the grantee.

The crown might claim to grant the whole of the gold in the country to a corporation, so as to secure the royalties more effectively.

The several patents and indentures here quoted, show very well the course of operation during the middle ages, and that the crown did exercise a monopoly over gold mines.

The act of Henry IV. against multiplying gold and silver, is only necessary to be here referred to, because the acts for its repeal were made the vehicle of new laws as to mines royal.

A feature necessary to be noticed in this period of history, is the number of general or extensive grants; as those to John, Duke of Bedford, to the Earl of Warwick, and to the two mining commissions of John Bottwright, and Jasper, Duke of Bedford.

Such being the powers of the crown previous to the charters of Elizabeth, they were only modified by the statute of Edward III. allowing owners to work gold within their own land. It is necessary to comprehend the status previous to those charters, because if those charters are void, the status becomes the same, except so far as modified by the acts of William III.

Queen Elizabeth, as already stated, granted various patents and charters which are now merged in the one subsisting corporation of the Mines Royal. One of the most important of those grants, is the first patent to Humfrey and Shutz, given on the 26th September, in the 7th year of the reign. The patent is a long one, but the most important parts only are here given.

The patent recites a grant to Cornelius de Vos for mining and digging alum and copperas in England. It then recites a grant to Daniel Houghsetter and Thomas Thurlind for digging and mining for all manner of ores of gold, silver, copper, and quicksilver within the counties of York, Lancaster, Cumberland, Westmoreland, Cornwall, Devon' Gloucester and Worcester, and the Principality of Wales. The patent goes on to state " and we now being minded that the said commodities and all other treasures of the earth, in all other parts of our realm of England, and also in the parts called the English pale, within our realm of Ireland, should be searched out for the benefit and profit of us, our said realm and subjects of the same. And having received credible information as well of the great industry travail and expense that our faithful and well-beloved subject William Humfrey, Assaymaster of our Mint, within our Tower of London, hath, in and about the mines, mineral ores, and matters metalline of long time bestowed and borne, and yet doth, whereby there are found out, in divers and sundry the said other of our said realms not only divers ores of metals very likely to prove rich and profitable, but also at and by his diligent procurement and charges there are now brought and won into this our said realm of England, workmasters of great cunning, perfectness, knowledge, and experience in all kind of mineral works, and of water works for the draining of all manner of mines. Know ye, therefore, that we of our especial grace, &c., for us, our heirs and successors, do give and grant full power, license, and authority to the said William Humfrey and to Christopher Shutz, their heirs and assigns, and every of them, for ever, by them, their servants, labourers, workmen, deputies, and assigns, to search, open, dig, mine, and try all earths, grounds, soils and places of and in our kingdom and realm of England, and of and in all the dominions, territories, borders, and confines of the same, together with all and singular so much of our realm of Ireland, territories and dominions thereof, as are within the limits and borders of all, that is, or hath been commonly called, known, or taken to be of the English pale, except only the principalities and counties hereinbefore expressed."

This recital seems to bear the meaning that William Humfrey had found out minerals in Ireland, but there is nothing further to guide our opinions on this head.

The patent goes on to say, " and to convey, carry, and work in waters and water works belonging to the said mines, in all places and territories of and in our said realms, and either of them, as afore is mentioned (except before excepted) for all manner of ores simple and pure, or mixed and compound of the metals of gold, silver, copper, quicksilver, and for all other minerals and treasures likely to be found in the said earths, grounds, places and soils, or any of them, and for tin and lead in such sort as by the laws or customs of our said realms is or hath been lawfully used, copperas and alum in this our realm of England as afore is said only except. And the same ores, simple or mixed minerals, metals and treasures, to drain, break, stamp, wash, boil, and roast, and melt, and otherwise to give and bring to best perfection of metals, and them and every of them to course, take, enjoy, or use to their most commodity and profit and to the profit of them and of every of them for ever. And any house or houses, or houses by their discretion meet and necessary and convenient for the working and manuring of the said ores, &c. at their pleasure, at their own proper costs and charges to erect, build, set up and use, s well in and upon the lands, grounds, and possessions as also in and upon the lands, grounds, and possessions of any of our subjects within our said kingdom of England, &c., without any manner of let, perturbance, or molestation of us, our heirs or successors, or of any other person or persons. Nevertheless, the said Humfrey, &c. shall not search, dig, or mine under, or work in any houses, edifices, on lands, courts, grounds, inclosed within any walls, or courts joining to houses in any manner belonging to any of our subjects, without the goodwill and consent (first obtained of such as have power either to impeach or license them so to do), or in or under or near to any castles, forts, fortresses, house or houses of access of us, our heirs and successors, without our special license had for the same. And the said William Humfrey, &c. shall also reasonably satisfy, recompense, and make amends to all and every owner, farmer, or possessor of all and every the lands, grounds, and possessions aforesaid, of and for all such damages and losses as by them or any of them, from time to time shall be committed or done to the detriment of any grass, corn, woods, quarries, or other profits or commodities whatsoever usually before taken and enjoyed, or that lawfully might have been taken and enjoyed in or upon the same grounds or soils. And in case where the parties cannot agree among themselves for the said damage and losses, then four indifferent men to be elected between them shall assess and rate the recompense of and for the same, as they shall think in conscience to be reasonable. And if it shall happen the said four men elected indifferently as aforesaid, not to agree in the rating and assessing of the recompense as aforesaid, then the matter to be brought before us, our heirs or successors, and by our and their privy council to be determined according to the laws or customs of the realms where the same may be."

The patent afterwards provides, " We do strictly prohibit, charge and command all our loving subjects, and every other person and persons whatsoever not to attempt, take in hand, or go about in any manner of way, directly or indirectly, in any of the lands, grounds or possessions aforesaid, within either of our said realms, or within the dominions, territories, borders or confines of them or either of them, at any time hereafter, to dig, open, mine, melt or work any of the said ores, metals, treasures of the castle, or other the substance aforesaid, or for any of them, to make search, contrary to our grant above mentioned."

Further power is given, " And further our said will, pleasure and commandment is, that no person or persons do attempt or enterprise of evil will, or envious intent, to hinder, stay, let or disturb the aforesaid Humfrey, &c. occupied or to be occupied in or about the said works, or any of them, upon pain of imprisonment of six months, without bail or mainprize, and the forfeiture of one hundred pounds of lawful money of England, the one moiety unto us, our heirs and successors, and the other moiety to the said Humfrey, &c., for every time that such attempt or offense, contrary to the tenor of these presents, shall be committed or done: And also upon such further pain, punishment and imprisonment as we, our heirs or successors, by the laws of this our realm, and by our prerogative and royal jurisdiction may any way tax, assess or appoint, or cause to be taxed, assessed or appointed."

Power is given to take up, at reasonable wages and prices, all workmen, instruments, stuff and necessaries for the said works and buildings.

It is recited, " And we are content and pleased that whensoever we, our heirs and successors, shall think meet to have any other part of our realm of Ireland than the English pale to be searched, digged or converted to the use of any minerals abovementioned, that then the said Humfrey, &c. shall have like privilege, power and authority, and shall have like profit and commodity in such other parts of Ireland out of the English pale as they have, may or shall claim, have and enjoy in the parts called the English pale, by virtue of these our letters patents, to all intents and constructions as though the same had been specially expressed in these grants."

The said grants are to remain in force, any act, statute, &c. had made or done, or hereafter to be had, made or done to the contrary, notwithstanding: " Provided always, notwithstanding any clause, article or matter in the premises, that if, at any time after the term of twenty-one years, to be counted from the date of these presents, we shall be disposed to take or resume into our own disposition this former grant and license expressed in the premises for the searching, digging, opening, roasting, melting, stamping, washing, draining of waters or otherwise working or melting down of the said mines or ores of gold, silver, copper or quicksilver, that then we shall and may resume and detain the same power in our possession, to be used only to our own proper use, and not to be granted over to any other person or persons, so as before we shall take and resume the same, the said Humfrey, &c. , shall be well and sufficiently recompensed and satisfied of all their charge, cost, expense, losses and interest, in such manner and with such sums of money as shall be adjudged by six persons, citizens of London, whereof two shall be aldermen of the city, and three of the said six to be named by us or the Lord Treasurer of England, and the other three by the said Humfrey, &c., and those six to be charged or sworn before the Mayor of the City of London for the time being, to consider and understand the truth of the demands and petitions of the said Humphrey, &c., whereof the said six persons so sworn shall make and deliver in writing to the Lord Treasurer of England for the time being, a certificate of such sums of money as they shall judge reasonable to be paid by us for the said recompense, and satisfaction as above is mentioned; and thereupon the said Lord Treasurer shall have full power, by force of these presents, without any other warrant or order from us, to make full and present payment, out of the receipt of our Exchequer, to the said Humfrey, &c. And if we, after the resumption of the premises aforesaid, shall be disposed at any time to grant the said power or authority abovementioned to any other person that then the said Humfrey, &c. , shall have the preferment to have the same before any other, upon such conditions as any other, without fraud or covin, offer to our benefit or commodity."

The rights of the grantees are further defined in the indenture made on the 17th Sept., 1565, between the queen of the one party, and Wm. Humfrey and Shutz of the other part. After reciting the letters patent, the indenture goes on: " Nevertheless it is now covenanted, granted, condescended, and agreed, between the said Most Excellent Princess and the said Wm. Humfrey, &c., that no other person shall be allowed to dig or work, &c., except Humfrey, &c.; and that the queen shall, by her prerogative, uphold the grantees. And also, that Her Highness, her heirs, and successors, and every of them according to their prerogative royal will, from time to time, and at all times, after the date of the said letters patent, overthrow, deface, and utterly destroy, or cause to be overthrown, defaced, and utterly destroyed, all and every such tool and tools, instrument and instruments, engine and engines, building and buildings, stuff, and other thing or things whatsoever which shall be brought, provided, begun, built, had or made within any the said kingdoms or realms of England and Ireland or the territories, &c., contrary or prejudicial to the said privilege."

The indenture then goes on to provide that the queen shall have of all pure gold, &c., the full tenth part of the same forthwith upon the finding thereof, and of all gold and silver ore to be found holding in every hundred weight eight pound weight or above in fine gold or fine silver by the assay, the like full tenth part. The queen further to have the pre-emption of the remaining gold and silver at *8d.* per ounce for gold, and Id. per ounce for silver, less than Her Highness may or shall then buy, without fraud Opera Mineralia Explicata, p. 26. or guile, of any stranger or other Her Highness's subjects within their mint.

Power is given to the grantees to export copper ore beyond seas for the purpose of smelting.

Privilege is granted to the patentees, that they may bring into the country as many foreign workmen as they please, and that they may become denizens on payment of the ordinary fees only, but for no longer time than they shall continue and be occupied in and about the said works.

Further privilege is given to import, duty free, all victuals and provisions for the workmen, and all tools, instruments, and other necessaries and furnitures, only for the said works in and about the said mines or minerals, &c.

The first charter of incorporation of the Mineral and Battery Works, was dated the 8th May, in the 10th year of Elizabeth. It begins by reciting the letters patent to Humfrey, and proceeds,f "And whereas, for the better search, finding, and working of the mines and minerals within our said realms and dominions, and to the intent that many of our subjects and others thereby may get their living, which trade of living heretofore was hidden and unknown to the great discommodity of this our realm and subjects, for lack of knowledge thereof: Our pleasure, &c., is, that the said Wm. Humfrey, &c., might assign, and thereupon they have since the making of our said letters patent, assigned and conveyed to Sir Nicholas Bacon, Lord Keeper of our Great Seal, and others divers parts and portions of the licenses, &c., aforesaid. Therefore the Queen confirms the previous grants, and incorporates Sir Nicholas Bacon, &c., as the governors, assistants, and society of the Mineral and Battery Works. " The charter gives power to purchase lands, tenements, rents, reversions and hereditaments. The Opera Mineralia Explicate, p. 39. t *Mi*-P-52.

S usual powers are conceded of choosing governors and assistants and of forming bye-laws.

The charter especially grants, " That every officer and minister of the said society, and every workman and labourer in the Mineral and Battery Works aforesaid, shall be, during the time of every of their said office, ministry, working or labouring, exempted, and not impanelled or put in any assizes or juries, or any inquisitions or attanits, against their will, although they do touch us our heirs or successors, or any other whatsoever. "

Power is granted to administer an oath to shareholders on their admission; persons judged to be unworthy may be dismembered or removed from the corporation. The governing body is further empowered to administer justice between all members, servants, and workmen, in all their causes, differences, or complaints, in anywise touching or concerning the liberties, privileges, works, or ores aforesaid, or the good order or rule of the said persons, ministers, officers, labourers, and workmen. The whole body of members have power to limit, set, ordain, and put reasonable pains and penalties, by fines, forfeitures, and imprisonments, or any of them on such members, ministers, &c. " Further, that if any of the said body politic or society shall be found contrarious, rebelling, or disobedient to the said governors, deputies, and assistants for the time being, or to any of the statutes, &c., that then the said governors, &c., may correct and punish such offenders, by fines, pains and penalties, or by imprisonment, within any of the jails or prisons of us, our heirs and successors, as the quality of the fault shall require, according to their good discretions."

Power is given to the Court of Assistants to constitute one officer or divers officers, as well within our said city of London, as also in any other place or places within our realm of England, which officer or officers will be named the sergeant or sergeants of the Mineral and Battery Works; and that they have full power and authority to take, receive, levy, and gather all manner of fines, forfeitures, penalties, or pains of every person or persons of the said body politic, that shall be convicted upon or for breaking of any statutes, &c. " That the said officer shall have power and authority, if need be, to set hands, take and arrest, as well the body and bodies, as also the goods and chattels, of such offender or offenders and transgressors, in all and every place and places, being no town or city corporate, but in towns or cities corporate, when a precept to them, directed under common seal of the society, shall, by their mayors, &c. attach the body, goods, or chattels of such offenders, and return and deliver to the said officer of the corporation."

The bye-laws of the society are of a similar tenor. By No. XII. it is enacted, " that any member of the society, upon any cause or passion of mind, giving any disordered or unseemly language or word of provocation to any of the said society, shall forfeit twenty shillings; and also that none hold communication or talk with other when the governor deputy, or any other of the said court shall be in speaking or declaring any cause or matter to the said company, under pain of twenty pence."-f

There is a curious provision allowing the court to issue bills in advance for calls unpaid, such bills being secured in the lands, goods, and chattels of the defaulting members, and on their shares in the concern.J

A charter similar to that of the Mineral and Battery Works was in the 10th of Queen Elizabeth, granted to the society of the Mines Royal,§ by which title the united corporation is now known. There is the like power to create a sergeant or sergeants, to be called sergeant of the Mines Royal.

The charters of the Mines Royal, and of the Mineral Opera Mineralia Explicata, p. 52. t *I*-P--J -P-§ *Ibid.* p. 101. *Ibid.* p. 143. If *Ibid.* p. 101.

and Battery Works, was exemplified and renewed in the 1st year of James I.

These charters and privileges were confirmed by the law authorities on three memorable occasions. The first case was that of the Earl of Northumberland's copper mines at Keswick, in Cumberland, said then, as now, to contain gold. These were resumed on the most flimsy pretexts, solely to favour the new grantees, to whom they were made over. Judgment was given in Hilary Term, in the 10th year of Queen Elizabeth. The following is the judgment. The arguments, as already stated, it so happens, are fully given in Plowden's Reports, this being considered an important trial:—

" There is a diversity between a mine of copper containing in itself gold, and a mine of gold containing in itself copper; for where the mine is called a mine of copper, containing in itself gold, it is intended the copper is the greater and the gold the less; for everything contained is less than the thing containing, and that which comprehendeth a thing is greater than the thing comprehended; and therefore, where the copper is the greater, the mine takes its name from that, and is called a mine of copper containing gold; and by the same reason, if it be called a mine of gold containing copper, the gold, whereof the mine hath its name, is the greater, and the copper the less. And this agrees with their opinions who have treated of metallic matters, and with the records of the Exchequer, which prove that the king hath the mines of copper containing or holding gold or silver, although the gold and silver be the less.

" But how it shall be esteemed the greater or lesser is the dispute; that is, whether it shall be taken according to the quantity, quality, or value thereof. Some are of opinion, according to the quantity, saying, that thing which comprehendeth another is greater than the thing comprehended: as Opera Mineralia Explicata, p. 141.

a hogshead of wine or a barrel of beer; for the hogshead (in quantity) is greater than the wine, and the barrel than the beer, but not in value, and yet it takes its name from the greater, and therefore is called a hogshead of wine. And the mine of copper containing gold hath its name from the greater in quantity, but not as from the value; for in the mine of copper containing gold, the gold may be of the greater value. And herein regard ought to be had to the value of the gold or silver; for if there be but a quillful of gold or silver in a great quantity of copper, there is no reason that that small quantity should be respected; but the gold or silver ought to be of some value of itself over and above the base metal consumed in getting thereof; for if the quantity of the value be not respected, then the gold or silver (how little soever there be) shall entitle the crown to all the base metals in the realm. For the writers of metals do agree that there is naturally some proportion of gold and silver in every metal, and the smelters and refiners do make it evident, that there is in copper naturally gold and silver, and in lead and iron there is naturally silver. And so, if there should be no regard had to the quantity of gold or silver which is in the base metals, the king should have all the mines of base metals in the realm, and the subject having mines of base metals in his own lands, they are of no effect; for there is not (according to the said authors) any such mine, either in this kingdom or elsewhere, which hath not some gold and silver in it.

" And therefore it seemeth reasonable to consider the nature of a poor mine, and the value of the gold and silver in the base metal, and that the product be of such value that it countervail the charge of getting it; or otherwise there is no reason that it should draw the property of the base metal to the crown; but, if otherwise, then it is to be a Mine Royal. " Plowden's Reports; Opera Mineralia Explicata, p. 99.

Upon such subtleties and frivolities does this judgment rest, and it has therefore been looked upon with less respect in latter times. The decision is made to turn upon the question whether the copper at Keswick contained gold, it being assumed, as a matter of course, that all gold and silver is the prerogative of the crown, though at that date there was no evidence of any such prerogative being exercised before the time of Edward I., but the age of the Virgin Queen was that of high prerogative notions. She had already undertaken, with her patentees, to overthrow and destroy the tools and machinery of any who might attempt to work in competition, and had given them the power of taking up or impressing workmen and materials at what the patentees might choose to consider reasonable wages and prices. She had likewise granted to the corporations the right of imprisonment and distress, of having sergeants or bailiffs of their own, and of issuing precepts to the magisterial authorities of the country.

The charters of the Mines Royal, and the decisions or opinions upon them, are of chief importance in this respect, that they show what are the claims that have been put forward and would still be arrogated by the crown on the lawyer's normal rule of precedent.

Before dismissing the judgment in the Earl of Northumberland's case, it may be as well, on the grounds just stated, to refer to the arguments of which an abstract is thus given:—

" The king shall have all the mines of gold and silver and other valuable metals and minerals in the lands of his suDjects, by the prerogative of his crown, and not by the propriety of the soil, although it be not recited in the Treatise of Prerogatives, and albeit the ore thereof is in another's land, toucheth others freeholds and inheritances, which is proved by three reasons.

" First, for the excellency of the matter, which, being more excellent, is appropriated by the law to the person most excellent; namely, the king. So the king hath, by the common law, whales and sturgeons, because they are the most excellent fishes that the sea or water renders, so that the ' Treatise of Prserogativa Regis cap. ii.' which sayeth, *Rex habebit Balneas et Sturiones,* is but a declaration of the common law before.

" Secondly, for the necessity of defending his people, and preserving the commonwealth against foreign hostility.

" Thirdly, for the commodity of Tiis subjects, that they, by the coin made thereof (which the king only may make), may have between them mutual commerce and traffic; because if the subject shall have gold and silver found in his own land, he might convert it into coin; for falsifying or counterfeiting money was treason at the common law; and for that cause a woman was burnt, *23* ass. pi. *2.* Also, it would be inconvenient that a subject, which is proprietor in the land, should have the metals and minerals; for that he thereby would exceed the king in treasures, which would be perilous to his estate."

The second proof was by precedents of three sorts.

" First, commissions, grants and demises by which the king hath granted such mines in other lands, viz. in Annis 32nd Edward III., 8th Richard II., 5th Henry VI., 15th Edward IV., *aniprimo* Henry VI., and in some of them the king gave license to dig in another land without license of the owner, and where some of them saith, *habita licentia fodiendi,* which is intended land of subjects where they give amends for the digging, or assign part to the lord of the soil; this is of courtesy and clemency of the prince, and not of necessity.

" Secondly, actions of the grantees of such mines.

" Thirdly, information and impleading of them which have disturbed the grantees, or imported their ore; also the king may punish him that taketh ore in another man's soil. And so charters, actions and pleas against the takers of gold and silver or other metals and minerals in the soil of another, proves strongly those mines to belong to the king by his prerogative; for the records of every court are the most effectual proofs of law in matters treated of in this court; and action lies not against an executor except for the king. Litleton, fol. 28. The king may seize the land of his debtor which he hath by what means, or into whosoever's hands it cometh after the cause of the debt. Sir Wm. Candish's case in the Exchequer."

The third proof is upon authorities of law, viz. " The book called ' Exposition of Terms of the Law,' and the reading of Hescot of *Charta Foresta,* and the laws of St. Edward the Confessor and William the Conqueror; and so these authorities and the said precedents and the reasons aforesaid for the excellency of metal, and for the necessity of it, and the public good, agreeing in one, That the king shall have all mines and ores of gold and silver, and other metals and useful minerals, for preparing, working and manuring them in land where is treasure found. *Thesauri terrce* taken for gold and silver in land is Treasure Trove; the use and continuance ratines this prerogative by prescription, although that it need not be contained in the treatise of *Prairogativa Regis* for the king. The common law hath many which are not there recited, as tenants of the king, aliens without license; it was a forfeiture before the statute of 1st Edward III. cap. 12, 9th Edward III. cap. 26., although it be to the prejudice of another freeholder; yet because the law gives those mines to the king, it giveth to him all necessary means to have it, by digging with all incident thereunto. For every prerogative contains in itself prescription, for it is in usage; and as prescription and usage will give title or interest to the king in the freehold of another, as by prerogative the king might enter into the woods of another, and take trees for to repair his castles, before the statute of Magna Charta, cap. 22, so he might afforest another man's woods before the statute of *Forestce,* cap. 2. So 7 Henry, he might break a pond and take the fish for his provision. So 27 *ass. pi.* 49. The lord might not take his villain (yet is his freehold and inheritance), in the presence of the king; for it is a protection to him for the time. So 13th Edward IV. cap. 6, the king may distrain for his rent charge in all the other lands of him which ought to pay it; so the prerogative of the king chargeth his other freehold to the king's distress.

" The king shall have, by his prerogative, mines of copper containing gold or silver in the lands of another; because they are as a thing entire by the commixture *et magis dignum trahit ad se minus dignum* as 41st Edward III., cap. 32; 36th Henry VI., cap. 26; and 3rd Henry VII., cap. 14. The heir shall have the charters with the box if it be sealed; so carts to which horses are tied if it fall upon a man the king shall have all; Stamford, fol. 20 (before 243), because as one thing they altogether occasion his death; so the king shall have all the obligations and horses where one of the joint tenants is attainted; because a thing entire proves that the king shall have all, where gold or silver, mixed with base metal, by commissions of Edward III. and 17th Richard II., 7th Henry IV., 17th Henry VI., 30th and 31st of Henry VI., proved also by accounts for silver and base metal. No mine of copper void of gold or silver, no mine of tin, void of silver; and therefore those of Devon and Cornwall, for digging in their land and other land for tin, and to have this to their use, derive their power from the kings of this realm, made unto them, and giving them such liberties as by charter 33rd Edward I. confirmed by Richard II., but the power given to them for to dig in another's land, and to pull down houses of another was restrained by the statute of 50 Edward III. Derbyshire and other places prescribes to take lead of mines sterile, which is without gold or silver, without paying anything except coplot and tolldish, which privilege, 10th Elizabeth, was granted for ever to the Society of London for the Mineral and Battery Works, and they only, to employ, govern, and pay the miners and workmen in all mineral affairs, *prout grant. ' On the part of the Earl against the Queen.'* " The thing of the most in value is worthiest, where the quantity of copper exceeds the quantity of gold, yet the less is the most precious, quantity for quantity; the gold or silver ought to be of more value than the charges of separating of it from the base metal cometh to, otherwise, this *aliquid nihil est* if he hath lost by it. Wast, of 2d is dispunishable, because *de minimis non curat lex,* 7th Henry VI. cap. 36, 38th Edward III., cap. 7, by this reservation upon the said demises it is intended a good quantity of gold or silver. Also because the information showeth not what value of silver or gold is to defray the charge, which is uncertain and bad; because this is the declaration of the king. Also commissions are not of great estimation, but show the obedience of subjects, and are made at their requests for whom they are granted; and many of the said commissions and leases were limited. That the grantee should make to the owners of lands in Cornwall, used for the digging of tin before the said charter proves by the words themselves, viz: That for the amendment of our stannaries, &c., and other words in the charter; and albeit, the king had some profit of tin or lead in some places as a tolldish of ore, that was not only in respect of the interest the king had, but also for bearing the charges of officers, as he had of merchants of some part of their merchandises for the searchers, comptroller, and weigher, because he had appointed officers for that purpose."

The Earl's counsel contended that the Earl held the mine by his original grant.

The third point argued by the Queen's counsel. " First, by the King's grant *ex mero motu, certa scientid et gratid speciali* mines of gold and silver or other mines of metals will not pass, although that it appeareth that it was hidden at the time and appeareth afterwards; otherwise of base minerals, yet those pass not, but not Mines Royal, which are collateral things to the soil as are hidden treasure, which passeth not by the gift of the king; nor wreck, strays, waifs, &c., pass not, nor do liberties pass by the grant of a manor."

After J further collateral argument on these grounds, the case proceeds, " The King had the secret mine of copper mixed with gold and silver in land given by his ancestors to the prior of Wenlock, and there it passeth not by the grant of the soil *ex mero motu,* &c., yet it was of the foundation of the King, and religious favoured. *Fitzh. nat. ir. 332."* " Secondly, by the King's grant *de omnibus et singulis mineris ex certa scientia,* &c., Mines Royal, namely of gold and silver, or of base metal, containing in it gold or silver passes not, because the King had them *ratione corona,* not of the land, and because appropriate to his crown, passeth not without special words; base mines here, as those which consist only of base substance, namely, copper, tin, lead, iron, or coals, and not having in them gold or silver, and patentees shall have things fit for subjects; yet the terms of the patent to the Earl comprehend things of the basest degree, the basest minerals, and needful to manure the soil 22 *ass. pi.* (several cases are cited in support of this doctrine as of grants of palatine right, *jura regalia,* &c.)"

The next case in favour of the Mines Royal Corporation, arose in the time of Charles I., concerning the mines at Talabont, claimed by Mr. Richard Price, when an opinion was given by a number of leading lawyers of the day, " that any mine containing gold and silver enough to repay the Plowden's Reports; Opera Mineralia Explicata.

charge of refining is a Mine Royal, and as well the base metal as the gold and silver in it, belongs to the prerogative of the crown. On Februrary 9th, 1640, this was signed by John Glanville, E. Herbert, Ralph Whitfield, and Oliver S. John; on the 25th, by John Herne, Christopher Fulwood, Harbottle Grimston, and Edward Bagshaw; on the 26th, by John White, John Glover, and James Haward; on the 27 th July, 1641, by Eusebius Andrews, Edward Prideaux, John Maynard, and Thomas Culpeper.

Strengthened by this decision and opinion, the corporations proceeded, with a high hand. Their course against what they called aggressors, was as follows: They first sent a summons to the party to attend their court, to answer to what should be alleged against him, who refusing so to do, and would not submit or obey the authority and order of the court, it was customary to crave a warrant from the Council Board to empower one of His Majesty's pursuivants to seize the body of the offender or offenders, and to bring him or them before the council to answer the said contempt and trespass which he or they must there make full satisfaction for or go to prison. These affairs were heard before a committee of the Privy Council summoned for that purpose, who, according to Stringer, were the lords of the Cabinet Council, who were also members of the Corporations. The Lord Chancellor, the Lord Chief Baron, and the Lord Chief Justices were also summoned as barriers or guarantees " to keep the societies from being too severe upon or oppressing the subject." Armed with such a jurisdiction, and provided with such a tribunal, the Mines Royal prevented any landowner from working his mines.

The Mines Royal Corporation was not successful in the next case; towards the end of the century, in King William's time, Mr. Anthony Shepherd then farmed the Cardigan Opera Mineralia Explicata, p. 148.
shire silver lead mines of the corporation which was then in a decrepid condition, and in want of capital. The mines being inefficiently worked by him, Mr. William Waller endeavoured to obtain a lease from the Mines Royal, but was refused. He then applied to Sir Carbery Price, the owner of the soil, to grant him a lease as for a lead mine. Mr. Shepherd then sent to Hugh Webb, the clerk of the corporation, to defend him, the crown's prerogative, and the corporation privileges. By some mal-address of Webb's, it is stated, he did not put the general court in operation. In the course of the proceedings Webb died, having in his hands the corporation books, records, patents, charters, &c., so that it is stated the corportion suffered, and Mr. Shepherd too; for they could not get at their records, nor assemble in due form till the lawsuits were over.

Stringer, to whom implicit confidence is not to be given, alleges that Webb was bribed, and that the cause was taken into court upon a wrong point, namely, whether the mine was a royal mine or not, and contained so much silver in such a quantity of lead; whereas Stringer contends, that, as a lead mine, it passed in the grant of such mineral to the Mineral and Battery Works. Mr. Shepherd produced very rich lead ore, containing much silver, while Waller and his party produced very poor lead ore. The verdict was that the mine was not a mine royal.

By the act of the 1st of William and Mary, a material change was made in the law. It is styled " An Act to repeal the Statute of 5th Henry IV. against multiplying gold and silver," which it does repeal, but it includes a clause, providing that no mine of copper, tin, iron, or lead shall hereafter be adjudged, reputed, or taken to be a royal mine, although gold or silver may be extracted out of the same.

By the 5th of William and Mary, this act is explained, and by it the law, as at present affecting some gold claims Opera Mineralia Explicata, p. 223.
was enacted. After reciting that doubts and questions have arisen upon the said statute, it goes on:—

" Wherefore, for the better explanation of the said statute, be it further enacted and declared by the King and Queen's most excellent Majesties, by and with the consent of the Lords spiritual and temporal, and the Commons in this present Parliament assembled, and by the authority of the same, that all and every person and persons, being subjects of the crown of England, bodies politic or corporate, that now are or hereafter shall be the owner or owners, proprietor or proprietors of any mine or mines within the kingdom of England, dominion of Wales, or town of Berwick upon Tweed, wherein any one now is, or hereafter shall be discovered, opened, found, or wrought, and in which there is copper, tin, iron or lead, shall and may hold and enjoy the same mine or mines and ore; and continue in the possession thereof, and dig and work the said mine or mines or ore, notwithstanding that such mine or mines or ore shall be pretended or claimed to be a royal mine or royal mines, any law, usage, or custom to the contrary notwithstanding: Provided always, and be it enacted, that their Majesties, their heirs and successors, and all claiming any royal mines under them, shall and may have the ore of any such mine or mines in any part of the said kingdom of England, dominion of Wales, or town of Berwick on Tweed (other than tin ore in the counties of Devon and Cornwall), paying to the proprietors or owners of the said mine or mines, wherein such ore is or shall be found, within thirty days after the said ore is or shall be raised and laid upon the bank of the said mine or mines, and before the same be removed from thence, the rates following, that is to say: ' For all ore washed, made clean and merchantable, wherein is copper, the rate of £16 per ton; and for all ore washt, made clean and merchantable, wherein there is tin, the rate of £2 per ton; and for all ore washt, made clean and merchantable, wherein there is iron, the rate of *£2* per ton; and for all ore washt, made clean and merchantable, wherein there is lead, the rate of *£9* per ton; and in default of payment of such respective sums as aforesaid, it shall be lawful for the owners and proprietors of the said mine or mines, wherein such ore is, are, or shall be found, to sell and dispose of the said ore to his and their own uses; any law, statute, or custom to the contrary notwithstanding.' "

The act concludes with a clause saving the rights of the Stannaries.

It is stated, but the date is not assigned, that the Mines Royal Corporation seized and worked the gold mines at Little Taunton, in Gloucestershire, and that at Pollux Hill, in Bedfordshire.

The only other facts necessary to be cited are the action of the crown with reference to the Devonshire gold mines and the Welsh gold mines in Devonshire. The Duchy of Cornwall have granted leases of mines having gold ores, and the crown compounded with the North Wales Mining Company for the royalties in crown lands at ten per cent., on private lands at five per cent. , and for preemption rights at five per cent.

The law affecting gold-working at present is derived from five chief sources:—

The common law, custom, or right of England. The prerogatives of the crown as asserted in the middle ages and since claimed. The act of Edward III. The grants to the Mines Royal Corporation. The acts of William and Mary. The first point however, to be considered, is the Mines Royal Corporation, for if the patents to that body remain in force, then all the gold and gold-bearing ores are in the power of that corporation.

These questions arise:—First, as to the validity of the charters, depending on the power of the crown to make such grants.

Second, as to the power of the crown to resume such grant.

Third, as to the voidableness of such patents, &c. for nonperformance on the part of the patentees.

Fourth, as to such patents being void from non-user and desuetude, and from license of infringement.

The first of these questions will be discussed further on, and is not necessary here to be considered, as the other points are sufficient for the determination of the powers of the Mines Royal.

The second question is as to the power of the crown to resume the patents and indentures. It is true the grants are to Humfrey and Shutz, their heirs and assigns " for ever," but it is expressly covenanted " That if, at any time after the term of twenty-one years, to be counted from the date of these presents, we shall be disposed to take or resume into our own disposition, this former grant &c., that then we shall and may resume and detain the same power in our possession." It is not, however, likely that the crown will avail itself of such provision to put a stop to the claims of the Mines Royal, should they be set up again, for by other provisions the crown must take to the property of the corporation at a valuation, must only use the resumed powers for the proper use of the crown, and must not grant them over to any other person, but must give the refusal to the corporation upon such conditions as any other parties may have tendered.

The third question relates to the conditions on which the corporation have received the patents, and how far they have complied with them. They are fortunate enough not to be bound to the payment of any rent or royalties, and have not therefore failed in their discharge. The patents were, however, made on a future consideration that the patentees should discover and work mines of gold, silver, &c. Whether they have done so will best appear by this work. They received from the crown the mines of Keswick, but have not obtained any gold from them. The only gold they ever worked was in the two mines they seized on the discovery of other parties, and although gold is known to be found in fourteen counties of England, and in half a hundred places besides in Wales and Ireland, they have not even attempted to work it. The only gold working is carried on by other companies. Any claim of the Mines Royal Company would, therefore, at once be met by the proceedings of the Attorney General to quash the charters and patents.

The fourth question is whether these patents are not virtually void by the non-user of the patentees, and whether they have not by long neglect, licensed encroachments.

For two hundred years they have not worked a gold mine.

They allowed the legislature, without remonstrance, to license the working of Mines Royal.

Under the statute 5th William and Mary, they acquired, as claiming royal mines under the crown, further rights to the preemption of copper, lead, tin and iron ores which they have not exercised.

They have allowed the Duchy of Cornwall, without remonstrance, to grant leases of Mines Royal.

They have allowed the crown to act as to Mines Royal as if their corporation did not exist.

First, in respect to the Wicklow mines, within the English pale in Ireland, where the government acted irrespective of the Mines Royal Corporation.

Second, in the case of the second grant or working of the Wicklow mines. T

Third, in respect to the Cwmheisian and Berthllwyd mines, in Wales.

Fourth, in respect to the Prince Regent or Britannia, and the Poltimore mines, in the Duchy of Cornwall, just referred to.

The charters of the Mines Royal Company have been treated by the government, the legislature and mine owners as a dead letter, so that the enforcement of the claims founded on them becomes impossible, though in case of the resumption of gold-working in Britain, the present members of the corporation may be disposed to trade on their privileges. They can, however, no longer put their sergeants in action, issue precepts to mayors, obtain the assistance of pursuivants, or try rivals before a judge and jury of members of the corporation.

The acts of William and Mary allow all mines of base metal to be worked, containing gold and silver, but they do not, as was held recently in the case of the Cwmheisian mine, allow of the working of a simple gold ore, nor necessarily of working native gold in dry or wet diggings.

It will be observed that the act makes no mention of royalties on gold and silver, and according to the tenor of the act, such royalties seem to be commuted for the preemption right of purchasing the ores of mixed metals at fixed prices, within thirty days of being brought to grass, or any time before removal. As these rates of preemption are founded on the class of base metal, they do not apply to gold ores or native gold.

It is this preemption right, it is to be presumed, which the crown commuted in the case of the Berthllwyd and Cwmheisian mines, unless the crown on earlier precedents claim a preemption right for the purposes of the mint and coinage, but there is no precedent for such preemption below the market price of gold.

In the case of the Berthllwyd mines, the crown could claim royalties on ores of any kind raised on its own lands, but it does not appear on what ground royalties could be claimed on the Cwmheisian ores raised on private land.

It must be noted that the crown has no fixed rate of royalties on gold and silver. The rate in the various patents and licenses of the medieval period varies, as will be seen in the table, most materially. There could, therefore, be no fixed royalty reserved in the 1st and 5th of William and Mary. To have reserved a fluctuating royalty would have been under the plea of reserving the rights and prerogative of the crown, and would have been fatal to the policy of the act. The acts themselves are acts affecting the prerogative. They go directly to limit it; they strike off a large class of mines royal, and only leave as mines royal ores and deposits of gold and silver. The prerogative as to the other classes of mines royal being repealed and abolished, the prerogative royalty absolutely ceases. The crown has only a prerogative royalty on mines royal, and a copper mine bearing gold is no longer a mine royal. For the abolition of this prerogative the crown received as a compensation the new prerogative of a preemption right of copper, lead, tin and iron ores, except tin ores of the Duchy of Cornwall.

Since the passing of those statutes, the working of silverlead mines has proceeded without any claim of crown royalties, as was intended by the statutes, nor has any attempt been made to claim or exercise the statutory right of preemption of such silver-lead ores. The procedure as to silver-lead ores is clear.

The case of goldbearing copper or lead ores rests on the same ground as that of silver-lead ores; namely, the 1st and 5th of William and Mary, and except from confused ideas on the part of the public, and part of the ores being simple gold ores, it does not seem that the crown had any right to claim royalty on the Cwmheisian gold lead ores, or that, in accordance with its own practice, it could commute its preemption right over the gold-lead ores any more than over the silver-lead ores of the same mines. It seems very desirable that this point shall be settled by the mining interest, as it will relieve a large class of gold mines. It is true that copper ores, containing a small quantity of copper and less than four ounces of gold, cannot profitably be purchased by the crown at the rate of £16 per ton, nor lead ore having less than two ounces, but all the rich ores are claimable by the crown at the fixed rate of the statute.

The crown has foregone its preemption rights, except so far as they have been commuted in the two cases cited; and if the Treasury or Woods and Forests refuse to forego their claims, an explanatory act might be introduced on behalf of the mining interest.

The act of Edward III. only gives the right of working gold to landowners on their own lands, but under inspection of officers to be appointed by the crown. This act leaves untouched all crown lands and crown claims, as the beds of rivers and so forth, in which gold might be wrought.

The common law, custom or right of England as to gold mines or working, apart from the doctrines imported at a late period as to prerogative, knows of no right to minerals, or royalties on minerals. No proof can be shown of any title to royalties on minerals, or grants of minerals, previous to the times of the Edwards, and no mention of such right or royalties is to be found in the treatise *Prcerogativa Regis* or any old authority. The laws of St. Edward the Confessor, have no such recognition. No distinction was made until the middle ages on the scholastic distinction between royal and base metals, and therefore royal metals went with base metals, that is, with the soil.

With regard to the common law right of the people to work minerals on uncultivated lands, and which has been very little considered, that is shown by the uniform tenor of the action of the tinners of Cornwall and Devon, the lead miners of Derbyshire and Somersetshire, and the iron miners of Gloucestershire, as determined by the several laws recognized by Edward I.

It is open for discussion how far those mining laws, limiting or privileging the miners of the several districts, at all touch the common law rights of miners in other districts. A limitation of the lead miners of Derbyshire would not affect the right to mining in Cumberland or Northumberland. The practices of mining existed previously to such grants of privileges, as they are entitled, and the nature of them is shown by the evidence of the charters. They include the right to search for minerals in all uncultivated land, of using the water of rivers for washing ores or stuff, of setting off ground claims and water claims. If no prerogative of gold or silver attaches to the crown legally or conditionally, then there is a public right of searching for and working gold in any of the English gold fields.

The prerogative of the crown, as supposed, stands in the way of all free action, if sustainable. Nothing can be clearer than the assertion of this prerogative by the judges and lawyers; but, nevertheless, a prerogative of the crown is not sustainable on technical and simply legal grounds, if it has no constitutional existence. Theoretically, it is said, *nullum tempus occurit regi,* that no limitation of time affects the rights of the crown; but, practically, no right of the crown is sustainable which is a usurpation, or which is contrary to the rights of the community. A prerogative of any kind must be sustainable upon other grounds than the claim of it, its exercise, or any period of sufferance, as the fate of many old branches of the prerogative shows.

The right of the crown to royalty of gold can only be said to be admitted, because never considered or contested. In the case of the Earl of Northumberland, his counsel did not oppose the crown claim to royalty or monopoly of gold; they admitted the crown claim to mines royal, and only contested whether Keswick was a mine royal within the proper definition, nor in any other case has the question arisen.

It may therefore be as well to see on what grounds the crown claims to gold rests.

The argument for the crown was made in the Keswick case, though no argument was made against it.

The first argument is, " For the excellency of the matter, which, being more excellent, is appropriated by law to the person most excellent—namely, the king."

In the nineteenth century, this argument cannot be put forward, either as to gold being more excellent than anything else, or the king more excellent than the meanest person, nor that what is most excellent is appropriated to the person most excellent.

The proofs adduced on the queen's behalf were no proofs at all. The king has not by common law whales and sturgeons, but by encroachment. King Alfred's works give no evidence that whales were royal fish, or that royal fish were then known, or the whale fishery prohibited to Englishmen; nor is it now. There is no necessity for the preservation of the commonwealth against foreign foes, that the king should have the gold and silver, nor has he. There is no convenience to the public as to the coinage, because the coinage does not depend upon English gold or silver, because no English gold or silver is now used in the coinage, because no English gold ever was used, and because no silver has been used for nearly two hundred years. Therefore all grounds of public policy fail.

The second argument was from precedents, by the recital of the several commissions, grants and demises of mines of gold and silver. To these may now be added the patents of the Mines Royal, and to these the answers of the earl's counsel strictly applies that they show concurrence or license on the part of the public, but no absolute right of the crown. Such commissions, &c. were only formally grantable on the grounds of public policy, as those of the Mines Royal were, but it has to be proved that, by subsequent legislation, the crown retains the power to issue such commissions, &c. A proof relied on, is from the law proceedings against those who have disturbed the grantees or removed their ore, to which may now be added, the proceedings in the Keswick case. To this must be answered, that the crown has not exercised, nor has such power, in the present day.

The third argument is upon authorities of law, but that utterly breaks down, for the treatise on *Prcerogativa Regis* says nothing as to such claims to gold and silver mines, nor do any of the others cited. Treasure trove has nothing to do with minerals.

The claims of the crown.embrace—

The monopoly of gold.

The preemption of gold.

The commutation of royalties.

The issue of prospecting and digging licenses.

So far for the arguments for the crown: among those against the crown are the following:—

First, there is no antecedent proof of such prerogative, and that the absence of testimony for it, is against it.

Secondly, that such prerogative has become obsolete, like other branches of the prerogative, and that the crown has no such royalty or monopoly for silver or copper.

Thirdly, that such prerogative has been abolished in part and wholly by the Statute of Monopolies, by the Bill of Rights, and by the 1st and 5th of William and Mary.

Fourthly, that such prerogative has been abandoned by the grant of gold mines to the Mines Royal Corporation, without the exaction of royalties.

The present state of the law in England seems to be this,

That mines of copper, lead, tin and iron, containing gold, can be worked without license or royalty.

That the crown cannot grant licenses for prospecting and working gold on private lands.

The points remaining to be determined are—

Whether the crown can exercise preemption rights on gold bearing ores under the statute of William III., not having enforced such rights with regard to silver bearing ores?

Whether the crown has any prerogative right to royalties on gold?

Whether the population have the right to work gold on public or waste lands?

Whether the crown has any rights with regard to native gold on private land, beyond appointing inspectors to superintend the working, pursuant to the act of Edward III.?

CHAPTER XVII. ROYALTIES OF THE CROWN. *Wales. — Scotland. — Ireland. — Berwick-upon-Tweed. — Man. — Channel Islands. — Orkneys and Shetlands. — Heligoland,*

B. Royalties In Wales.—Wales of course follows the law of England, except so far as the crown can claim only prerogative rights as succeeding the princes of Wales, but there is no evidence of any such.

All the gold in Wales was granted to the Mines Royal Corporation, through Houghsetter and Thurland, but the crown, in the cases already cited, has acted without regard to such claim.

C. Royalties In Scotland.—The history of the crown prerogative in Scotland as to gold is more obscure than that of England. There is no proof that the kings of the Scots or invading race of the Highlands, or the kings of the English in the Lowlands, had any such prerogative. The constitutional history of Scotland moreover is obscure. There is no original common law of the people of Scotland except so far as the English invaders and settlers of the Lowlands could be held entitled to English rights. There is not, as in the case of the English of South Britain, original constitutional rights descending from the remotest antiquity. It may, however, be a question how far the south part of Scotland, being part of the kingdom of Cumberland, is subject to the incidence of English law.

The exercise of jurisdiction over gold mines in Scotland in the middle ages, is open to the same objection as in England, that it was only by sufferance.

The act of parliament of James I., passed in 1424, seems to ignore any original prerogative to royal mines in Scotland, and grants a royalty on silver only in lead. It provides that wherever gold or silver mines are discovered within the lands of any lord or baron, if it can be proved that three halfpennies of silver can be produced out of the pound of lead, the mine shall, according to the established practise of other realms, belong to the king. It will be seen that this is only an attempt to imitate a foreign prerogative.

D. Ireland.—The law relating to Ireland may be first considered with reference to the English pale and the district without the pale.

Henry II. would succeed to any claims of the Irish kings, and could further claim his own English prerogative, but it has yet to be proved that the Irish kings had any prerogative as to gold, or that the Plantagenet kings had.

There is no common law right on the part of the Irish people to the working of mines or ores, and it is questionable whether Englishmen in Ireland would have any right to the working of gold. The gold, therefore, goes with the soil, and belongs to the owners of the soil, except so far as there is any statutory limitation.

The law respecting Ireland depends upon three measures.

First, the statute of Edward III.

Second, the grants to the Mines Royal Corporation.

Third, the Wicklow case.

The statute of Edward III., although passed by the English parliament, became law in Ireland by Poyning's act, and gives the right of working gold and silver to owners of lands subject to the inspection of officers of the crown. It confers no right to the crown of royalties on P. F. Tytier's History of Scotland, vol. 3, p. 63.
gold, unless the English crown had, at that time, such a vested prerogative.

Queen Elizabeth undertook to grant to the Mineral and Battery Works all gold mines in Ireland within the pale. It may be assumed that, under the circumstances of the country, she had sufficient power to do so, though the crown would not have such power now. The corporation never have exercised these privileges in Ireland, and the crown paid no regard to them in the Wicklow case.

In this latter case the crown took upon itself to seize into its own hands the Wicklow gold district, on its supposed inherent prerogative, which was undisputed, but may not be so on the future working of the Irish gold fields. Indeed, at a former period, no one thought of disputing the right of the most excellent prince to the most excellent of metals, any more than his claim to touch for the king's evil. It is to be observed, the statute against monopolies is not in force in Ireland.

Ireland, without the pale, was not included in the Mines Royal grant, but the patentees are guaranteed the preference of such grant. The patentees of the Mines Royal, as in England, did not discover gold fields, nor, when discovered, did they attempt to work them. There is such a clear case of neglect of duties, that the Mines Royal Corporation would experience no better fate in Ireland than in England in the assertion of their claims.

The English government did, in the middle ages, attempt to exercise a prerogative of mines royal in Ireland, for there are writs relating to silver mines of 1276, 1289, and 1303. In 1360, Edward III. issued a commission to search for gold and silver mines, and in 1543, the Lord Deputy St. Leger.

E. Berwick-upon-tweed.—Berwick-upon-Tweed follows the law of England, and was included in the Mines Royal grant.

F. Man.—In Man there is no inherent prerogative, but the crown will claim English prerogative. The owner of the soil has the right to the gold found within it.

The Mines Royal patents include this island.

G. Channel Islands.—It is questionable what is the law in the Channel Islands. The prerogative of the crown there is that of the Carlovingian and Capetian kings of France, who certainly did claim mines of gold and silver. In 786, Charlemagne made a grant for prospecting and mining gold.

The grant of the Mines Royal Company extends to these islands.

H. Orkneys And Shetlands.—The prerogative of the crown in these islands is derived from the kings of Denmark, as to whom, there is no record that they had the prerogative of royal metals any more than they had of whales. Otherwise, they are subject to the law of Scotland.

I. Heligoland.—Heligoland lies at the mouth of the Elbe, which is a gold-bearing river, but there is no proof that gold will be found within the tidal range.
Jacobs on the Precious Metals, vol. 1, p. 258. CHAPTER XVIII. GEOLOGY OF GOLD. *Theory of the Constitution of Gold, and of its Combinations with other Metals.—Electric Conditions of Gold.— Gold Quartz.— Clay Slates.— Gossans.—Electric Action as Governing the Elevation and Depression of the Earth's Crust.*

It is to be regretted that little has yet been done to ascertain the laws, in pursuance of which mineral deposits and formations take place. This, however, is in a great degree owing to the undeveloped state of geology, and of those sciences which treat of the great instruments and operations of nature. Geology has done very much, but it is chiefly in the direction of the observation of facts, rather than of induction from these facts; and, indeed, when we come to consider how little is known of the earth's surface, geologically, with any degree of comprehensiveness, we shall be the more surprised at the progress which has been made in geology, and which has enabled its professors to determine the position of coal measures, and to point out the auriferous or metalliferous characters of particular formations. Nevertheless, for the proper and sound progress of the science, geology must, for some time, remain to a great extent a science of observation. It is by continuing to collect facts that we shall make ourselves acquainted with the phenomena of tin and copper and other lodes, and with the circumstances under which the other metals are deposited. A great help to this will be the corresponding progress of terrestrial magnetism, and of the electromagnetic sciences, which will give us an insight into the machinery by which the structure of this planet has been effected, and that by which its operations are maintained. We shall then have a new view of the world, or rather as the tendency of human thought is, an old view brought to life again. Instead of looking upon the earth as a dull, dead, inert mass, we shall witness it as an active body, moving with the well regulated automatous action of a steam engine, and approaching nearly to those notions of the ancients, which endowed it with a soul and an intelligence. We shall ascertain the laws, in virtue of which the ancient geological formations took place, and so obtain a satisfactory theory for the phenomena, and we shall see how far these operations continue with greater or less force to influence the constitution of the globe. At present, so far as the subject, we are considering, is concerned, we have only vague indications. We see lodes and courses, and veins, adopting a polar direction, we obtain evidence of their magnetic vitality, and synthetically we can, on a small scale, procure the deposition and concretion of metallic lodes; but these are our limits.

My course of observation has led me, independently to the same results in Australia, as many men of science have obtained in Europe and America. Of the views so formed, I shall, in this book, treat briefly, and chiefly for the purpose of explaining, so far as I can, the circumstances under which gold has been distributed, and where it may be reasonably expected to be found with a prospect of profit. It is necessary to put this limitation, for gold, like most other elements, so far as our knowledge goes, is extensively diffused. Such a diffusion of iron, for example, is patent; as we see it in the soil around us, so we are prepared to acknowledge its existence in the human frame, but the fact is not so palpable as to gold, because gold is diffused in smaller proportion than iron, and is truly a rarer metal, and its bulk, in proportion to the globe, or the surface of the globe, is infinitesimally small. Gold is seldom present in sufficient bulk, like iron, to make itself visible, and thereby more easily escapes notice; but, as attention becomes directed to the subject, and as minuter analyses are made, gold will be no doubt found to play a general and important function in the economy of nature, as other rarer elements, iodine for instance.

It is upon this general presence of gold, from the earliest geological periods of formation, that we are enabled to account for the existing phenomena of gold distribution. These phenomena vary according to the locality, but, nevertheless, there are certain prevailing types, which will afford us some insight into the general system, of which the several examples are modifications. Let us go to Australia, California, the Ural, or Lanarkshire, there we shall find rocks of what are called the paleozoic class, clayslates, for instance, which have been subsequently acted upon by the intrusion and protrusion of enormous masses of the so-called crystalline or igneous rocks, as granite in its several varieties. On examination we shall convince ourselves that these intrusions have not been mere temporary and forcible incisions, making a way through, and simply disturbing the clayslates, but a considerable concomitant action has occurred, leaving evidences behind it, which we cannot fail to recognize: Thus the granite, where it has come in contact with the clayslates, has its structure altered, a gradual transition and metamorphosis of character takes place, and, except to the eye of the geologist, who can, upon scientific grounds, safely comprise the several varieties in one system the rocks appear to belong to various classes and denominations. So, likewise, the clayslates are operated upon, their structure is altered, veins of granite are run into them, and, as I hold, their metalliferous character is affected. Whatever gold previously existed in such clayslates, its present quantity and direction have reference not to the clayslates, but the intrusive rocks.

In putting forward such a proposition, I offer nothing really strange, for scientific men have established the like doctrine with reference to other metalliferous lodes, but gold is distributed differently from copper and lead. Gold cannot be said to be found in separate lodes like other metals, and it is independently distributed in various rocks, and precipitated in those forms, popularly known as gold fields or gold diggings. This ideosyncrasy, or proper constitution of metals has yet to be studied to a great extent. I have observed chiefly that of gold, as others have of copper, but we want, in the interests of mineralogical science, a good account of the position and habits of each metal. There is no general mining character which can be attributed to all metals, and the general laws which govern them can only be ascertained from the dissimilarities and individual peculiarities of each, the modifications of which, and the interrelations constitute a general law. Gold, copper, and iron, have each a distinct mining character, and for any practical purposes must be separately treated, and yet each has influenced the deposition or precipitation of other metals, as for instance, both iron and copper, under certain circumstances, become indications of gold.

It is this characteristic constitution of metals, which will in time assist us in their discovery, and in a scientific point of view it will lead to very considerable results, for one of the most important steps towards determining the age of rocks, is by the direction of the minerals in their neighbourhood. Hitherto, the observation of fossils, or paleontology, has much engaged the attention of the geologist, and naturally so, for by such evidence he connects the remains of the latest formations with existing organisation, and he is enabled to trace up, as it were, from the roots, a tree of evidence. The study of fossils will, however, only do this, and no more; we get, as it were, to the top of the tree, and then the indications of organized life become rare and indistinct, and serve us but little. The traces of organisation are fragile, creatures that live but for the hour or the day cannot be embalmed in the gossamer shades of their form for the hereafter of millions of years, and even those of stronger make subjected to the operations of accident, time and nature cannot be preserved in their integrity. It is just at this point that the mineralogical character which, in the superior formations, is still feeble, comes strongly to our help. We no longer depend on the shell of a nautilus or the wingcase of a beetle, but we have the history written, as we may say, by the hand of nature, with pens of gold and copper. For the footsteps of an unknown animal, we have the gigantic lines of elvans and veins, cross-courses and lodes, indelibly impressed, and giving as secure a determination for the earliest periods, as a recent shell does for a river alluvium. Indeed, without the evidence here spoken of, the gold mineralogist would, instead of a sound and well established art, be, without rules for his guidance. The commonest gold digger, however, knows, by the traditions of his art, or by his own experience, as does the copper miner the favourable indications for the metal sought. The gold worker in Hindostan follows a practice, which had its origin before the existence of history; he, in South America, is guided by the manipulation of the Spanish conquistador, perhaps of the Romans, perhaps of the Phoenicians; and the occasional gold seeker of Clydesdale, in his small operations, adheres to the timehonoured principles of Greatbeard and Sir Bevis Bulmer.

By observation not only do we learn that each mineral has its habitual or characteristic forms of depositary, but that each has a particular direction in which it is more easily precipitated than in any other. Thus a north and south direction is not a general direction for all metals, but each has a distinct and characteristic direction, having a relation to u all the others, and they reciprocally to it. This relative direction, in my opinion, has been always the same from the earliest geological epoch; but the general direction of the whole system of metals, or what may be termed the axial or polar direction, has been subjected to variations, and these variations are now recognizable, dependent on the age of the operations, in virtue of which the deposition of metal has taken place. Thus the line of deposition adopted by copper may in one district be found east and west, yet in other districts, or in the same district, as determined by another geological direction, be north-east and south-west, yet the relationship of the Other metallic depositions will be constantly the same to the line or direction of copper deposition. On a small scale this has been observed with regard to copper in our western mining districts, and in Germany.

Metals, having their own directions of deposition, have their affinities and their oppositions, and it is in virtue of these that the combination of ores takes place and the deposition of masses of mineral, for precipitation never takes place but when metals meet their antagonistic metals, or those coming at an oblique or right angle. Gold has this peculiarity, that where precipitated it is a surface precipitation, in the nature of what may be called a determination to the surface. This is a characteristic which will be readily recognized by the gold digger, and it is one of great importance to be borne in mind in all scientific and economical considerations of the gold subject. From inattention to this fact many erroneous theories have been entertained, and a prejudice has been thrown on gold workings. The imagination that gold, like some other metals, would be found in veins or lodes by going down deep, has caused in many instances a useless expenditure of capital and labour, and produced most serious disappointment, because the object sought for was unattainable, being nonexistent. On the other hand, where gold might have been obtained, it was not sought for. The gold sands of Siberia, the diggings of California and Australia offered examples of superficial deposits on a large scale, very different from the conventional ideas as to the metallic formations, and the working of which has enormously increased the supply of gold.

On examining the clayslates in the examples already referred to, gold will be found on their surface, because the electric current passing off from the intruded rocks, and bearing gold has there met an antagonistic iron current and a low temperature, which have favoured the precipitation of both metals. It is thus that we so often find a ferruginous earth attending an auriferous deposit. If by any accident, of arrangement the iron was encountered before reaching the surface, then precipitation would have taken place, but this is only exceptional.

Gold sometimes meets opposition from tin, when the tin must become an oxide, and they may be precipitated together. As however both of these metals have a determination to the surface, they will generally be found there, and mostly on the flanks of granitic ranges or granite moors where there is sufficient moisture to keep battery power at work. Thus, under such circumstances, the tin at the surface often takes the place of animal and vegetable remains, and often the form of large pebbles and boulders, corresponding to what takes place in the transformation of such remains in their geological positions into silex, or into phosphates or carbonates of lime. Gold will be sometimes amalgamated with, and sometimes in distinct crystals in the tin-stones or ore (I often found it in this state in the vast tin deposits of the Tumut, Hume, Mitta Mitta, Ovens River, and many other places in Australia,) and sometimes independent, but in the immediate locality; as many of the tin streams of Cornwall show us.

The efficient cause for tin and gold taking this superficial direction is that the geological conditions, and perhaps those of neighbouring antagonistic metals, are too violent and vigorous in their electric alterations for such sensitive and delicate metals. Another reason is, the deficiency of the opposing current, iron, which is so much more powerful and active at the surface. Gold is more in opposition to iron than tin;—copper being the chief opposing medium to tin.

Now, tin having a double capacity, viz.: forming itself in lodes (which gold does not), and having a determination to the surface, it will be oftener found rich at a great depth, than gold, and will be worked profitably in the immediate vicinity of copper, especially when setting against it or jammed in by it, when the term may be used that the copper has made the tin in the manner that blende and copper often make lead. This accounts for the metals being found rich in the neighbourhood of their opposing metals, because in an electric state they cannot co-exist after they come under the immediate influence of each other; therefore, one or the other must precipitate. If both precipitate, the ores will be of different chemical constitution, one may be an oxide, whilst the other may be a sulphuret; but those metals which are not various in their chemical bases, such as gold, and generally tin, will always produce the same ores or chemical combinations in contact with other metals, gold will thus precipitate iron in an oxide (for the oxidation of iron is favourable to the accumulation of a precipitated nucleus of all gold in a secreted state in the neighbourhood), whilst the oxide of tin will cause copper generally to form in a sulphuret.

In some of my experiments I have obtained results elucidatory of what I have practically observed, that is, I have compelled the mass to precipitate its various undetermined metallic constituents in the same order of succession in which the various opposites are arranged or brought to bear upon it; and so powerful is the electric operation of precipitation when two antagonistic metals are brought in contact, that a forcible explosion ensues, and a great resisting power is evinced. Although I do not wish to dwell upon this subject here, as I can more conveniently develop it in a separate work, yet a few words relative to my views of the physical laws governing the elevation and depression of the earth's crust, will help to show the reader on what a grand scale the alteration of metallic masses is even now going on, and for what reason, very much that is attributed to igneous operations I consider to be incidental to other causes. The greatest moving cause acting on the earth's surface is the law of gravity under the various alterations of the electric conditions of the geological mass surrounding it. Now it is apparent to all who choose to watch what may be seen going on in the gradual distribution of metallic lodes and accumulations around any intruded granitic mass, that as the metal becomes developed around, it naturally impoverishes the primary matrix or mass from which it originally sprang, and helps to repel the iron current which would naturally have pervaded the mass below the surface, and which, under those circumstances, being partially cut off, could not be acted upon equally by the laws of gravity, they being wholly dependent upon the electric state of the mass acted upon.

Now, when we take into consideration the grand counteraction always at work, viz., the battle the sea maintains to keep its mean level against all the invasions into it in the form of the enormous quantity of detritus daily and hourly washed into it by thousands of rivers, steadily and uniformly working to one great end, and when we know that the sea does keep its mean level, we must presume that something must give way, or be forced up, to allow of the sea rearranging its basin, or making room for itself. Of course it would be the mass the least open to the operation of the laws of gravity. Again, on the other hand, all accumulations of alluvial and more recent formations, must, in their turn, be subject to depression, as they become impregnated with matter more congenial to the iron current.

This current, however, being in most vigour at the surface, and iron most given to precipitation and accumulation there, this would account for many depressions that these masses have to undergo coming under the conditions of the laws of gravitation which are very consistent on the surface and on the sea where they meet with a more even resistance throughout, in consequence of the sea being generally of the same mineral composition and of a uniform electric condition.

These facts are not generally made very apparent to us unless we experimentalise and bring to light points that were before hidden, but which are often led to by deductions from the theory based upon the observation of the laws of nature. These laws tend to show us upon what a grand system and circle nature is at work. Rivers bring down by their levelling process, vast accumulations of mud and sand; these in time, assisted by the action of the sea, and the laws of gravity, become dry land. Again the internal heat of the accumulated mass and the altered electric condition engendered around it, assisted by the great counteraction of the bed of the sea, all help to submerge the rising mass, as it is elevated and the distance becomes lessened between the level of the sea and the heated volume below. Vast masses are by those means caused to alter their temperature, and cooling, form extensive volumes of granite, and in such cooling having thrown off their various metallic constituents, these latter generating around them in their precipitated form engender conditions of opposition and absorption. The surrounded mass is by these means deprived of the electric conditions necessary to the carrying out to the full extent the laws of gravitation upon it; therefore it naturally rises. Now as all granitic cooling masses affect the neighbouring strata, or if vent should be given to them, thereby allow igneous intrusions and eruptions, the solid crust being so much thinner, would be the first to yield to the combined conditions already mentioned. These are the intrusions which constitute the mountain ranges of the world; again these are worn down or levelled by water and electric decomposition; the levelled mass then, may either be attacked by the encroaching influence of the sea, or by the changed electric conditions may become depressed under the re-action of the electric influence on gravity. The chain of events now completes the circle, and that which has been dry land, is again immersed in the sea, and so if we were to follow out the various evolutions of nature we should generally be brought back to the point from which we started. For this reason I would prefer, in the difficult subject of classification, a circular one as being most analogous to the laws of nature.

Before I leave this subject I must notice what an important agent in the physical alteration of the earth's crust is that great electric conductor—water. It acts in many different ways, sometimes connecting one geological mass with another, thereby causing the alteration of the local poles, by bringing in contact that which before was separate, and insulating that which before was connected; sometimes the overflowing of a river will so alter the relative electric state of the surrounding geological conditions that upon a sudden alteration or reversion of poles a slight shock or earthquake may often be felt.

Thousands of tons of granite, or other substances, will sometimes be under decomposition at the same time. So powerful a battery will serve as a unit to estimate the magnificent scale upon which the whole system of a metalliferous country, or a number of lodes may be undergoing electric alteration, one metal giving place to another, and as they alter their relative position the various chemical bases become affected and changed. Sometimes these operations result in the formation or precipitation of large silicious crosscourses, for some miles in length. Now all these incidents have their greatest operating agent in water, but of course the great electric medium engendered by the internal heat of the earth has a combined influence.

I will now endeavour to show in what manner heat and fire concur in the elevation and depression of the earth's superficial crust, and how much such an influence stands in the way of mineral development whenever it comes too near the surface.

First, with regard to the laws of elevation. It is a well established fact that temperature increases as we descend into the earth's crust, so that if the increase is in a regular ratio we should have all the known solids entirely dissipated at a limited distance below the surface. These phenomena lead to important inferences, and in fact, prove that there must at least be a belt or band of heated matter below the superficial crust, and if heated according to the laws of expansion creating deficiency of the electric medium, an equilibrium being required with the surrounding masses not so affected, it must necessarily rise when the space is lessened between it and the earth's surface, or where the gravitating power immediately above it is partially neutralized or weakened; those parts offering the least resistance to the grand counteraction of the sea, and a proper regulation of matter according to the laws already referred to.

When, too, these heated masses come so near the surface as to get vent, then there will be a fiery mass engendered which I believe will not exist in life or activity anywhere but at the surface. So great a heat as this will not be congenial for the precipitation or formation of any large metallic bodies, merely because the intense heat assists to dispel them into electric, gaseous, and atmospheric states, chiefly at the vent or outlet; but if there is no outlet, and the temperature is milder at the surface or surrounding the heated or cooling volume, then although the same matter has to pass off and pretty nearly in the same electric state, yet it meets with negative conditions, opposite mediums, and lower temperatures, in passing through the vast masses of clay slate or other rocks surrounding the cooling mass, and will be detained in one form or another as already explained. My space in this work does not allow me to enter into sufficient detail perhaps, even to explain my views upon a subject so grand, important, and so neglected; but I hope soon to lay before the public the accumulated result of years of labour and of study in the collection and digestion of these facts and observations.

The conditions under which the formation and secret dissemination of gold take place may be thus classified:—

A. When precipitated.

I. When precipitated on the surface.

II. When precipitated beneath the surface.

B. When in cryptothesis.

I. Circumstances under which gold is precipitated on the surface. I have already stated that whenever the gold-bearing current comes in contact with the iron current at the surface of the clay slates, precipitation of gold takes place. The chief forms may be thus divided:—

a. When gold is precipitated on the surface of the clay slates, having passed through the clay slates from the igneous mass at a corresponding angle to the cleavage.

b. When gold is precipitated at the surface and at the sides of quartz dykes, which have been the conductors through the clay slates. *c.* A surface precipitation is found in the clay slates, which may be styled an after or surface precipitation of the gold. *d.* Quartz is a well known vehicle for gold, and quartz veins are looked to as profitable sources of gold, and I believe they will be found so, but I doubt if the formations are true veins. Where schists have been transmuted by crystaline rocks, numerous clefts and vacua were created, by the baking and contraction of vast alluvial mud deposits. These coming in contact with the vast heated volume, the silicious portion was thrown off in steam, and electrically guided through the cleavage of the slates, meeting at the surface in many instances the infiltration of water, and a cooler temperature which assisted in filling up the clefts created in them at the surface, and thus forming the numerous quartz dykes. These forming or cooling dykes again acted as favourable conductors for electric currents charged with gold and iron, and these currents, according to their direction, possessed an affinity for the several metals. Thus the current bearing gold would, directly it came in contact with the cold ferruginous clays and earths at the surface, precipitate the gold, which would take the many partially granular and crystaline forms, in which it is now found when washing the original clays, in which it was left. On the other hand, the quartz dyke having cooled at the sides and surface, arrested the progress of the after current, and often caused the gold to be left imperfectly precipitated. When such is the case, the gold is in two forms, in its metallic state, and in what I shall call its electric secretion, deposited in infinitesimal particles, appearing when partially precipitated through a strong microscope in the form of a cauliflower head and generally of a green colour in the quartz. In this form mercury will not always collect it, and in most cases the ordinary modes of reduction fail. The gold will sometimes be found precipitated on one side of the dyke, but near the surface. If, however, there were no opposing iron current, or if such current were weak, and the quartz dyke were sufficiently cool, the gold would be in cryptothesis or secretly disseminated throughout the mass of quartz, at a much greater depth than the previous conditions would allow.

It is from these peculiar conditions that rich quartz specimens must be accepted with caution as indications of the auriferous character of the dykes, as rich specimens are more likely to be examples of a. surface incrustation than of the general quality of the rock.

Gold is seldom precipitated below the surface in clayslates, because it has not there met with the iron current, and because the electric cleavage of the clay slates has afforded a good conductor.

Gold is found at the surface of the clayslates, taking in many cases the exact form of the interstices.

II. Circumstances under which gold in certain conditions is precipitated beneath the surface of rocks.

First. Whenever the gold would meet iron in its upward course. This is the mode in which the gold gossan and mundic ores have been produced.

Second. When the gold current has come in contact with two metals under such strong electric action as to interfere with and overpower its course.

Third. When the gold has been held down by its metallic affinities through amalgamation with other metals.

In the case of lead lodes, the silver having an affinity for the lead, and the gold having an affinity for the silver, the progress of the gold current would be arrested by the amalgamation or association with the silver, the latter leaving the lead for the gold, for which it has a stronger affinity, and the gold and silver being thus deposited alongside of the lead, and thereby cause the gold to be found at a much greater depth from the surface, than it would be found under any other condition. Under the circumstances stated the lead ores become worth working for gold.

Copper, in its original direction, is not a favourable medium for gold, but sometimes becomes so in its subsequent deviation. Gold may be extracted from certain copper ores very profitably.

Many of the iron deposits of England and Wales contain gold, and some of them in the neighbourhood of lead would be likely to contain silver; but by the present modes adopted for reducing the ore, these are all lost. The blast furnace, for instance, would naturally engender a very strong opposition current, which would repel every atom of gold, throwing it off in a gaseous and electric state, whereas, by a little ingenuity of arrangement, it might all be caught upon an opposing plate. This would allow some of the poorer oxides to be worked profitably, as they are occasionally rich in gold. A similar construction, by a slight alteration in arrangement and direction, might be brought to bear very profitably upon the blackband ironstone, when containing silver.

Gold becomes mechanically associated with various metals, viz.: the sulphurets of copper, iron, zinc, antimony, silver, and some others.

Gold becomes amalgamated with, and, in its native state, has a great affinity for, metallic mercury, silver, and copper; but it partially loses that affinity when these metals become sulphurets; for when the chemical base is altered, viz., in iron, zinc, and others, although gold may be overpowered by the iron assuming a sulphuret character, and sometimes causing it to become chemically associated with it, yet it would be directly the reverse in the oxide of iron; there would be no chemical affinity, and it would be the opposing action of the iron upon the gold which would cause the gold to be native precipitate, and distinct from the iron, although disseminated throughout in independent particles. As these two ores — the oxide and sulphuret of iron — will be found to be of the greatest mercantile value, the way to treat them as gold ores will naturally call for a little attention. Up to the present time, amalgamation with mercury has been the grand medium for treating all ores; but this will attack gold when in its native malleable state only, and even requires great care, and is a most delicate process. For instance, many things have to be considered, viz.: electric affinity of the two metals under certain degrees of temperature and atmospheric changes. To create a perfect amalgam with all the gold in a native state would require the crushed ore to undergo a change of temperature twice whilst with the mercury, once as a wet, and then as a dry process. Now, as I have before said, this would do very well for ores where the gold is native and malleable, as in the oxides of iron and tin, quartz, some granites, and auriferous earths, &c.; but in the sulphurets of iron and copper, or when secreted in quartz or granite, that process would be of no avail. In some experiments I have been trying upon mundic, or sulphuret of iron, containing gold, by oxidizing the mass, in company with a sufficiency of mercury, I obtained a perfect amalgam with the mercury and gold, by returning the mercury again to its native state; but, with regard to rocks containing the electric dissemination of gold, I believe there is no way of treating it but by my electric process, for no chemical analysis will touch it.

It may be observed, that I have found sulphurets of iron of two classes—one in which the gold is found distinct, and as a mechanical combination, and the other, where it seems to approach more nearly to the character of a chemical combination. The best paying sulphurets seem to belong to the former class. In the course of some years, and particularly since I have returned from Australia, I have paid particular attention to the sulphurets and oxides of iron. I have examined nearly two hundred specimens of the sulphuret of iron from different localities, and find that by far the greater part contain gold, but the average varies considerably; but is highest where the combination is mechanical, and generally in decomposing matter. The specimens that have lately come under my notice have varied from two pennyweights to seven ounces per ton. I have never found gold in the character of a distinct sulphuret.

As to the combination of gold with tellurium, although I discovered that metal in Australia, yet it is not of sufficient present importance to induce me to encroach upon my limited space here; I will save what I have to say for a chemical work on the subject.

B. Gold in cryptothesis.

The *cryptothesis,* concealed or impalpable electric dissemination of gold arises under several conditions. One chief condition is the want of an iron current, and the want of an adequate temperature in the mass of granite subjected to new intrusion to admit of the thorough passage of the gold.

Granite or crystalline rock of an early formation will commonly be found to have parted with its gold into the surrounding paleozoic formations, but where the crystalline rock has been subsequently displaced by other intrusions it becomes charged with gold throughout certain portions of it, these portions having the true electric direction for gold relatively to the intruded mass. This gold, however, is not visibly developed or palpably obtained by any ordinary analysis, except when the granite decomposes under certain electric or atmospheric influences and happy conditions.

Metals generally may remain for an indefinite period in a state of *cryptothesis,* on account of their not meeting their opposing currents when thrown off from the later igneous intrusions into older formations, but when the masses containing them are subjected to decomposition and the operations just referred to, the metal becomes developed in an It was by noticing these influences that I was led to adopting my electric process for the assaying and reduction of gold, by means of which I have succeeded in obtaining a greater amount of gold than by any other process.
appreciable form, either on the spot or in the immediate vicinity.

Metals belong to two classes, those determining themselves into lodes, as copper, lead, &c., these would not become developed on the spot, but would travel some distance in the form of veins, and those which have a surface determination and general dissemination, as gold, &c., and under certain circumstances tin. These would develop themselves on the spot, unless the battery engendered by the decomposing mass were either too strong or of an uncongenial character, by which means the metal would be thrown off, and would not precipitate until it arrived within the sphere of another electric medium of sufficient power to neutralize the force that had rejected it. This would generally happen either at the surface,—or at the side of some vein, dyke, or junction of two different formations; and, wherever the infiltration of water, the bed of a river, or creek met its progress, the tendency to develop and accumulate would be greatest.

Gold is cryptotheted in quartz when there has been only a partial operation of the iron current, or when a cooling of the upper portion of the dyke has interfered with the passage of the gold to the surface.

In some cases of quartz dykes the gold has turned off and followed the wall of the quartz dyke, and so precipitated itself partially oh the wall and partly on the surface. If, however, the quartz vein had been at a sufficiently high temperature at the surface, it would then have passed out into the surrounding clays, there forming into pure masses.

It may, perhaps, be useful here to state that the electric functions of lodes are always in operation, as observers have ascertained, and starting from this principle I wish to draw some conclusions affecting gold formations. Thus there is a continuous electric action; there are suspensions of this action, and, on the other hand, new connections are formed, the polarity of lodes is altered, and their conditions materially affected, old elements being removed and new elements being introduced; while new causes of attraction and repulsion are thus brought into activity.

One circumstance resulting from this is that in a given lode a metal may undergo a great variety of changes, acting as a base to other chemical elements, and the quantity of metal greatly varying at several periods, and at one time disappearing altogether, and being replaced by another metal.

When the relative position or polarity of a metallic lode has become affected by geological causes or l6cal circumstances, the metal becomes electrically decomposed and is deposited in an altered direction forming strings and diverging veins. This may result from a variety of circumstances. The connection of the lode with neighbouring lodes, crosscourses, and dykes, may be broken by the lode becoming dry, by the infiltration of water, or by the altered electric character of some neighbouring vein or string which ceases to act as a conductor from its impoverished character or altered condition. On the other hand, new connections may be opened with other neighbouring lodes, cross courses, and dykes by like causes, and a neighbouring vein or string may become so altered in its metallic or chemical constitution as to originate or bring into operation a powerful electrochemical action.

Where a long level is driven and a large portion is laid dry, the progress of action is partially arrested in the portion above the level, or a new course of action is developed by the operation of atmospheric influences. Nature, although a slow miner, is ever active, and would therefore in a relatively short time, make great havoc in a very valuable lode.

While such operations are going on, which is sure to be the case when various metallic masses are in proximity, the "country," in miner's phrase, supposing it contained gold or some other metal in cryptothesis might be subjected from the introduction of some new constituent into the lode at a right angle, electrically speaking, to the precipitation in the lode of the self-contained gold or other metal.

Gossans are often the residuum or impoverished remains of former metallic masses, which having undergone change at the surface, have been chiefly re-charged with iron, which has imperfectly allowed the new metal entering the lode to penetrate to the surface. The same cause which would prevent copper from reaching the surface of the lode would favour the precipitation of gold in those gossans or oxides of iron.

CHAPTER XIX. PRESENT STATE OF GOLD WORKING IN BRITAIN. *Gold Mining Companies. — Commissions of Survey. — Gold Licenses. — Gold Prospecting. — Gold within the Tidal Range. — Commutation or Abolition of Royalties. — Assays.—Deficiency of.—Fluctuations of.—Loss of Gold. —Bad Sampling.—Public Assay Offices.—Managers of Mines. —Stamping.— Washing.—Fusion. —Amalgamation.—Electric Treatment of Gold.—Local Reduction Works. — Will Quartz Companies pay ? — Causes of Failure.— Yield of Gold Ores.*

From what has been already stated, it will be seen that there is evidence enough of the existence of gold in these islands, but that the present production is inconsiderable. I propose, now, to consider the state of gold mining and working.

As to the diggings or working of the deposits, nothing is being done except the picking up a chance nugget in the tin streams or at Lead Hills, and what is got from the South Wicklow gold field for the Dublin goldsmiths.

As to the gold mines which have been opened, or are now at work, there are:—

The North Wales, Cwmheisian, Dolfrwynog, and Berthllwydd.

The Prince of Wales.

The Exmoor Wheal Eliza. *J*

The Arundell, near Ashburton.

Inney Consols, near Launceston. Of these the operations as yet are inconsiderable, but they show the foundations of a large gold-working interest if properly directed. Indeed, nothing more shows the progress of gold mining in this country than the fact of the existence of a dozen gold mining companies at this time, and the actual production of gold. It matters little what the opinion may be as to the present profit of these undertakings, for it is so far a concession that there are gold ores, and that these ores can be worked.

I shall proceed to consider what is requisite for the proper development of the auriferous resources of the country.

In the first place, I shall take the gold deposits, and urge the expediency of the home government pursuing the same course as that of New South Wales, and appointing commissioners to examine and discover gold fields. I would respectfully suggest that these commissioners should not be taken from those men who have pledged themselves against gold-working in England, but from those who are at any rate desirous to find it. Messrs. Hargraves, Clarke, and Stutchbury, cost the Sydney government very little, and they have incalculably repaid the outlay by discovering what will long be sources of wealth to the province.

These explorations, I therefore consider, should not be appropriated to the ordnance geological survey department, as they have enough to do, and have not hitherto exercised themselves in gold mineralogy. The official report on Londonderry says nothing on the known localities of gold in that district, the official report on Cornwall and Devon has two pages about it, and the ordnance map has one gold locality marked in Wales. It will be much better to employ persons who have made themselves acquainted with gold in the Brazils, Columbia, and Australia; but here care must be taken that they are not fettered by theoretical views, looking for quartz veins where they should find good diggings, or neglecting gold mines for the search of alluviums. The investigation should be directed to the twofold object of finding alluviums and gold rocks and veins, and individual commissioners may be employed in the research at pleasure or as their experience best qualifies, in either department.

There are now here a great many experienced diggers returned from Australia with practical proofs of their success, who might be very usefully employed in examining known gold deposits by sinking and cradling, and if anything can be done they will give practical instructions to the population.

The next thing is to organise a department of commissioners for the issue of licenses, again on the model of the Australian gold department. This would be consequent on the regulation of the claims of the government and the public to the gold. Whatever the opinion of the crown lawyers may be as to the prerogatives of the crown, the public will not allow a crown monopoly while royalties are abolished in our Australian Colonies. It will be necessary to define the rights of the public as to the search for gold on public and privatelands and river beds, for if the claims of the crown to the monopoly of gold be abandoned the public cannot consent to surrender to landowners what cannot be said ever to have belonged to them. There must be an adjustment of the claims of the crown, of landowners, and of the public under the two heads of alluvial deposits and mines.

By means of a proper system for licenses, the productiveness of the gold fields would be effectively proved, and without loss to the government, as thousands will take out licenses though the results of their operations may ultimately prove unremunerative. Many deposits have been examined in the Australian provinces, which have proved either destitute of gold, or for the present not adequately remunerative. Were proper arrangements made, there are many old Australian diggers who could be induced to try over again the Clydesdale, the Wicklow, or the Cornish old diggings, or some new diggings to which they might take a fancy.

In searching for gold deposits, it becomes a question how far such should be sought within the tidal range. There has been an impression that the sea-sands are auriferous, but beyond their general participation in gold as an element, this becomes very questionable to my mind. There are, however, many situations, where, there being a known or supposed bed rock beneath the tidal range, it may be desirable to sink down to it. This I found on the analogy of the tin deposits, which so much resemble gold. Thus the Carnon, which is both a gold and tin stream, has been successfully worked for tin at Restronget Creek, in Falmouth Harbour, and the tin stones were found beneath the sill and sands of the estuary.

Gold mining I shall examine more at length, because the working of a digging is a simpler matter. When the gold is found, it is readily got out, and can be put into the hands of the refiner, but gold mining requires a great variety of processes.

Having already urged the appointment of commissioners of investigation for finding out gold veins, I would earnestly submit that, although in Australia, royalties have been reserved on gold mines, it is most inexpedient to enforce them here at present, if at all. If the royalties, being legally recoverable, which is questionable, are to be maintained, and Delabeche's Report on Cornwall, &c. p. 401.

to be constituted a source of revenue, the most effectual way to make them so is by giving a present bounty for the working of gold mines. Royalties of eight and a half, ten, and fifteen per cent, are a heavy tax in the present infant state of gold mining. In the case of the Poltimore, on one cargo of ore producing £429 *9s.,* the cost of reduction was £179 1 *Is.,* the dues to the landowner £28 12s., and the crown dues £35 15s., leaving to the proprietors to cover the cost of raising £185. The royalties at present are taken on the gross amount of gold, so that in the case just given, while the crown dues are eight and a half per cent, on the gross amount, they are fifteen per cent, on the net amount after reduction, and on such amount, less the lord's dues, are nearly seventeen per cent.

The crown must be urged, for its own sake, to abolish its claim, and it'must be pressed by the combined action of the owners of gold mines, while some joint arrangement or modified arrangement should be made as to lord's dues. Between thelord's dues, one fifteenth, andthe crown dues, one twelfth, 15166 per cent, of the gross produce is taken, and in the case just cited about twenty-six per cent, of the produce, after paying the cost of reduction. If, according to old practice, the crown dues and the lord's dues had been delivered in ore, instead of in value, the company would not be subjected to such loss, as, instead of £185 lis., they would receive £212 as their share, after reduction. It is clear, therefore, that, as a matter of fairness, the royalty must be taken on the ore, or basis of the ore, and not on the gold after reduction. With charges so oppressive, none but very rich gold ores can be worked, and a modification is essential in the public interest. The production of silver has of late years become an important item of metallic produce in England, and there is no reason why the gold should not be so.

If gold working be properly followed up, I am convinced that many very poor ores of copper, lead, and zinc may be advantageously worked; I may say, that even the richer ores may be made more profitable. For such a purpose, the assays of ores must be conducted on a different system. The assays must not be special assays for copper, lead, or silver; they must be general assays, or, at all events, they must be specially assayed for gold. It has been very well remarked, that it is too general a practice of mineral proprietors and mine owners to send up ores to be assayed for copper or some other metal. The fee paid to the assayer is a limited one, and he returns a quantitative assay of the leading metal in the ore. Thus a minute portion of gold, very valuable in itself, will not be reported, and it may be an ore that, with a joint produce of copper and gold, or lead, silver, and gold, would be remunerative, is neglected. Mr. Mitchell, who has a very extensive practice in assaying for the mining companies, says, expressly, that very many of the samples of iron pyrites he has seen contain both gold and silver, but the working of them is neglected. Some of these pyrites are employed in the manufacture of arsenious and sulphuric acids, and the gold is dissipated."

Other evidence is distinctly given, and on which I have already dwelt in the second chapter. Ores of the class just stated, and containing sixty ounces of gold to the ton, have actually been thrown away, and never manufactured for any purpose. Some of the gold, however, instead of being dissipated or thrown away, is sent out mixed with other metal. " There is no doubt," says Mr. Abbot, " but that there are now many mines throwing away silver ores, as copper has been, and no doubt gold. "-)-Mr. Thomas Rowlandson, C.E., speaking of the Poltimore mine, says:— " The non-discovery of gold by the adventurers who cleared out the mine during the period intervening between the years Mr. J. Mitchell in the Mining Journal, 1847, p. 266.

t Abbot's Essay on Mining, p. 16.

1841 and 1846, is perfectly compatible with the fact of its existing in large and remunerative quantities; for it has fallen within my experience on many occasions, that argentiferous and auriferous ores have been thrown away and neglected as ' waste,' which, if selected and dressed at the time of raising, would not only have paid well, but in many instances have converted unfortunate speculations into remunerative ones."

The character of the assayer is an important consideration. The local assayer is chiefly employed on a few metals, even where he has sound elementary knowledge; but Mr. J.Y.Watson observes, "The Cornish assayers, generally, have not the slightest notion of the theories of chemistry or metallurgy, and their assays are not very accurate. Ore, which, according to their assay, gives a produce of seven, will often, upon a stricter analysis, yield more, and the difference goes to swell the already enormous profits of the smelter."

Even with practised assayers great discrepancy will be found in assays of gold ores, and mine proprietors must neither be discouraged by unpromising assays nor buoyed up by very high per centages. The average produce at the end of the year, on a large quantity of ore, is the true test. Gold ores vary so much in the distribution of the metal in the ore, that it is difficult to send corresponding specimens to the same assayer or to several assayers. A very good practical example as to this occurred this year to the Poltimore Company. To make sure, they employed three assayers, Mr. John Mitchell, Messrs. Johnson and Matthey, and the Sheffield Company, and they weighed out to each two pounds of red gossan ore, two pounds of brown gossan ore, and two pounds of the two ores mixed. This last was intended as a further check on the several establishments. The return was:— Compendium of British Mining, p. 20. Here it will be seen that apart from the fact that all reported the red gossan as the richest, the greatest discrepancies exist, and the assayers cannot be suspected of any neglect or want of skill.

Where metals exist in a large per centage, as in ores of copper, iron or lead, very wide differences are of less importance, and a few assays are enough; but of all gold ores many assays must be made in order at all to ascertain their character. The ores likewise vary so much in different portions of the vein. Thus in a case cited of the St. John del Rey ore, which near the surface yielded only three pennyweights per ton, and the working of which might have been abandoned, it improved in the course of following the vein to seven pennyweights eighteen grains.

In assays, I have made myself, I have recognized these diversities according to the process I employed, or in comparison with the assays of others, and I would further observe, that the assay in different hands will yield as wide results as the reduction process will with which it is intimately connected. In gold mining the assay is for a double purpose; first to determine whether the ore is worth working, and next to compare the absolute quantity existing in the ore with that obtained in the reduction and to reduce the loss, which in the present state of gold reduction is nearly always found in the ores treated. Mr. Berdan, the inventor of an American machine asserts that he has obtained more gold from the tailings than others have from the whole ores.

This too must not be lost sight of with gold ores; they contain the metal sometimes in particles extremely minute.

The average quartz of California yielding by the present processes from seven to fifteen pennyweights per ton, will, by the more careful and better understood management of the native Chilean process, yield thirty-five pennyweights per ton generally, and, with a very careful average made by myself, under my process, of the very same ores, give fortyseven pennyweights per ton.

If it be considered what is the proportion of gold in gold ores, it will be seen that great variation existing between the particles in size, they are reduced to a small fractional proportion of the whole mass of mineral. A common rate for Australian and Californian gold quartz is fifty to sixty parts of gold in one million of quartz. In St. John del Rey ores it ranges from five parts to twelve, fourteen and fifteen parts in one million, which latter is a high average, but a remunerative rate. The proportion in Macugnaga ores is similar.

It will be seen, therefore, that it is desirable the quantities of ore subjected to assay should be large. Picked pieces of an ounce weight are of no use. It is seen that even with two pounds very discordant results are obtained.

One consequence of the minute dissemination of the metals is, that it is frequently not visible to the naked eye, and many ores are neglected on that account. Thus many valuable ores or portions of a lode are rejected.

At Santa Rita, near Marmato, in Columbia, the gold can sometimes be seen in the quartz freely disseminated, and again, large blocks of quartz have been broken from the rock, in which no gold could be traced. Many tons of hard quartz were, in 1840, conveyed to the mill, that on inspection, showed no gold to the naked eye, and yet the Company obtained daily a fair quantity of gold from this quartz.

Masses of quartz, with no external indication of gold, afforded by hand-washing, an average of about fife ounces of gold to a ton of rock.

Looking to the importance of the assay, I would strongly recommend the establishment of assay offices, supported partly out of the crown royalties and partly by subscription and fees in each of the gold regions, and would urge on the companies the desirability of more frequent assays. London is well provided by means of the Government School of Mining, and its College of Chemistry, and by the many experienced assayers, and there are many towns in which there are good laboratories and assayers, but there ought to be two or three assay-offices in Cornwall and Devon, others in Wales, and public offices in Dublin, Glasgow, and Edinburgh. A system of licensed assayers might be desirable. If properly organised, several local mining schools might be established by appointing licensed assayers, mineralogists and surveyors, who should act as gratuitous professors of chemistry, metallurgy, mineralogy, and mining engineering. The private practice obtained by an authorised professional man would compensate him for his professional duties.

A process analogous to assaying, is the sampling of ores, a kind of local or mine assay, which is very inefficiently conducted, as those connected with the mining districts well know.

On the works of the National Brazilian Company at Cocaes stones of gold ore were thrown away as rubbish, picked up by the negroes, and the gold sold from time to time in the village. This took place in 1835, and it was not till 1846 that the directors found it out. They remark, " One of the greatest faults in the character of the Cornish miner is the disinclination to sampling, which is scarcely ever done Ansted's Gold Seeker's Manual, p. 84.

unless the ground appears favourable for gold; and had this common sense plan been adopted, it might have been the means of saving the fearful outlay of money expended in the various explorations at this mine."

At the Columbian mines, in 1839, there was no assay apparatus.

Now, if gold mining is to be profitably conducted in England, there must be good sampling, and there ought to be some one on the premises able to make an assay. With the present extension of education, if companies would only insist on captains and clerks having a competent knowledge of chemistry, there would be no difficulty in finding qualified officers.

A great difficulty encountered by gold mining companies at present is that they employ captains of copper mines or lead mines who prefer working what may be called their own ores, and neglect other ores however rich, or at any rate, do not pay proper attention to gold ores. It has taken a long time for the English companies in South America to break in their officers, some of the most efficient of whom have never been in Cornish copper mines. A man, very able as a copper miner, able because brought up in a practical school, immediately shows his deficiencies when he is put in a new mining country or a new branch of mining enterprize. He has had no preliminary scientific education to imbue him with general principles, and enable him to discriminate between what is essential and what is merely formal in the range of his old experience and the new sphere in which he is placed. Thus many gold companies in England are perilled or neglected by their managers, and with the extension of gold mining, the same difficulties will occur. The great fault of the Cornish school of mining, and its great merit, is that it is too special. If it had not been so, its silver lead ores would have been sooner worked, its gold Report of the Directors, 1847, p. 7.
ores would now have been developed, and even copper would have been worked earlier than it was.

A great mischief to be avoided is sinking shafts or trial works on the advice of geologists to find the gold lode or the mother of gold, and going deep, when, so far as the experience of practical men goes, and I am able to confirm, so far as I have seen, gold is best sought on the surface.

In a mine which is worked for copper or lead, as well as for gold, it may be desirable to put the gold workings under separate superintendence, or the gold ores will not receive due attention.

On the ore being raised from the mine, there are various processes for reducing it, and as to which there is not yet a settled system of working. It is most likely that what succeeds with one ore is not equally applicable to another. These processes are:—

Stamping.

Washing.

Fusion.

Amalgamation.

Electric precipitation. Stamping is that process which, under the management of the Cornish captains, has received the greatest attention, and has been carried to what they consider great perfection. In this they have been assisted by engineers, so that the heaviest possible stamps are produced, and quartz rock can be crushed to impalpable powder in a very short space of time. Various patents have been brought out and directed to the same object. Now, so far as my experience goes, I am convinced that this minuteness of stamping is most generally carried too far, and that the small produce of the gold ores is to be greatly attributed to it. Nothing can differ more widely than the constitution of a gold ore and a copper ore, so far as regards stamping. The copper ore contains a large proportion of metal, say one hundred thousand or two hundred thousand in one million; the gold ore a very small proportion, perhaps ten in one million. In washing a copper ore the greater part of the metal must be saved, but in washing a gold ore, however carefully conducted, it may very well happen that the fractional contents may be dispersed instead of saved.

The result of stamping upon gold ores is one of two processes, either the metal is comminated or it is flattened. In the former case, the water cannot get at it in the mass of mineral to separate it, nor can the mercury always, without great care and expense. When, by the power of the stamps, the larger portions of metal are flattened, they are liable to float on the surface of the water instead of sinking in it.

Instead of all energy being directed to obtain the most powerful stamps, it is necessary that great care shall be taken to diminish the stamping effect, and limit it to the minimum power, which will extract the gold particles whole.

The next process is washing, which is conducted in various modes, and which it is questionable whether it should be applied to all gold ores. Rough stream washing will never do for them, and the tailings must be most carefully preserved. In my opinion much of the gold in the ordinary process of washing is floated away. It was noticed with some Cwmheisian gold that many particles floated on the surface of the water for three days and some for five.

At Marmato, in 1842, Mr. Chapman, the secretary, observed that a large loss was sustained in the dressing department. He says, " It is here that by far the greatest loss is sustained. It is in this department that the large heaps of dressing remains are collected; and in consequence of the expedition required to get a portion of free gold out of a large monthly supply of mineral, these remains may be supposed to contain about as much fine gold per ton as the average of the rough mineral extracted from the mines. This appears to me a great disadvantage. I am fully aware of what has been said about these heaps becoming decomposed by exposure to the atmosphere, but then there is this inconvenience, that every flood of rain washes a portion away, leaving a fresh surface for decomposition, which in its turn is carried away."

The loss on the extraction of gold at Marmato, belonging to the Columbian or Mariquita Company, in 1845, was estimated at fifty per cent.

The fusion process is another source of loss with gold ores. It is not generally thought of, but the gold becomes volatilized, and escapes in that form when combined with certain ores of opposite electric conditions, so that a great expense is gone to in fuel, in order to bring about the dissipation of the metal. Of this I am so well convinced, that my attention has been turned to a process for profiting by this fact of volatilization, and obtaining gold whereit isnowlost.

The amalgamation process has been hitherto the most effective, but it was very expensive. In this, too, my experience has shown me that many of the supposed improvements are inferior to the rude, practical processes, and result in the loss of the gold. I find this opinion confirmed by a very good practical authority, Mr. John Phillips, formerly of the Real del Monte mines, the author of the Silver Mines and Amalgamation Process of Mexico.

He describes a very rude process, but he lays great stress on the practical skill of the *azoguero,* or amalgamator, in choosing the proper time and temperature for applying the quicksilver. There is, however, a wide opening for improvement in the old amalgamation process. The amalgamation of gold is chiefly founded on the practice of silver ores, and the right temperature for gold has not been studied. There are many conditions under which mercury repels gold, and the mercurial affinities under various stages have not been sufficiently considered.

Railway Register, 1846.

Nearly fifty amalgamating and gold reducing machines have been laid before me for inspection, many of them possessing great merit. While experimentalizing upon Berdan's machine, I discovered some results which, in addition to what is claimed by the inventor as new, justify me in stating that his is the best machine that I have yet seen for treating gold ores. One advantage is, that the crushing being carried on at the same time as the amalgamation, engenders friction, which, together with the artificial temperature, results in an electric opposition. This condition is dependent on the constitution of the machine, the ball and basin being iron, and under these circumstances the gold is repelled, and the mercury acquires a decided affinity for it. In the case of large masses of ore, not containing iron, an admixture of ferruginous earth or other iron ore, may become desirable to assist in promoting the operation. The opposition of the iron element materially assists in perfecting the amalgamation, and this will, no doubt, be the quickest and surest amalgamation that can be effected, as it results from the happiest state of electrical affinity and opposition, coinciding with an efficient temperature and combination of the metals brought under operation.

Having long studied the laws of electric decomposition and opposite determination of metals generally, the electric treatment of rocks containing gold and other metals in cryptothesis has naturally occupied my attention to a great degree, and has allowed me to bring that branch of electricity to greater perfection than has been yet attained.

I have several modes of electric analysis, one by decomposition, another by electric blast; the first is slow and a work of time, the last instantaneous; in both these instances I require a combined opposition (to determine a precipitation) of metal in two states, one in precipitation, and one in electric solution.

Generally, I would say, in all that regards gold, it has suffered from the want of a special treatment, though, with enlarged experience, this evil will be remedied. We want a distinct gold mining and gold metallurgy, and not to treat gold on the basis of silver or copper, any more than we would treat iron on such a basis.

I know no measure which would contribute more effectively to the promotion of gold mining in this country than the establishment of district reduction works. It is true that gold ores have been successfully treated at Hawarden, in Flintshire, and now at St. Helen's, in Lancashire; but there should be local establishments. The Britannia Company feel the necessity of this so strongly, that they have proposed to form reduction works on their own mine at Molton; but there are many mines which will produce only a few hundred pounds' worth of gold in a year, and to which a separate establishment becomes impossible, on account of the expense. When we get to regular gold reduction establishments, the amount of business will be greatly increased, and the processes improved.

At the present moment a strong opinion prevails in many quarters that gold mining, or what are called quartz companies, will not pay in California, Australia, or England. The only reason that can be assigned for that impression is, that gold mining companies did not formerly pay.

The reasons for this I will first briefly state. The failures arose from—

Bad managers.

Bad processes.

Many of the managers sent out by the South American mining companies were broken down merchants or knights, with extravagant salaries and extravagant habits, and who did nothing but expend the money of their shareholders. Under them were Cornish captains, who knew nothing of gold mining; were puffed up by high wages and a higher position than they had been accustomed to, and who were

Y given to drunkenness. They treated the native processes with contempt, and those they introduced themselves were ineffective. Of the results of such management a specimen has been already given. The companies failed, not for want of gold ores, or because the ores were poor, but because the companies were mismanaged, the waste enormous, and the expenses too great.

In answering the grand question, whether quartz companies will pay, I should say that they do not pay, but that they may be made to pay. They generally fail from want of knowledge of the right kind of ore; and, secondly, from want of knowing how to treat it when found. Those quartz rocks from which rich specimens are obtained at the surface are, in nearly every case, mere incrustations, and delusive indications, so far as the lower part of the vein is concerned. Although such a vein does, in many instances, afford profitable employment to the man, boy, and mule, working the old Chilian mill in California, who work surface quartz, yet companies on a large scale always, with the idea of diving into the vein leave untouched the smaller but more productive resources left to the smaller capitalist. I would, therefore, point to many veins which have little or no surface indications for gold, and to various other metallic combinations, in reality with a low percentage, but of which there is an unlimited supply which will afford the best paying and the only remunerative source of employment. There are many of these ores in England which I place under this head, and which serve as an indication of the scope open for gold mining throughout the world. These include:—

Granite containing gold in cryptothesis. Decomposed granite containing gold in precipitation. Quartz with partially precipitated and secreted gold, giving it a greenish cast throughout.

Quartz with various metallic combinations. A few slates near the junction of other rocks with sandstones, but confined chiefly to the surface.

Gossans, oxides of iron, &c.

Magnetic iron pyrites.

Sulphurets of iron.

These last are very various in their assays and if some samples I have examined were of uniform character with the mass would lead to almost extravagant estimates, but I do not point to these as localities to be preferred to some of the others of less promise.

I do not undertake to be responsible that all the Californian and Australian companies will pay, for many of them are bubbles under insufficient management, some of them have worked out their capital in buying lands, mines, veins, and which either have no existence or which the sellers had no right to sell. Some of these will go through the career of the old companies, but I have no hesitation in saying that gold mining will pay, if properly conducted.

The St. John del Rey is a company originating in the mania of 1825, and which sank its capital in the usual way. Its ore is very poor, and, nevertheless, it has now for some years been paying good dividends, and if the St. John del Rey Company pay dividends there are plenty of English companies which can do better.

I am obliged to repeat here that the yield of the St. John del Rey ores ranges from 7 pennyweights of gold to 9 pennyweights per ton of ore, less than half an ounce.

The ores of Marcugnaga, in Savoy, are not better.

The yield of gold from the prepared sands of the Ural, is only one twelfth of an ounce per ton, somewhere about *2* pennyweights probably.

Ansted's Geology, Vol. 11, p. 267.

The Devon mines are working ores with 1J ounces, and the Cwmheisian worked richer ores. As to Australia, I have seen abundance of quartz and other ores of great richness.

FINIS. APPENDIX. ASSAYS OF GOLD ORES OF GREAT BRITAIN

Made while the present volume was in the press; out of many assays these were the best; I classify them according to the electric conditions that gold generally is found in, viz.: when metallic or precipitated; when partly precipitated, in electric solution, or secreted; and when in cryptothesis. The following is a list of ores or rocks, where no gold was visible with a microscope, treated by two processes—chemical analysis, and electric analysis.

PRECIPITATED. Chem.anal. Elec.anal. Chem. anal. Elec. anal, ozs. dwts. ozs. dwtfc.

Cumberland.—Oxide of iron, near High Ireby.0 3.... 0 3

Lead, Caldbeck Fells... 0 13.... 0 13

Silver-lead Goldscope...1 0 1 0

Sulphuret of copper, Goldscope. 0 17.... 0 17

Slag, Goldscope....03 03

Quartz, near Crumnock Water.0 19... . 1 3

Sulphuret of iron, near Keswick. 1 0. ... 1 6

Westmoreland.—Oxide of iron....7 0. ...7 0

Derbyshire.—Quartz 1 17 2 1

Sulphuret of iron....3 0 3 4

Earthy iron ore....2 3....2 3

Devonshire.—Oxide of Iron 7 0....7 0 3 3.... 3 3 *n* 1 8.... 1 8

Sulphurets of iron....6 0 6 18

Slaty pyrites 217 3 4

Silver-lead 2 0....2 0

Sulphurets of copper...1 2.... 1 4

Oxide of iron, Poltimore.. 1 12.... 1 12

„ „ Arundell.0 3.... 0 3

Oxide of tin ore, Dartmoor.. 1 13.... 1 13

Decomposing granite... 3 19.... 4 16'

Cornwall.—Sulphurets of iron, decomposed.8 3.... 8 3 .7 10.... 7 10 .0 13. ... 0 13

Sulphurets of iron....3 2 3 4 10.... 1 2 copper...1 4.... 1 5

„.... 0 17.... 0 17 Decomposing granite...3 0.... 4 2

Sulphurets of iron, Redruth.. 3 17.... 3 17

'"" „ „ near Lostwithiel 2 3.... 2 8

Oxide of iron „ „.1 0.... 1 0

" ' Ferruginous quartz „ „.4 3.... 4 3

Quartz, near Bodmin...2 0.... 2 3

' ' Sulphurets of iron, near Bodmin. 1 3 1 5 ' Silver ore, Inney Consols..16 not tested.

'"' SECRETED.

Quartz, Dolfrwynog, Wales 0 3 0 7

„ 0 11.... 1 1

„ Bodmin, Cornwall..... 0 14.... 1 5

„ Cumberland......07 0 10 i. Devonshire 0 19 2 13

„ „ 0 11 1 14 CRYPTOTHETED.

Granite, Dartmoor. 0 0....30

„ „ 0 0 3 19 , „ 0 0.... 1 1

„....... 0 0.... 1 7 0 0.... 0 3

„ Castle-an-Dinas..-...00 about 0 2

„ Aberdeenshire...... 0 0.... 0 1

Sienite, Cumberland 00 0 4

J. c.

INDEX.

Lightning Source UK Ltd.
Milton Keynes UK
UKOW07f2021140116

266449UK00007B/250/P